The Feast of My Life

KENNETH LO

THE FEAST OF MY LIFE

Doubleday

LONDON · NEW YORK · TORONTO · SYDNEY · AUCKLAND

TRANSWORLD PUBLISHERS LTD
61-63 Uxbridge Road, London W5 5SA

TRANSWORLD PUBLISHERS (AUSTRALIA) PTY LTD
15-25 Helles Avenue, Moorebank, NSW 2170

TRANSWORLD PUBLISHERS (NZ) LTD
3 William Pickering Drive, Albany, Auckland

DOUBLEDAY CANADA LTD
105 Bond Street, Toronto, Ontario, M5B 1Y3

Published 1993 by Doubleday
a division of Transworld Publishers Ltd.
Copyright © 1993 by Kenneth Lo

Chinese calligraphy © Hong Zuojia

A catalogue record for this book is
available from the British Library.
ISBN 0385 404506

Typeset in 10/13pt Bembo by
Falcon Graphic Art Ltd,
Wallington, Surrey
Printed in Great Britain by
Mackays of Chatham Plc, Chatham, Kent

To all the moments of friendship and kindness I have known.

Author's Note

When writing any piece concerning China, the author has to choose a system for romanizing the Chinese words. This is never a simple choice. Certain well-known Chinese concepts, places and people may already have a romanization that has become standardized through common usage, but belong to different systems.

I have chosen to adopt the Pinyin system that was developed in post-revolutionary China and is most commonly used around the world today. As this system has gained popularity since my youth, I have inevitably encountered problems and have had to make numerous exceptions.

The first and most obvious exception is my surname, 'Lo': it has been romanized in this way for over a century, so I have chosen not to adopt the Pinyin way of spelling it (Luo). Other more obvious pre-Pinyin usages that I have retained for clarity are Foochow, Peking and such widely known names as Chiang Kaishek and Sun Yatsen.

Many of the lesser-known names of my childhood were spoken in the language of the Foochow area and are also not readily rendered in Pinyin.

There are other grey areas where I have had to make a considered judgement as to how much a particular romanization has become common currency. But as far as possible I have tried to stick to the Pinyin version.

Much of the history related in my autobiography is as it was passed down to me through family stories and makes little attempt to be objective. I have used it to try to convey the lives of people suspended between two ages in China. Wherever I have discovered wild inaccuracies in those stories, I have amended them.

Similarly, in translation, I have chosen well-known Chinese poems and pieces of literature and have translated them loosely and in a way that pleases me or reflects my memory of them and the way that they were handed down to me.

Finally I would like to thank all those who have given me encouragement in the writing of this book. In particular I would like to thank Ruth Herd and Peter Raby for their invaluable comments and criticism, my daughters Jenny for typing the manuscript and Vivienne, without whose natural enthusiasm and unremitting editorial effort this book would never have been completed.

EASTERN CHINA

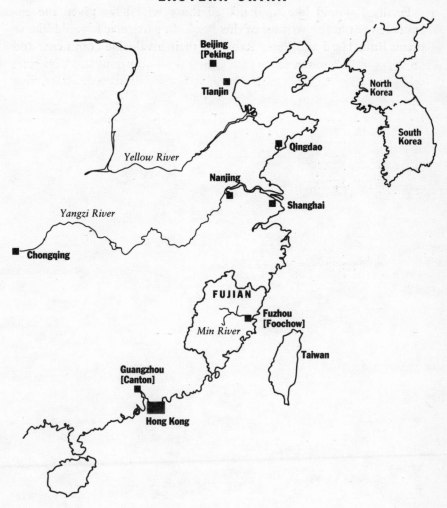

Beijing
[Peking]

Tianjin

North
Korea

South
Korea

Yellow River

Qingdao

Nanjing

Shanghai

Yangzi River

Chongqing

FUJIAN

Fuzhou
[Foochow]

Min River

Taiwan

Guangzhou
[Canton]

Hong Kong

When Ban Gu divided Heaven and Earth, three emperors put the world in order and five rulers settled the moral principles. This world then separated into four large continents and beyond the seas was the land of Ao Lai. Nearby and out of the sea grew the famous Mountain of Flowers and Fruit. On the top of the mountain was a magic rock. One day this rock split asunder and gave birth to a stone egg the size of a ball. Fertilized by the wind, the egg changed into a monkey whom they called the Stone Monkey. The Stone Monkey possessed all the five senses and all four limbs, he quickly learned to climb and walk and he bowed to the four quarters.

The Monkey then leaped and ran in the hills, feeding on grasses and barks, drinking from the mountain streams, gathering mountain flowers, looking for fruits. He was friends with wolves and the fallow deer, he ran with the tigers and panthers, and all the apes and monkeys were his family. At night he made his bed under the rock cliffs, by day he wandered over the hills and in the caves. He had no idea of time and thus one winter followed another, year succeeded year . . .

Chapter 1, *Journey to the West* (*The Monkey King*],
Wu Chengen. *circa* 1500–82

CHAPTER ONE

Journey to the West

There flows through the middle of this city a great river, which is about a mile in width, and many ships are built at the city which are launched upon this river. Enormous quantities of sugar are made there, and there is a great traffic in pearls and precious stones. For many ships of India come to these parts bringing many merchants who traffic about the Isles of the Indies.

The Travels, Marco Polo. Foochow, 13th century

THE WATERS OF the Min River pour out of the mountains of north-west Fujian and, passing south of the city of Foochow, split into two swift-flowing streams – measuring up to a mile wide during the rainy seasons – to reunite again in a vast pool called the Pagoda Anchorage. Pagoda Anchorage was not only a vast expanse of water, it was also deep enough for ocean-going liners and the first Chinese dockyard was built upon its banks. When I first sailed the pool in my early youth, it seemed to be an ocean upon which our sampan-tethered-to-a-motor-launch was tossed like a leaf by large and frightening waves.

For nearly six years I had lived in the suburbs of Foochow, close by a world that buzzed with maritime activity. Junks with great gaudy eyes painted on the prow sped about the river with their tall fanned sails billowing in the breeze. Closer to the water sampans beetled around, propelled by a rudder that sliced diagonally through the water while the women, under bamboo awnings, vied with each other to sell local produce. As evening drew on they moored side by side on the north bank, spontaneously creating little river villages that would disperse at dawn with the same ease that they had appeared. Through the night the hooting of small steamboats punctuated the silence as they tugged along their heavily laden vessels.

The river ran deep and clear, except during the rainy season when it carried down yellow sediment and loads of debris, simultaneously flooding the cultivated land and the narrow valleys. Whole boats and dwellings were washed away and shattered against the two stone bridges that joined the river isle and the city. Daqiao (the Great Bridge) was one of the wonders of my world. It had been standing on its twenty-ton granite pillars for over a thousand years. From the top of the hill above our house I could see its one hundred arches stretching a mile to the other side.

Sometimes the water upstream from the bridge was ten feet higher than the water below so it would cascade down in thundering torrents. In full flood it was dangerous for junks and sampans to shoot these short 'rapids' but some daring boatmen did so. In quieter times I liked to listen to the boatmen chant in unison. They sang in one of the eleven lyrical tongues of Fujian and poled long stretches of pine trunk rafts – many of them over fifty feet long – to the Japanese sawmills on the lower reaches of the Min.

It wasn't always the bustle of the river that had attracted our attention. Nor did we know much of life in the city of Foochow. But what we did know was that Foochow was brim full of 'ghosts'. There was one ghastly pair, the 'Tall Elder Brother', and the 'Short Younger Brother'. The tall one was probably the victim of hanging: he was all of ten feet, with a long, red, swollen tongue hanging out of his mouth. The short one had probably drowned, being large and squat with a bushy bloated head. During the festivals the idols were paraded around in the streets and lanes of the suburb, preceded by blaring trumpets, clashing cymbals and the flickering of torches. I used to hide anxiously behind the adults' skirts until the procession turned the corner. The glare of torches reflecting off the whitewashed walls would suddenly blind us and those two hellish figures towering above would seem to bear right down. Then I'd rush indoors, only to re-emerge in an instant peeping, scared out of my wits, to watch from a safer distance as the ghoulish procession passed by and became shrouded by the darkness of the street.

As my brother and I lay in bed recovering from a bout of measles, I imagined that the Elder Brother had grown even taller and bigger and was peering in from the back garden through the first floor window. Only when my mother came to comfort me did I dare to emerge from under the bedclothes. It was during the convalescence that I learned to appreciate Nestlé's condensed milk and found myself licking it from the lid of the half-opened can.

Those were the days before the great journey. As I scampered about the banks of the Min and watched the sampans swarm around the ocean-going liners, hawking their wares down at the Anchorage, I had no idea how soon I would leave the humdrum backwater of Foochow and, in the tradition of the coastal people, make a break for the freedom of the seas.

It was 1919 and I barely six years old. We weren't sure why our father was taking the whole family to Britain. Happily his resources weren't completely exhausted and when, in the autumn, we first set sail for the West we did so in style. My father loved style! A month before we embarked our house was already a hive of activity. Mountains of foodstuffs were being nailed down in crates on the veranda. There were little ones two and a half feet square and huge containers that probably weighed nearly a quarter of a ton. Each crate was stuffed with straw to ensure that the precious bottles of soya would arrive intact. We took all our provisions with us for fear we might starve in a strange environment where noodles were unheard of and the trees were not laden with heavy bunches of 'dragon eyes' (longyan fruit). We stocked up as if we were going on a Himalayan expedition. Apart from the crates there were some half-dozen ribbed sea trunks of the sort with which British colonials always travelled. My mother saw to it that all the linen and clothing stacked inside was so perfectly washed and ironed that it would not need to be laundered again when we arrived in distant Britain. Who could tell how people ironed over there?

Luckily Qingqing, our most capable houseman and cook, was on hand to help out. Not only was he impeccably clean in his crisp, white, Western-style jacket, he was also extremely efficient. But his greatest asset to us was that he was a story-teller extraordinaire who would bring joy to the dullest moments. He specialized in the classic epics of the *Journey to the West* and, as we grew older, the *Romance of the Three Kingdoms*. He told them with such enthusiasm and illustrated them with imaginary battles and such flying kung fu kicks that he breathed life into the classical heroes so that they danced before our eyes. In fact Qingqing, with his thin wiry body and bony face, looked rather like a monkey. My daydreams were filled with the Monkey King's exploits. I could picture him as he entered the Dragon King's palace at the bottom of the sea. I knew how he had uprooted the magic cudgel and I revelled in his insolence as he left havoc in his wake. We listened enthralled to Monkey's battles with the Heavenly Generals, to how he stole the Peaches of Immortality from the Grand Patriarch and fought off countless wicked demons on his journey to India to fetch back the Buddhist scriptures.

On the day of departure all our trunks and crates were loaded into a massive house-boat lashed to a motor boat at the wharf near the Great Bridge. It sped its way down to the Pagoda Anchorage and the ocean-going vessel which was waiting to take us to Shanghai, 450 miles up the coast. For some reason we had started late and it was getting dark when we reached the Pagoda Anchorage. From more than a mile away the vessel was a bank of shimmering lights topped with a huge funnel belching smoke. At twilight it was true romance. The waters of Pagoda Anchorage swelled dangerously and I was glad to get off the small boat and on to the stability of the sea-going vessel. The ship loomed above me like a walled castle with winking rows of portholes, all ablaze with lights that danced on the surface of the water, sitting solidly amid the swell and sway of the world. Once we had boarded the big ship we were all tucked into bed, and before long all the excitement of the day and wonder of the ship melted away and we fell fast asleep.

Shanghai was where my mother's family, the Weis, had settled. I had never imagined that I could have so many aunts, uncles and cousins. My mother had six sisters and eight brothers. Our eighth uncle and seventh aunt were as young as we were. A couple of middle aunts had married into the Mao family and produced a string of cousins and some, we were told, were wild and unruly. Our parents cautioned us that we must not grow up like them: they threw ice-cream parties at the Majestic, the top hotel in Shanghai. My mouth watered. The leader of our gang of cousins was one Mao Fei and he was the most wild and unruly of them all. He had to be kept at arm's length to avoid damaging our rustic innocence. But during the few weeks in Shanghai we made catapults and fought mock battles in the side streets off Heishalu (Haskell or Black Sand Street) where they lived.

My maternal grandfather, Admiral Wei Han, was a very grumpy, severe old gentleman whom everybody held in reverence. In fact Wei Han was only an admiral because the family styled him so! In 1911 two of his Mao family sons-in-law were captains of gunboats on the Yangzi River. On hearing of the onset of revolution, they both declared UDI and raised the Republican flag. When they arrived in Shanghai, they went to pay respects to their father-in-law, declaring him then and there Admiral of the New Republic.

Most of the time he reclined on a twin couch, propped up by

firm, round cushions, occasionally pulling on an opium pipe to relieve him of his arthritic pains. The pipe was set on a tray on a low table which was arranged between the two sides of the couch, so that he could relax face-to-face with his guests and prattle on interminably. All opium smokers, I observed, talked too much. My grandfather sometimes filled his own pipe, but more often it was filled for him by a young cousin. I watched, transfixed by how she did it. Opium was like treacle. By turning a thick pin in it, enough of the treacly stuff would stick on so that one could roll it into a tiny blob of a ball against the broad face of the pipe. She would pierce the ball through the centre and roll it against the pin-hole entrance of the pipe over a small flame. This made a sizzling and sucking noise as the smoker puffed and billowed out a sweet, heavy fragrance. They said that smoking opium made a person feel good and gave him beautiful dreams. I was entranced. One day I checked carefully all around the house and seeing that there was nobody on the same floor I picked up a pipe. In a precise re-run of the cousin's method I prepared my first taste of opium. But after three or four puffs I recoiled: it was truly disgusting. The taste was bitter and cloying and no treat for my sensitive taste buds. I gave up smoking opium for good at the grand old age of five.

I do not remember the day we left Shanghai, but I was very proud of the ship in which we were sailing. It was the biggest flagship of the Messagerie Maritime line, the 27,000 ton *André Lebon*, and we were travelling First Class. The government treasury was well stuffed with French francs. For several years 200,000 labourers drafted from the northern province of Shandong had been impressing the Europeans with their lofty six-foot stature while digging the trenches on the Western Front. They had been paid in francs, at a time when the exchange was favourable, so naturally all the foreign exchange had gravitated to the coffers of the Ministry of Finance in Peking. Temporarily China was in the black, at least as far as her diplomats were concerned.

The furnishing of the First Class dining-room was French Mediterranean. The adults danced to Viennese waltzes amid luxurious palm trees but most of the time we drank tea. Father, who barely spoke a word of French, taught us that the word for tea was 'Du thé'. In Foochow dialect 'Du' means pig and 'té' sounds something like trotters. So we rang for the French steward, and when he arrived in our cabin we all shouted 'Pigs' trotters' in Foochow French, and collapsed into fits of giggling. But the tea I enjoyed most was the 'tea' that they gave us for a nightcap: this was a kind of beef bouillon which British travellers to the Far East enjoyed last thing at night for over a century while reclining on the decks of P & O liners. Fortified by the same beefy strength that had braced the British Empire we were well set up to take the West by storm.

As we steamed southward our first port of call was not Hong Kong but the coastal port of Hanoi, Haiphong. After all, our ship was a French liner and Vietnam, then Indo-China, was a French colony. To get into Hanoi required a lengthy steam up the Hong River, the banks of which were dense with tropical jungle. As I peered through our porthole in the early hours of the morning when all the adults were sound asleep, for a moment I thought I saw a tiger prowling through the bushes. My hair stood quietly on end. And then, in an instant, it was gone and the ship steamed on.

Saigon, or Xigong (Western Tribute) in Chinese, was a large town, with no tiger-ridden rivers, and here we disembarked to drink coffee and lemonade in the open air. Then the ship ploughed its way, once more, into the South Seas. We had already been sailing for a week and our next stop was Singapore which was well known to us. One of our younger aunts had married a local millionaire and settled there. Tan Subin's fabulous wealth was substantially increased by the sale of his garden to the British, who built a naval base on the site. But our aunt hated the environment so much that she went half crazy in her exile so far from the civilization of Foochow and her home on the banks of the Min River. Well before our arrival she had pined to death leaving two sons, George and Robert, and several other youngsters. Craning our necks over the deck railings and looking down the perilous heights of the prow we saw that they were all there to welcome us. We could hardly miss them. They had a fleet of five shining motor cars in attendance. The glistening array of motor cars impressed me much more than the diamonds which the women wore on their slippers or between their toes. My brother counselled me that such ostentation was in poor taste. Early on I was learning to be a snob, although there was nothing much to be snobbish about. All the same we knew that these things were not in good taste.

From Singapore our ship headed towards the Indian Ocean. The tropical sun beat down mercilessly on us. We gulped down glass after glass of iced lemonade. In another three days we had docked in Colombo, where the coastline was thick with coconut palms. In the heat and humidity of these fertile tropics our hair seemed to have grown more rapidly than when we were at home. Our straight bushy hair was rivalling the coconut trees and mother thought that we should get it cut. Father seemed to know exactly where. He took us to the Metropole Hotel. A huge black stuffed elephant with long, white tusks towered over us in the reception hall as we entered. The barber chopped off our spiky locks and then brushed our heads with a revolving brush which whirred in our ears. The faces that stared back at us from the mirror seemed peculiarly foreign.

More tropical ocean and more iced lemonade and we were among the leaping fishes of the Red Sea and its luminous waves at night, then through the Suez canal where, sandwiched between deserts, the ship seemed to be sailing on dry land. We stopped for an afternoon at Port Said and sat around in a café on a dusty street. Scruffy children gathered around and insisted on brushing our shoes. Our shoes didn't need brushing so we had to shoo them away with as much composure as we could summon. As Father disappeared down the street and into a shop to make some purchases I prayed that he would return quickly. He might disappear unaccountably, leaving us boys and our mother in this dreadful spot. We had lost sight of our ship behind the alleys of this alien port; perhaps it had already sailed and we would be left to fend for ourselves to the end of our lives. How would we ever earn money to eat? I was gripped by a terrible foreboding. How relieved I was when Father returned, parcels bulging under his arms, and we could head back to the security of our floating castle.

At Brindisi we were told to watch out for erupting volcanoes. We watched all day but didn't see any. After another day or two of sailing, and a total voyage of one month, we landed in the noisy port of Marseilles and took the train to Paris.

If post-war Paris was drab, I didn't notice it. But I did notice that there was no sugar. You had to shake some kind of syrupy liquid out of an upturned bottle to sweeten cups of tea or coffee. The bottle had a heavy lead stopper, rather like a perfume bottle from which the perfume was eked out in drops. It was very frustrating. The only other thing I remember about Paris was that it was very cold at the top of the Eiffel Tower. Mother was re-packing in our hotel room. In these chilly northern parts we began to wear combinations, woollen socks and thick coats with velvet collars. Britain was going to be cold and also very foggy. I braced myself to bear the shock. The crossing to Dover was uneventful but for putting on lifebelts as a precaution against the unswept minefields that might lurk below amid those millions of gallons of cold, grey water.

Britain, as expected, was not very welcoming. When we docked in Dover it was already dark and drizzly. But there was one thing which we had not expected – we had landed in the middle of a strike! With inflation rising at twice the rate of the war years, continued food rationing and a threatened reduction in wages, the railway men, transport workers and miners had tried to resurrect the pre-war triple alliance in what was to be a precursor to the General Strike. We did not know what a strike was. All we knew was that we might have to be put up in a cheap hotel before some form of transport could be found to take us to London. Besides, all that luggage had to be cleared through the customs first. We were, however, able to get unlimited hot sugared tea. There was plenty of sugar here and, thankfully, no frustrating bottle of syrup. Hot tea sustained us through the wait.

What were Mother's feelings on her first evening in Britain? She was sitting stoically on a hard bench in the waiting-room shed and, with her three sons gathered all around, could still create an atmosphere of good cheer. My elder brother's face was pale and pinched. Qingqing was watching over our huge mound of luggage in case some foreign devil might snatch a bag and disappear into the darkness. My father, the only English-speaking person in our company, was scurrying around, trying to find either accommodation or some means of conveyance to London. I was very impressed with him. Time passed and, at about our usual bedtime, he came rushing into the waiting-room to announce that we could go up to London by motor car. What he should have said was motor coach, but there wasn't such a term in the Foochow dialect. Foochow had neither seen nor heard of a motor coach.

In fact it wasn't even a coach. It was a *charabanc*! A charabanc was a topless coach with about ten rows of seats behind the driver; each row was entered from either side of the vehicle, thus giving it the appearance of having innumerable doors. My first problem was the height of the car. It was like climbing on to a camel's back. In the end I was thrown in with the greatest of ease by some invisible helping hands. All the seats in our row were occupied by the Lo party: three adults, including Qingqing and three children, with the addition of one British army officer who was returning on leave from the Western Front. He was in a good mood and invited me to sit on his lap, showing me how to lift up the tarpaulin and cover my knees to keep warm. It was getting on for midnight, in early November, when we rumbled out of Dover into the wide open spaces of Kent. My mother was pleased that a British officer was looking after me. His uniform was somehow reassuring. He proceeded to button me inside his huge greatcoat which, covered with the tarpaulin, certainly helped to keep us both warm. Before long, as the warmth of our bodies intermingled, a strange smell began to fill my nostrils: it was the smell of the goat milk we sometimes drank, or the goat meat that we frequently cooked in the hilly regions of Fujian. Amid these homely odours I soon slipped into a doze. Many decades later I realized that this was the normal smell of Europeans.

But it was a long ride through the howling wind and the fine rain with only the tarpaulin and the British army greatcoat to keep me warm, and I could sleep only fitfully. Finally we were in Victoria station, disembarking from the charabanc, and that warm, sweaty army officer bid us farewell. The night was dark and we were in a strange city, once again on our own. Would my father be able to guide us to the right house in this huge sprawling metropolis? All around were sooty buildings. The Grosvenor Hotel loomed gloomily out of the darkness. We waited, as we always seemed to be waiting, while Father sorted things out. Before long he had managed to hire two cabs. They were like sedan chairs on the inside and a source of great comfort in this hostile environment. I counted the gas lamps as we passed them and concluded that they must stand quite far apart, perhaps more than one hundred and fifty paces. As I counted I imagined everyone must be fast asleep. I also watched the red rear light of the taxi ahead which was belching smoke, deliciously.

The cabs drew to a halt on an incline. Could this be the right house? Qingqing raced up the steps. A light flashed on on the first floor and through the brightly lit window we could see a dark-haired figure, who threw on a fur-lined gown which was undoubtedly Chinese – only Chinese wore gowns with the fur lining on the inside. I was elated, as we all were, for at last we were 'home and dry'. Then my little brother fell out of the door on to the pavement. We had arrived at number 18 Fitzjohn's Avenue, a large Victorian pile of a house which still stands today on the hill between Hampstead and Swiss Cottage.

After ascending the steps we were shown into the front dining-room where a long dining-table was laid out with huge chunks of roast beef, a boiled chicken and lots of other goodies. This was my kind of Heaven. In the background a fire was roaring in the grate. A huge pot of tea was brought in and the adults were all given hot cuppas and some beef sandwiches. I was longing for a bite. But instead we were only given hot cocoa, biscuits and no sandwiches. The adults felt that cocoa was good, at least good enough for children, when I could have eaten a whole leg of beef by myself. My eyes smarted with the injustice of it.

As I drank my cocoa and munched my dry biscuits, I surveyed the adults. There was second uncle Yi, who was thin as a stick, and his pretty wife who was also my mother's fourth sister (mother being the fifth of seven sisters). There was their daughter, Becee, who was a double cousin – her mother was my mother's sister and her father was my father's younger brother. I was only vaguely aware of these family complexities as I gulped down my cocoa, my attention being fixed on those succulent sandwiches.

There were murmurs that 'the children must be very tired, having had such a very long day', and shortly we were all sent upstairs to bed. But I wasn't tired or sleepy at all; I was very much alive to the sandwiches, at the very least to another cup of cocoa, and an exploration of the house before retiring. But that was not to be.

Instead, my elder brother and I trudged reluctantly upstairs to the attic where beds had been made up for us. The attic was quite cold despite the gas fire. We undressed and changed into our pyjamas in front of the fire, and were tucked into bed. The sheets felt crisp and freshly laundered. Reaching down towards the bottom end of the bed I was surprised to feel something warm. I was told that it was a hot water bottle. We had never needed hot water bottles in Foochow but they were welcome to me here. We simply lay there and looked at the reflection of the gas fire on the corners of the ceiling and the yellow glow of the street lights which seeped in through the edges of the drawn blinds. Tucked into our twin beds, my brother's nearer the window and mine nearer the door like two little boats on Pagoda Anchorage, we were adrift in a big sea. We didn't know where we were in this strange house, not to speak of the city beyond. There was so much that was new to us: when you pulled up the handle beside the wooden toilet seat, torrents of water came swirling around the shiny white bowl like the water under the Stone Bridge, and on our way up to our bedroom we had passed several stained glass windows which had pictures of long-haired gentlemen in long robes. They carried crosses like the crazy Taipings that Qingqing had told us about. These Taipings, 'the longhairs', had swept over the country and stolen the Empire, praying to someone called Jesus and performing magic rituals. Could it have been those very men I saw depicted there?

After such an inhospitable reception by the British weather it was no wonder that my elder brother Xiaochao, my younger brother Xiaoyue and myself, Xiaojian, all caught the dreaded 'flu which had killed more than twenty million Europeans that year – a figure that rivalled the casualties of the Great War.

Our names were all prefixed with the character Xiao Filial as was customary in the Chinese family, where each generation was distinguished by a common character that appeared in the second or third syllable of their name (the surname comes first). My father's generation were called Zhong (loyal), my children's Qian (forward), and my grandchildren's Hong (*grand*); the sequence of words being taken from a poem adopted by the family for the specific purpose of naming (see page 39). These subtleties of naming were lost upon the doctor in attendance during our affliction. In order to differentiate between the bottles of medicine he was administering in varying potencies to the three of us, he had to come up with something, and belaboured with the problem of pronouncing, let alone romanizing, our queer names, he labelled us Charles, Kenneth and Walter, and so we remain today.

We Chinese love festivities. That first Christmas in London was an ideal pretext for us to enjoy a prolonged family get-together. First of all it would be an occasion to celebrate our safe arrival after the long voyage from Foochow and would help us settle into this foreign country. Both Father and Uncle Yi had jobs. They were reasonably well installed, although my father's job as Vice-Consul was that of a very minor functionary. All he ever seemed to do was stamp passports. His younger brother's job as First Secretary at the Embassy and occasional Chargé d'Affaires was second only to the Ambassador. The clan in London consisted of more than just our immediate family. My maternal uncle, Uncle Long, together with a nephew of his, were studying engineering in Glasgow, and my youngest paternal uncle, Uncle Arthur, and Uncle Cecil were at Fitzwilliam and Magdalene Colleges in Cambridge. They all came to stay at Fitzjohn's Avenue during vacations and this Christmas was a special occasion. There were already quite a few people in residence: six of us including the cook, and our aunt and uncle's family with their two maids, a servant and a nurse to look after their only daughter. The house at No. 18 was large enough to accommodate a convergence of the clan and we were all delighted to see everyone. We children were most pleased of all. With so many friendly faces sleeping in every room in the house we felt both excited and secure, as, with such an onslaught of sallow heathens, surely no foreign spirits would venture out from the dark nooks and crannies of those Victorian rooms.

Everyone pooled together their resources to make Christmas a lavish one. People arrived in large cars. The Christmas tree was glittering with stars, hung with baubles of silver and gold and festooned with multicoloured streamers. There were dolls and teddy bears galore; I pulled Christmas crackers with all and sundry and collected all the 'priceless' gifts which dropped out of them. We thundered the steep mile down Fitzjohn's Avenue on go-karts and pogosticks that we had discovered wrapped beneath the tree. Surely we were the only pogoing Chinese of 1919! We had been initiated into Wonderland and on the

London Chinese social circuit I made many friends of my own age and discovered my nature to be a gregarious one.

On the table in the dining-room was not only a turkey but also a huge chunk of roast beef and a mountain of hot-tossed Chinese noodles from our food crates. We helped Qingqing break into crate after crate and store away our precious Chinese stock. This was the start of our underground life with the servants in the basement kitchen. As I tucked into the noodles, turkey and roast beef I was soon full to bursting point. Our increasing immobility and bloated stomachs attracted an early dismissal and we were sent upstairs to bed. This time I was content to retire to the attic. I had enjoyed every minute of the day and evening, and tasted enough fare for many weeks' happy reflection – indeed I had more than tasted it, I had wolfed it down! What more could I ask for?

The next morning I awoke just as a glimmer of light was creeping through the sides of the window-blind. There was hardly a sound from outside; it was too early for anyone to be out and about on a winter's morning. I could feel the freezing coldness seeping into the room. Suddenly the stillness was broken by the rhythmic clatter of horses' hooves. I listened to the noise approaching quickly down the hill like a smooth roll of drums gathering to a crescendo. 'Horses!' Calling out in a loud whisper I woke Charles who was sleeping nearer the window. I watched him sit up, push aside the blind and peer through the window. 'Cavalry soldiers!' he said. I rushed over to his side. Mounted soldiers were riding in formation, trotting their way down the hill. 'There must be a cavalry camp nearby,' he said. 'It must be freezing outside,' I replied. 'See the steam from the horses' nostrils.' The steam was also flaring out of the noses of the soldiers. We were deeply impressed by the effect of hot breath on freezing morning air. Perhaps those steaming troops were coming back from the Great War. I was vaguely aware that there had been war of unprecedented proportion. I had seen the pictures of British tanks in Father's *Illustrated London News*.

After Christmas the days passed in murky succession. On those grey winter afternoons we would often spend cosy hours down in the basement kitchen with Qingqing, who would tell us more tales from the *Monkey King*. He would jump and kick his feet high in the air. I loved the kitchen as here we did not have to behave as the grown-ups thought we should. Besides, with a fire kept burning in the burnished grate, it was always warm. I watched to see how fires were built and lit. One morning I rose early and made a pre-dawn foray to the basement to brush and polish the fireplace myself and then to build and light the fire. I proudly displayed my achievement to the adults when they finally appeared. But I was told never to do it again. I might burn everyone in their beds. I was crestfallen, but tea and biscuits soon soothed my wounded pride.

We would often come here for hot refreshment after accompanying baby cousin Becee and the nurse on their dreary stroll across the Heath. The sky was always drizzly and the winter sun hung desolately on the horizon. We were never going anywhere on these strolls, except mostly, it seemed, in circles. Apparently it was good for us but, clad in the local uniform of grey flannel shorts and socks with our knees exposed to the British wind, it seemed to us no wonder that large sections of the indigenous population were felled by the 'flu.

One day in January, after having recovered from the 'flu, my elder brother, Charles, and I, clad in our grey socks and shiny black shoes, were taken down to the bottom of Fitzjohn's Avenue where we were enrolled in the kindergarten of Kingsley School. There we were introduced to the Head, and handed over to a Miss Orman, who took us up to the first-floor playroom. When our uncle left we felt unaccountably deserted in this strangest of worlds where nobody spoke a single word of the language of Fujian. For a while we wondered what to do next – I consoled myself that nobody looked hungry enough to eat us. There were a little over a dozen youngsters in the room. Some had yellow hair, and others quite dark hair, although it all seemed quite artificial to us, brown being nearer to yellow when the world as we had known it was entirely jet black. Miss Orman showed us to the sand pit where a few children were making sand dunes, towers, and castles. She said, 'Here are Charles and Kenneth,' but the children took scant notice. I dug my fingers and hands into the sand and found it wet and unpleasant. I preferred the plasticine, or drawing with coloured crayons. I felt that I could draw well. In fact I could draw almost anything: houses, birds, cats, dogs, people, trees, cars, almost anything in the world. This new competence gave me a greater sense of ease and provided a way to get to grips with this new world in which I was living.

As I was absorbed in play, time passed quickly and soon the bell rang lustily to announce that it was time for lunch. We were all to go and wash our hands first, and then we marched in a crocodile into the basement dining-room a few doors away. We sat at the head of the long table on benches next to the teacher. She probably thought that, being strangers, we required special coaching in the use of the knife, fork and spoon. In fact we were already experts but too polite to say so. We did learn that in Britain soup was spooned away from the body, unlike the Chinese custom, and when you had finished eating you had to put the knife and fork neatly together rather than leave them cross-swords on the plate.

British ways were easy for us to pick up, as we Chinese children were always attentive as to how to be polite. What was not easy was to sit at the table and eat beetroot and potato washed down with cold water day after day. Beetroot was strange to my palate: it coloured the rest of the meal a hideous purple hue and was not quite sweet enough to be a fruit nor the right colour for a vegetable. With its cold slippery texture it was a strain on the stomach, even for a well-behaved Chinese boy. The cold water was tasteless; Qingqing, the fountain of culinary wisdom, said that too much coldness brought on stomach cramps. As for potatoes, well, they were an utterly tasteless food which we wouldn't give to the pigs in China. All in all it was a kind of culinary purgatory. Still we endured and endured with all the stoicism our young palates could command, but meal times went slowly. The only consolation was that my English was improving every day. Within a few weeks I was quite fluent!

Soon it was spring, then spring warmed into summer. During those early months in Britain the varied and fulsome life at 18 Fitzjohn's Avenue was beginning to deteriorate. When second Uncle was recalled to China we were obliged to move to a pretty little house with flowery wallpaper on a street called Briardale Gardens which ran on an incline from the Heath towards Finchley Road. After 18 Fitzjohn's Avenue it was like a doll's house. It had small rooms and a small garden at the back with loads of flowers. Everything about the place seemed floral and my memories of it are pervaded with sunshine. So long as we had our little family together it didn't matter who came and went. From here, to get to school, we had to take the bus to Belsize Park – probably more than a mile along the Finchley Road, so we became well acquainted with this stretch of road. We always looked into the ABC teashop, where the waitresses in bibs were serving tea and cakes to elderly ladies, and at John Barnes, the magnificent department store that always looked entrancing from across the way.

One summer's day at Briardale Gardens we encountered the first sharp edge of racism. A boy at the top of the street shouted, 'Ching Ching Chinamen. Your father's a Chinaman!' Unable to contain himself, Charles immediately leapt up and chased after him. He chased until the boy disappeared into a house. Charles was always fighting, he didn't seem to care. I always shied away from violence or at least tried to keep the peace. After this incident Charles always armed himself with a walking stick which was given to him by an uncle in Foochow.

We had to move again. This time it was to Canfield Gardens, just below John Barnes. It was a much bigger, four-storey terraced house that backed on to a rectangular communal garden. It was there in the communal garden that we met other children. One afternoon a friendly boy called Leonard invited us home to see his electricity generating machine which, when made to revolve at speed, would cause electric sparks to jump loudly between two terminals. It was all very exciting. I was filled with enthusiasm for modern science.

One day, on the way home from Leonard's, I was thinking fondly of my pets. It was in that house that we began to keep rabbits. We kept them in an unused room on the top floor for fear that they might run away through the communal garden or get killed by cats or dogs. It was feeding time and they were always in need of fresh cabbage leaves. I rushed into the house and mounted the stairs two at a time. Arriving at the top, I pushed open the door and raced into the room only to stop short in my tracks: no rabbits, no hutch! Where had they gone? I was searching for my beloved friends when it dawned on me that although the room was the same shape and size, the furniture was unfamiliar and there was a strange musty smell. Disorientated, I remembered seeing some people on the first floor who had looked at me a little strangely. I decided that I had better beat a retreat and crept down the stairs. Those same ladies were still sitting in a neat row on the sofa sipping tea. They looked a little peculiar so I didn't stop to say, 'How do you do!', but just rushed past and burst out of the house. All the houses suddenly looked the same. Unsettled, I cautiously entered the next house and mounted the stairs. Pushing into the room there was the smell of straw and there, to my relief, were all the rabbits! They looked at me as if to enquire, 'Where are the cabbage leaves?'

By this time it was the autumn of 1920 and my third brother, Michael, was born, although I didn't notice him much. Perhaps because of the trouble my mother had had in labour she was tired and he had been put out to a nurse by the name of Mrs Hooper. It was soon our second Christmas and the tree stood grandly in the corner of our drawing-room, festooned again with gold and silver baubles, crackers and glittering fairies. Many of our friends had returned to China, but we still felt we could put on a party. Toys were not so plentiful but millionaire Uncle Tan arrived one dark afternoon. After tea he called us together and pressed three crispy pound notes into our sweaty palms. We were startled. One pound was a fortune, never mind three! We stuffed them deep into our pockets where, charged with our excitement, they almost burned through our trouser pockets. Unfortunately soon after the guests left Mother and Dad confiscated the bank notes, saying that they were needed to pay the rent. Only then did I become aware that things were not easy for my parents. Money was getting tight.

Barely perceptible changes were taking place in the government in Peking and with a rapid succession of 'North China war-lords' in power, to whom the diplomatic service was of little concern, we found ourselves a long way down the pecking order when it came to payment of salary. As with all military governments the first to be paid were the officers and any tax collected was filtered through many pockets before it reached the Ministry of Finance. At the bottom of the hierarchy things were nearly high and dry. Although still young we quickly sensed the position: our parents must have been desperate otherwise how could they confiscate our pocket money?

Another move and we were at 31 Eaton Square. This was not the move up the social ladder it might seem. Eaton Square was where the Chinese Consulate General was situated. The top floor of the five-storey building was completely empty, and we could live there for free. In those days of political turmoil in Peking, business was slow in Eaton Square. In the spacious storerooms and empty offices we spent much of our time drawing pictures on the back of an unlimited supply of redundant visa application forms. Our drawing had advanced. I could make an expert representation of the motor car. Mother tried to teach us to write some Chinese characters, but with so many counter-claims on our time she had little success.

We were to be drilled into a squad of Chinese Cub Scouts. With four fully fledged scouts and a pack leader sent specially from China, we were to represent China at the International Boy Scout Jubilee to be held at Olympia. After a few days' drilling in the Square we were pronounced fit for service. It was embarrassing. We were not marching with precision, nor handling our boy-scout batons with ease. Moreover our green woollen jerseys were too long and the orange handkerchiefs were tied uncomfortably around our necks while the new brown caps swallowed up our tiny heads, perilously ready to fall off at the first gust of wind. But foolish or no, we were taken to the Royal Box at Olympia to be presented to some minor royal and a grand and decorated person whom I presumed to be Baden-Powell. Accustomed to prostrating ourselves and offering incense to the minor deities of the temples in Foochow, or to the spirits of ancestors resident in stone tablets in the ancestral halls, we were quite proficient in performing that part of the ceremony. After all this expert bowing and handshaking, one of the dignitaries was impressed enough to pin a bronze medal on to our uniforms. The engraved medal hung from a resplendent multi-coloured ribbon just like a real military medal. Armed with these Victoria Crosses we swaggered home.

Moving to Eaton Square necessitated our becoming boarders at the Kingsley School. The dormitory for the boarders was half a minute up the road from the school. We usually had our midday meal in the basement of the same building. Although they were not boiling down cabbage in the kitchen all the time, this dubious fragrance always assailed our nostrils.

Mother took us there and Charles and I both carried a suit-case containing our pyjamas, combinations, a change of clothing, a new toothbrush and toothpowder. We were always at pains to instruct people that Chinese also brushed their teeth every night before retiring. We were placed in a dormitory of seven to eight older girls. Kingsley was essentially a girls' school, with girls up to the ages of fifteen to seventeen. They took in boys only up until the second form. Each one of the half-dozen beds in the dormitory had full length surrounding drapes. The girls changed behind drawn curtains. Lights were out soon after 9 p.m., but we little boys were put to bed soon after 6.30 p.m. I had never been to bed so early, but they were even more barbarous; we had to change in broad daylight and weren't given an evening meal, only a couple of dry biscuits with a glass of cold slimy *milk* before retiring. This was not the sweetened condensed milk that we had learned to love in Foochow. Nobody in China drank pure milk or ate any other dairy product. Far from being a comfort to which we looked forward, the ritual became a kind of torture perpetrated by matron at bedtime.

It was mid winter when we moved into the dormitory, and by the summer we were still there, quarantined on account of mumps or measles. Being the only ones left in the dormitories, we were moved up to a small room on the very top floor. Since we were practically unsupervised we could climb up to the attic and poke our heads out through the skylight. On summer evenings, when a breeze blew in the waning sunshine, we let fly handfuls of down from a torn pillow, and delighted in the feathers being carried away in the breeze. At weekends mother would come and fetch us back to Eaton Square, making a detour to Piccadilly where we would have a Chinese high-tea at the Tanhua Lou (nowadays the Cathay Restaurant where the spring rolls and wuntuns remain much the same seventy years later), the very first Chinese restaurant to be established in Europe.

Before long we were on the move again. The Consulate General itself was moving to a place which could not accommodate the staff. Our new house was way out in the suburbs, at 174 Willesden Lane, Brondesbury – a long, forty-minute ride on the No. 8 bus, plus ten minutes' walk. It had a drive at the front and a long garden at the back, complete with a chicken run. After an initial exploration, we declared it was a suitable abode and not the social climb down we had been led to believe. There was much more space to run about. The chickens provided us with a job which we all knew well from Foochow and by climbing up to the top of the apple tree we had a good view over all the neighbouring gardens. It was early autumn and everything in the gardens appeared lush. The apples hung ripely in the trees and nature seemed rich and warm all around us.

Soon it was winter, and before long another Christmas. Father caught 'flu. I remember walking down to Kilburn to buy tangerines for him. The tangerines shone luminously under the glare of the gas lamps. Our bulk purchase necessitated flat wooden boxes which were awkward to carry home. The evening paper had to be bought from a newspaper vendor whose call was barely comprehensible, but by this time our command of English was nearly native and we could decipher most of his broad cockney. Down on the High Road was the State Cinema where we would escape in the afternoons when there was nothing better to do. There were round the clock shows with an orchestra or pianist improvising to the action. Sometimes the images were alarming and one showed someone tied down into a hole and drowned to death.

There wasn't any great celebration that Christmas. Father probably hadn't been paid for over a year and, only able to rely on his private means, was getting towards the end of his resources. On our last lap before retreating to China, we moved from Willesden to the wilderness of South London at the foot of Annerley Hill, Gypsy Hill. We also had to change our school. We attended the Junior part of Stoneleigh School. Judging from the school picture, I was, in those days, very thin with a long neck and large floppy ears like Fred Astaire.

Croydon Road, where we three boys and Qingqing took temporary lodging, was the last stop before we joined Mrs Hooper, with whom our youngest brother Michael was, for reasons we never fully understood, boarded out. The change of school was a wrench, but by now we spoke fluent English and it was not too difficult to make new friends. Besides, the house was not a humble shack and had the advantage of its proximity to Crystal Palace, where every Saturday evening there would be a great display of fireworks which we would watch from our bedrooms. In the afternoon we would visit the Palace and wonder at the great naval guns and the tiny biplanes which hung from the ceiling like kites. All these had recently seen action during the First World War. Just inside the Palace grounds there was a park with a winding stream and ponds, thick and overgrown with huge vegetation behind which monstrous dinosaurs lurked. Some prehistoric fear of these majestic beasts engendered in us a compulsive drive to make these afternoon trips and test the limits of our courage.

One early morning when there was no traffic on the roads Father took Charles and me up to the Crystal Palace Parade with a second-hand bicycle. Charles was always faster at learning anything new and in a leap he mounted the bicycle and was off. One spill and several trials later I followed on. Once I caught up with him, because of my superior stamina, I had no difficulty in keeping abreast. It always gave me great pleasure to feel his equal. Bicycling was one of the few things that father ever taught us.

When the day came for us to return to China I remember retracing our steps through France and boarding a Japanese cargo ship, the SS *Suwa Maru* in Marseilles. I wheeled my bicycle on to the deck to store it in the forecastle. Michael's absence did not strike us as strange. After all, our baby sisters, Anna and Mary, had been left with Granny in Foochow, so how did that differ from Michael's being left with Mrs Hooper? Besides, in our 'retreat' from Britain we were joined by Uncle Long who had come down from Glasgow. I was very pleased to have his company because his animated conversation made our voyage home something of a party. He prided himself on having been allowed to join the scrum of a famous Scottish rugby team. He also told me kung fu tales. To prove his toughness he asked me to hit him as hard as I could in the abdomen. I hurt my fist but he didn't even flinch. Secretly I thought I would like to become a kung fu master as well. What a worthy reason for returning to China. That was in 1922 and I was nearly nine. Long was a maternal uncle, a Wei. The Weis did not bend in the wind, they were too passionate. Forty-five years later Uncle Long died during the Cultural Revolution in a labour camp near the family coalmine in the Province of Henan, North China. In contrast, we Los were known to be unassertive (often to the point of inertia), occasionally brilliant, but always inscrutable enough to survive!

It was a breezy sunny day when our ship pulled out of Marseilles. I did not return again until the autumn of 1936, when the Civil War in Spain had been fought and lost by the Republicans, and in China the Long March had been marched by Mao's armies, and Japan was about to invade our divided country.

The *Suwa Maru* wasn't a patch on the *André Lebon*. But it still seemed grand to me. There was even a canvas swimming pool on the foredeck. We swam our way back to China. Uncle Long was our instructor. Although he was strong he had little grace and taught us to swim like frogs. We swam all the way through the Mediterranean and down to the Red Sea. We only stopped swimming when the roll of the sea in the Eastern Indian Ocean threatened to throw us out into the ocean like the baby with the bathwater. But by the end of the voyage we were confident enough to swim under water from one end of the pool to the other. Although we never progressed beyond swimming like frogs, we returned to China with no fear of water!

CHAPTER TWO
Lo Lodge

Red berries grow in the South Country,
When spring bursts with a few sprays,
I beg you to gather a few more,
For these, I most long for.

Wang Wei. AD 699–759

AT ITS BROADEST, Nantai island, the stretch of land between the two branches of the Min River, is about seven miles across, and from end to end about twelve. It is covered by gentle undulating hills and criss-crossed by canals and streams that connect the many villages of the southern suburbs of Foochow. In the northern part of the island, nearer the city, the population becomes more dense. Crowded together, the tall wooden dwellings often, as if by spontaneous combustion, burst into flames, so, from Yantai Shan (Smoke Platform Hill), the highest point of the district called Cangqian Shan (Hill Fronting the Warehouse), a fire watch is constantly maintained. It was on the top of the highest slopes beneath the shade of the pine trees and far from the city heat that western merchants and tea-planters came to stay. But with the decline in the tea trade in the last quarter of the nineteenth century, many of the British migrated to Ceylon and Assam, leaving their villas which were bought by the Chinese bourgeoisie or at least those who chose to emulate the foreigners.

Here amid the foreign settlement, superbly situated on the northernmost slope of the island overlooking the river and the city, my father managed to acquire a desirable property. He had been invited to tea in the house by a British estate agent and, discovering how cool and breezy it was, had settled the matter there and then for $10,000, an astronomical sum to pay for a house in those days. But with its echoes of British imperial splendour, the neighbourhood was the natural habitat for my father. Moreover, it was a decent distance from the milling crowd of relatives who still inhabited the original Lo family compound in the centre of the city. By retreating to the suburbs he would only have to see them at annual celebrations. Thus it was a safe haven where he could pass his time in pursuits befitting a gentleman who had been born with an ivory chopstick in his mouth. He named his newly acquired property 'Lo Lodge'.

My father, being the first-born, had inherited my grandfather's money, but not his passion for education. Not that he was illiterate: he had studied for three years at St Catherine's College, Cambridge and spoke some English with a heavy Tianjin accent. But his mind was never set on study and he had idled away his time at Cambridge punting on the Cam and rowing for his college. He had coxed for his team at Henley Regatta and had several glass-bottomed pewter cups to prove it. On the rare times that he became animated he would speak of wild parties after the team won and of how the boats would be ritually burned. It all seemed rather wasteful to us.

We wouldn't have believed his stories, but he had all the regalia of an Edwardian gentleman. He was the first student in Cambridge to own a motor car and had several yellowing, sepia photos of himself at the wheel of an open-top car, surrounded by a bevy of young ladies in long Edwardian dresses and wide hats. He must have been popular, although he never said so. His modesty did not stretch to his wardrobe. He had half a dozen Saville Row suits and dozens of hand-made shoes that he kept in immaculate condition by stuffing them with wooden shoe trees. And on Sundays we had roast for lunch and every day at 4.30 p.m., without fail, tea was served on the verandah. He had a silver teapot from which he poured a smoky-flavoured tea which was probably Earl Grey, a brand not easily purchased in Foochow.

Lo Lodge was easy to find on account of the four great trees that rose imperiously above the rooftops. One of these, a South American *Agathus danmara* at the bottom of the garden, had been planted as long ago as the 1840s. Eighty feet high, it was clearly visible against the horizon from a couple of miles down river. As there were no branches on the lower half of the trunk, it was a problem to climb. We could climb another South American tree that grew in the centre of the back garden. Its branches grew at regular intervals like radiating steps, so in this tree we built a tree house. From there we had a panoramic view of the river and could watch the fires which, from time to time, consumed the city below. I never knew why there was so much South American flora in Lo Lodge, although it must have been planted by the British. Pomelo trees with fruit as large as grapefruit lined the courtyard, lending a comfortable air of opulence.

Up the hill and along the leafy main street from the river, Lo Lodge, among a nest of sturdy, whitewashed Victorian mansions, stood out from the wooden homes. The walls were built three feet thick to guard against typhoon. Being fronted by the American Consulate, flanked by the French Consulate to the right and the Japanese Consulate to the left, Lo Lodge provided us with plenty of opportunity to observe ways of life unfamiliar to the average Chinese. Although we had little to do with the Japanese Consulate it was through watching the afternoon games on their sweeping lawn that I first became an ardent tennis fan. By the side of the court stood a huge earthenware jar filled with ice and water into which they would sink bottles of lemonade. When the heat was on, the tennis players could help themselves to refreshment and douse themselves with freezing water. Such were the joys of a civilization Japanese-style!

Here, where the creeping English rose draped itself over the iron railing high above the way and formed the barrier between our childhood world and the reality of traditional Foochow, was home.

Below us the teeming population went to and fro. For the most part the ordinary people went about their business as they had done for generations. Mostly from the farming community of the hinterland beyond, the men, women and children often staggered slowly up the incline bearing enormous mounds of food, vegetables and water on their backs. It was a long way from the city, over the great bridge, to the interior villages of Nantai island. Many were too poor even to afford a donkey and would have found their life's satisfaction in a couple of small fishing boats or a plot of land large enough to feed their family. From Lo Lodge their lives seemed quite remote.

From the railings we could watch the minute changes happening within our environment. With the memory of London taxis fresh in my mind, I'd watch with interest as the sedan chair was gradually replaced by the rickshaw. Some roadways were beginning to be constructed and ran from the suburbs to the city centre, providing a smooth track for the new wheeled vehicles. There was obvious pride among the rickshaw boys, for they were the new kings of the road and, sporadically breaking into a trot, they could keep up a pace 25 per cent faster than the sedans. The rickshaws themselves were a matter for competition; with their well-upholstered seats and gleaming, oil-fired lamps, they shone like beacons, and would dazzle you if you met one noiselessly turning a corner in the half light.

Ascending a little further up the hill towards the house, and passing along the full length of the front garden, the lane rose to the level of the main gate. When travelling by sedan chair our climb would seem simple, but the bearers would have a hard time of it, especially during the rains when the lanes became slippery.

Our house was rectangular, with green-painted shutters and a broad terracotta-tiled two-storey verandah which ambled the full hundred feet length and forty feet width of the house. My father had a mania for building and rebuilding and in a very short time had had the verandah partitioned into innumerable sections, adding ten rooms on either floor. With three enormous ground floor reception rooms and three roomy bedrooms on the first floor, we had nearly thirty rooms!

Every single room in the house was different and held its own special mystery for me. The central hall of the house was an impressive affair decorated with evergreens and chinaware drums which we could sit on. It was held up by two enormous red lacquered columns which greeted the visitor with all the pomp and ceremony of a Confucian temple. To the right of the door hung a scroll written by the great reformer Kang Youwei; to the left was a biography of my grandfather,

Sir Lo Fenglu, in the unmistakable calligraphy of Chen Baosun, my great-uncle and a tutor to the last emperor. Despite the grandeur, here was not the place for ancestral worship, a practice confined to the first floor. The only ancient present was our grandfather clock, which had been brought from Britain.

Next to the central hall the three principal reception rooms on the ground floor were furnished palatially. The drawing-room had an Edwardian flavour. A grand piano graced one corner and a tiger skin, central to the room, guarded the fireplace. At least he did until his position was usurped by a polar bear who had made the long trip back to Foochow from Peru, in the company of Uncle Yi who had been posted as ambassador there. My grandfather's mementoes had place of honour and were displayed where they could be best shielded from the crowds who often milled around the house. There were some Japanese ceramic pieces from the Imperial Palace in Tokyo, personally presented by Prince Ito at Shimonoseki. Prince Ito and my grandfather had been fellow students at Greenwich Naval College in the 1860s. In a glass display case there was a signed picture of Prince Bismarck of Germany, some colourful military sashes from Tsar Nicholas of Russia, some decorations from Italy and Belgium where he had been envoy, and grandfather's British insignia, including the honorary KCVO. Altogether it was a resplendent collection that never failed to remind us of the importance of having an ancestor with international diplomatic status. After all, it was thanks to him that the family enjoyed the privilege that it did.

Summer days in these sub tropics of Foochow were often dominated by the racket made by innumerable cicadas which seemed to increase in intensity with the heat and stillness of the day. The only way to escape it was to hide behind closed windows and let down the shutters, both to shade off the glare of the sun and to muffle the incessant noise of the insects. We would curl up in wicker chairs or on the upholstered sofas where the fabric felt deliciously cool. Sometimes we would fall into a snooze, but as often as not we lay awake day-dreaming. By the late afternoon a storm might brew up, so strong that it frequently blew open one of our doors or windows. Then we would fling open all the rest of the doors and windows and go out on to the verandah to enjoy the fresh winds.

From the verandah the garden opened out into a well-kept lawn where, when the heat of the afternoon receded, Father played croquet with his many guests or watered the exotic plants that he lovingly nurtured in the greenhouse. Such lawns were exclusive to the foreign settlement and a far cry from the dusty courtyards of Chinese homes.

Clusters of bright red fruits peeping out from between the dark green leaves of the lychee trees hung invitingly, weighing their boughs down nearly to the ground. Longyan fruits (dragon eyes), although not as attractive to the eye as lychees, are much sweeter and leave a pleasant after taste in the mouth. Father piled them into large glass buckets full of chipped ice. Although you can eat no more than half a dozen lychees at a time, an unlimited amount of dragon eyes still sit easily in the belly. Longyan and lychees are the true flavour of summer time in Foochow.

My father took his imitation of the 'English gentleman' very seriously and had even adopted the habit of 'rambling', an idiosyncrasy that any self-respecting Chinese scholar would resist. Come rain or blistering noonday shine, every day, armed with a walking stick and often in the company of a veritable 'rambling club' of my uncles, also brandishing walking sticks, he would sally out into the hills. But in the hills of Foochow the walking stick was more than just a fashion accessory. It was a weapon to be employed against rabid dogs.

On those intolerable summer days the temperature would begin to rise from early in the morning. At 6 a.m. pools of sunlight filtered through the shutters, throwing an orange glow around the bedroom walls on the upper verandah where we slept. By mid morning it could rise to over 30 degrees centigrade. As we all walked out in the narrow streets and down the ancient stone steps to the river the walls radiated as much heat as the sun itself. Every stone and tree, even the very ground, throbbed with enough heat to cook an egg. It became a test of endurance. You had to bring yourself to enjoy it, otherwise madness might ensue. As a last resort we'd lie in the upstairs bedroom and fetch water from the adjacent bathroom to douse clothes, body and all. On the hottest days I lay in a wet bed fanning myself. Charles, in the next bed, was always at his wits' end with the heat. He never really managed to pass the test, but after he had followed my instructions the soggy bed would give him sufficient peace of mind to fall asleep.

Yet even in his sleep Charles was often plagued, especially when he was suffering from a high fever. One night I awoke to a rustling in the corner of the room. Sitting up to investigate, through the dim light I made out the figure of my brother slipping out of the bedroom into the hall. I followed him out just in time to see him clear the window sill at the other end of the hall as if it were a hurdle. Fearing the consequences of leaping thirty feet to the granite path below, I rushed to the window. But I need not have worried. Charles had cleared the drop and was curled up fast asleep on the roof of the servant quarters, ten feet below and across the way. In a short while

Qingqing appeared on a ladder, gently coaxing him down with a cup of tea. That time he only sprained his ankles. However deranged and alarming Charles's nocturnal antics might have seemed, I had had time to get used to them. At Mrs Hooper's home in Croydon he had already sleepwalked across the room and given his foot a good toasting in the blazing fire. After this last incident the two of us were made to sleep on the ground floor at night.

The eccentricity of the Los expressed itself most in my brother's daring. He was always much bolder than I. He would often walk on the two to three inch wide window ledges of our house, some twenty feet above the ground. Below was granite paving. But there he would be again, with his back pressed up against the wall, edging his way along, and his eyes staring at me as though to say, 'Look at me, I'll never fall!' One time he really scared me. He clambered along the branch of a huge walnut tree that grew over the garden railings far above the iron spikes. I imagined those blunt spikes piercing him through the chest and neck. It was surely going to be the end of him, but he carried on performing his inane antics with his legs loosely wrapped around the branch. While he was up there taking a break and relaxing before his next trick, I walked away to give my nerves a rest. When I returned a few minutes later I saw to my great relief that he was on dry land. He looked at me with his typical pinched, quizzical look, as though to say, 'Nuts to you!'. When an adult behaves in a peculiar manner he is generally described as eccentric, when an eight-year old behaves so strangely he is just plain 'nuts'.

But it was not always summer in Foochow. When winter came it was colder than one would imagine. Some winters were freezing. In many places there were no heating arrangements at all. Ours was an exception. As it was constructed by an Englishman it had a fireplace in almost every room, including the bedrooms. From my days in London I had learned exactly how a fire should be built and would light one in our bedroom where we would listen to ghost stories and watch the lights flickering on the walls. The thump of chestnuts falling to the ground in the garden, from time to time, was like the tolling of church bells.

What I enjoyed most was eating oysters by the blazing fires. We didn't eat raw oysters. Foochow oysters were cultivated on bamboo sticks, stuck into the sandflats in the shallow water. When mature they were harvested by simply uprooting the sticks which they clustered around. The easiest way of cooking the oysters was in their own shells. By turning the bamboo over a blazing fire the shells would soon pop open with the oysters ready cooked. We prised them from

their shells with a fork or chopsticks and ate them hot. By pressing
your lips, being careful not to scorch them, up against their shells,
you could lick or suck up some of that incomparable oyster liquor.
This way not just a dozen or a dozen and a half, but half a hundred
could easily be consumed in one sitting. Those winter evenings were
memorable indeed!

When spring came around the great clumps of bamboo that formed
the boundary to the east of the garden shot up almost an inch a day.
Before a month was out some of them were taller than me. Following
the bamboo hedge and rockeries down to the end of the triangular
garden you came to a courtyard where our lower kitchen and servant
courtyards were situated. Steam rose in a leisurely fashion from the
lower kitchen where huge pots were daily filled with rice and congee
(soft rice). Outside in the courtyard there was a disused well and a
slab of stone where the firewood was chopped with a heavy blunt-
edged chopper. This was the scene for acts of great martial prowess.
We would try to cleave several blocks of wood in a single blow. I
don't remember ever achieving this, though once I did kill a duck
with a single blow. Qingqing followed on by slitting its throat,
leaving it to flap all over the courtyard.

After their late night mahjong parties our parents didn't rise till
midday. We were thus on intimate terms with all the servants. They
looked after us when we weren't having lessons. They gave us our
breakfast of porridge, toast and jam, with Nestlés condensed milk.
Besides Qingqing there was Lingling, the eldest and most respected
of our household staff who, in his traditional white cloth socks and
ankle ties, had come from the Nanyang Lo family compound to be
the head servant. Then there was Yongyong, a younger servant and
almost a fifth son to my father, a new cook called Kuozui (Big
Mouth) and two sedan chair bearers called Gogo and Damei. Damei
was a muscly fellow and it was always a mystery that he had been
given a nickname that meant 'big sister'. But elderly men were often
so called in the local language. All these elder servants treated us as if
we were family, but still maintained a degree of respect, addressing
us as the 'Little Young Master'. I was 'Little Young Master 2'. But
many of the 'upstairs downstairs' distinctions had become blurred in
Lo Lodge. In every room there was a bell pull for summoning the
servants that registered the source of the ring on a dropping gadget
behind the back staircase. Over the years it had become decrepit and
when you pulled it it only gave out a muffled tinkle. The washing up
was done crouching over buckets outside the back door instead of at
the heavy porcelain sink that I remembered from Fitzjohn's Avenue.

In addition to these old hands there were numerous maids in my mother's and grandmother's service, making a household staff of some fifteen people. Some of them were still children and could only be regarded by us as playmates. They were all good fun and, hailing from the southern villages of Nantai island, always added an extra dimension to our sheltered lives. We learned from them about the lives of ordinary folk, and from their endless gossiping we could keep ourselves tuned in to the events that were going on outside Lo Lodge. Among them they had many connections and would bring all manner of people into the house. Sometimes we would listen to story-tellers on the verandah, and for parties they would bring in travelling entertainers who would stage lively tales of local gods and demons. Other times they brought in fortune-tellers. One told me that I would live to a great age because I had long earlobes and a large space between my nose and upper lip. I, too, had the feeling I would live to a great age because of the care I would always take in negotiating the stepping stones and trip-wires of this world. Charles would have a long life because he was charmed.

Being free of parental supervision during the mornings, we developed the habit of checking through Father's pockets to see if he had won at mahjong. He was always generous, and if he'd won at night would frequently give the servants a ten dollar note for opening the door. So we didn't consider it thieving, just sharing out the spoils.

On a good day we could siphon off a few crisp notes and go down town to buy sweetmeats, baked buns, olives and sesame snacks. It was half a mile to the great Stone Bridge, down a narrow street and past the many carpenters and street vendors. Life was not easy for the average native, but it was never without flavour. There were delicious foods: an endless variety of seafoods, succulent lychees, dragon eyes and juicy tangerines, not to speak of the city's renowned soya sauce that could elevate plainly cooked foods to *haute cuisine*. The local 'red wine sediment paste' that provided the soya with its distinctive flavour could be used to cook or preserve meat and seafood and added an appealing winy flavour. There was dried and powdered meat and fish which could be sprinkled over rice porridge for breakfast.

With continuous building and renovating of the wooden dwellings the street was full of the sound of chopping and sawing and the smell of fresh sawdust always hung in the air. When combined with pungent wafts from the earthen pots filled with wine sediment paste that were piled up high in great splashes of red and magenta, we barely noticed the general stench of the city streets.

When our pockets were flush with change we could go to one of the riverside bars and order several bowls of sesame paste noodles and a cup of tea. This was poor man's food, but we still considered it an indulgence. The plain boiled noodles tossed in a large spoonful of sesame paste, a medium spoonful of soya sauce, and a pinch of chopped spring onion made a snack to delight even the young connoisseur. When the fishing boats came home, for a few cents you could buy a basketful of the freshest crab claws. The crabs conveniently discarded their claws when caught; these needed to be boiled and cracked open and, with the tender pinkish white flesh dipped in a marinade of vinegar or soya sauce with chopped ginger or garlic, made for an orgy of gastronomic delight. Sitting at the tables we would while away the morning watching the ebb of the river reflecting patterns that moved lazily across the walls of the shop. In the background there was always the continuous ticking sound of the proprietor's fingers flicking the beads of the abacus back and forth, while on the sampan, parked nearby, his wife was busy preparing the family's meals or sorting the endless array of goods and chattels that were kept on board.

On our return and after our parents had come to and been served breakfast in bed, we were honoured with the leftovers – more toast and tea, although by this time it had generally gone quite cold. It must have been then that I developed a taste for cold tea. In the afternoons, when we weren't called to have hot afternoon tea with the adults and their silver teapot, we could play in the garden. The garden held many delights for us. We could picnic in the sampan swing, roller skate or charge up and down the concrete patio on our trikes. Our parents had bought the sampan swing when the Oswalds, a British family working in telecommunications, had returned to the West. The sampan had been hauled up the hill by ten servants and strung between two maple trees. On the day it arrived ten of us piled into the boat and had a great celebratory feast. Unfortunately the swinging of the sampan was too life-like, and as if picnicking on the high seas, all those without an iron digestion had to bale out to dry land, clutching their churning stomachs!

Before we went to school in 1926 we had very few Chinese friends. Having little contact with mainstream life on the Min River, we only came across Chinese children on the odd family occasions and then they were only our first and second cousins. So we contented ourselves with our little family of six brothers and sisters. Mary was growing into a pretty child and is most remembered for the speed with which she ran the circuit around the garden. Charles always staged highly competitive races giving the youngest a head start and finishing the race at the round Moon Gate in the wall. Not being endowed with powerful legs, Anna was always secretly disgruntled with her handicap and treated the regular contests with some suspicion. But Charles was insistent and, ever respectful of his greater age and authority, Anna always submitted without open revolt.

Michael came home with Uncle Yi, cousin Becee and the polar bear. Becee was no longer a baby, and was almost a western child, with a sophistication that could only be learned from an upbringing in the diplomatic service. Michael had been in England for six years in the care of Mrs Hooper, who hadn't been paid. On passing through London, Uncle Yi had remembered him and had to bail him out before bringing him home via Peking and Shanghai. It was never clear to us whether it was as a result of a birth trauma or ill-treatment by Mrs Hooper, that Michael became quite deaf, but the signs of that ailment were already evident. I first came across him again on the landing upstairs. He was pointing at the goldfish that we kept there in glass jars. His little mouth was gaping 'fish . . . fish'. I felt sorry and a little sad for this strange and lonesome little fellow who couldn't even speak his mother tongue.

In those early years we had as many European and American playmates as we did Chinese. There were friends in the French Consulate, and we shared the same French teacher with one Mary-Lou Price from the American Consulate. The teacher was a White Russian emigré who taught us to dance the hornpipe and Cossack dances on bent knees. There were Don and Bright Munson. Bright wasn't really bright but very cheerful, but Don was impressively big and could out-box me until one day I floored him with my greater speed and flexibility. Then there was the son of Mr Lacey the technical missionary, a cunning piece of work. Most of all I was taken with Marion Gossard, the daughter of an American doctor. With her beautiful complexion and lithe and voluptuous movement she was easily the most beautiful creature I had ever seen. The Walshams lived on the other side of the Japanese Consulate and appeared to be richest of all. This should have been no wonder, for China was suffering the indignity of having foreigners controlling its overseas trade and Mr Walsham was the Commissioner of the Maritime Customs in Foochow. He was in charge of levying all taxes, a proportion of which was deducted as a reparation for the Boxer Rebellion. They had a daughter called Joyce who was very well brought up but not half as beautiful as Marion. Joyce had two huge dogs, a golden retriever who went by the name of Kitchener and a fat, short-haired bitch called Betty.

By far the largest piece of ground on Cangqian Shan belonged to the British Consulate General. Mr Giles was the Consul General. He had a brother who was in charge of the Chinese section of the British Museum. We talked together about London and he took a shine to me, promising to be my guardian should I ever wish to go to Britain again. Every year on Empire Day they would hold a celebration on their huge front lawn to which we would be invited. There was a Three-legged Race, the Potato Sack Race and of course the Egg and Spoon. I loved the competition and took great pleasure in beating these foreign-devil children at their own games. Charles always won the sack race.

Charles and I never felt the least bit out of place with the English children. After all, we had spent most of our lives in London and, as far as class and education were concerned, our grandfather could not be bettered. Our dining-room was at the opposite end of the house to the drawing-room. It had an extendable dining-table capable of seating at least twenty people. There was a huge mahogany mantelpiece to the left of the window which had been carved into a multi-storey pavilion which scaled most of the wall. Although the 'pavilion' had a myriad of little shelves and display cases in the form of miniature terraces, not a single *objet d'art* had been placed into it and instead of fulfilling its purpose of adorning the room it gave off an air of barren grandeur. On the left was a portrait of Tsar Nicholas and on the right, where in British households a picture of a hunting scene or the 'Stag at Bay' would be hung, instead there was a hand-sketched picture of the House of Commons in session. Among the distinguished crowd in the Visitors' Gallery one could faintly discern a person, very like my grandfather, sporting a skull cap.

Although I was not born until nearly a dozen years after my grandfather's death there was an abundance of his possessions around us. Apart from his mementoes that took place of honour on the ground floor the fruit of his academic career was stored upstairs. Around the enclosed verandah in the north-east corner of the upper house was an L-shaped library which contained thousands of volumes, both in Chinese and English. It was said that some of the Chinese books were extremely valuable, rare editions. During his time at Greenwich Naval College and as envoy, my grandfather's favourite hobby had been foraging around book shops. The landau waited patiently outside while this Chinese minister, clad in his long high-necked gown, browsed at leisure. He must have had a pretty catholic taste: the library contained such books as *Jane's Fighting Ships*, a volume of the *Problems of Nautical Astronomy and Navigation* and a pamphlet on 'Indeterminate Equations', both of which my grandfather had translated into Chinese, *Encyclopaedia Britannica*, beautifully illuminated volumes of Tennyson and Dickens, some bound copies of *Punch* and a magazine called *Truth*. The bookshelves in the library mounted to the ceiling which, being a typical house of the semi-tropical region, was probably more than 18 feet high. Since I was not possessed of a catholic nature, most of the literature was of little use to me. The best entertainment the library could offer me was clambering up to where *Jane's Fighting Ships* was stored on the top shelf and then, with closed eyes, leaping down. And then there were the model ships. They were not toys but prototypes measuring six or seven feet long. All the details of the ships, including the detachable lifeboats, were crafted with meticulous detail. Perhaps they had been presented to my maternal grandfather when he was ordering merchant vessels and warships from British shipyards. My own favourite was a grey warship, equipped with rapid-firing guns, which resembled a modern-day frigate of the type that was not delivered to China in time for the 1895 Sino-Japanese War, and was so sorely missed in the sea battle off Yalu.

There was a lot of literature to remind us of my two grandfathers' early association at the Foochow dockyard and China's first Naval College. As the College was taught by a team of European supervisors, much of our library was in French and English. Admiral Wei Han had studied mathematics and ship construction in the French school, while Lo Fenglu had graduated from the English school, having learned arithmetic, geometry, algebra, rectilinear and spherical trigonometry, astronomy and the calculations of navigation. Lo Fenglu was the only Chinese person to be taken on to the teaching staff once the Europeans were disbanded in 1874. The academic example of the two men was both brilliant and daunting to follow. At night the library was unlit and took on a forbidding air.

In fact my paternal grandfather was ever present around the house. His presence could be felt all over the library, but his spirit seemed to reside more vividly in the stone tablet on the altar at the top of the stairs. Standing beside him were the spirits of other ancestors including my own grandmother. To look at, the stone tablets were no more than upright blocks, like large ink stones, displaying the name and official rank of their owners, but the degree of solemnity and respect that was conferred upon them made the atmosphere of the room austere. Moreover the chairs placed in front of the altar did nothing to alleviate the atmosphere. They were part of a suite of furniture made from the hardwood of my grandmother's outer coffin. It is not clear whether it was frugality, Anglophilia or some strange romanticism that possessed my grandfather to recycle the coffin that he had dutifully had transported from Britain in 1900.

On the birthdays and anniversaries of our ancestors, dinner was prepared for them. Five or six dishes of the finest fare were placed before the altar. Candles were lit and Father placed handfuls of burning incense sticks into the urn in front of the tablets. We children filed along behind him kowtowing and bringing more incense. From the way my father conducted the ritual I was never quite sure how serious he was, but the event was heightened by the stultifying fragrance around the altar and the consciousness of elders in the spirit world intent upon our performance. There was some compensation. The ancestors could improve our fortune by helping with the family business or in our examinations. Even better than this we got to eat the food, but only after they'd made off with the finest nourishing essence. Fortunately they didn't seem to care much about the taste. This was the part of the ceremony that my father took most seriously.

The oldest ancestress was my paternal grandmother. Although not my own grandmother she was my grandfather's second wife. My real grandmother was the one who had perished in London and whose coffin wood was now before the altar. Second Granny was still alive and lived in a granny flat, perilously close to the tablets, where she whiled away the time counting beads. She suffered with rheumatic pains and spent her days reclining on a couch. Her two personal maids, one still a child, were clad in blue batik jackets and loose trousers and fussed around massaging her aching limbs or pounding her with a soft pummel. Despite being only a step-grandmother she was held in awe by many in the family and I was her favourite. She always treated me kindly. Sometimes I would attend to her. She was a skinny little thing and seemed very old, even though she was probably no more than fifty. In the summer she would sit out on the verandah and then I would cool her with the swing fan. The swing fan had a six-foot wooden frame upholstered with thick beige woven cotton and was hung from the ceiling. When I operated the rope pulley it sent gentle gusts of wind back and forth along the verandah.

The afternoon was the best time to visit her apartment as she would take her supper early, and being quite advanced in age, her appetite had decreased so that she never quite managed to finish her meal, leaving plenty for us to scavenge. Being a practising Buddhist she was therefore mainly a vegetarian, although she did indulge in eating seafood. No doubt she felt that if she did not harm living things, when the time came, her chances of entering one of the better Buddhist heavens would be improved. Her maid prepared fabulous

vegetarian soups from turnips and mushrooms, of which I have yet
to taste the like. One of her favourite dishes for 'high tea' was a hot
pot of leeks, french beans, oysters and noodles, cooked freshly over
charcoal on the table. For a young hungry body this was one of the
most succulent treats available.

There was no greater mystery in the house than the contents
of Grandmother's tallboy. I knew that she kept her jewellery and
savings in there and when she felt like specially indulging us she
would bring out strings of Yuan Shikai silver coins which were four
times the size of British half-crowns. What other treasures were also
tucked away inside was a secret that she kept to herself. Despite her
age and frailty Grandmother still had a very astute mind, and was
at the helm of managing what was left of the family fortune.
Twice weekly the bookkeeper would report to her about her two
businesses, the pawnshop and the teashop. We would listen to her
issuing instructions and discussing stratagem with him. Occasionally
we would accompany her to town in a sedan chair to oversee the shops.

Being the eldest and therefore the most venerated of the members
of the household, my grandmother's birthday on 16 October was the
occasion for the most lavish of celebrations. My father, who loved
parties, saw that the occasion was conducted with the proper ritual
befitting to a woman of her age and status. Autumn was chrysanthemum season and he would bring in three or four hundred pots so
that the house was aflame with vibrant colour. From early morning
the whole household was on the move: the contract caterers would
arrive to set up stoves around the garden, a troupe of actors would
be ordered to perform local plays in the hall, while mother bustled
around overseeing the preparations. At noon the guests would begin
to arrive. As was customary, they would be greeted with a bowl of
chicken noodle soup, garnished with shredded ham. This was designed
to stave off their hunger and give them a taste of the delicacies soon to
come. Everyone came in their best costumes; the gentlemen in black
satin gowns and skullcaps with coloured topknots that denoted their
official rank. The ladies were clad in more colourful robes with rectangular embroidered panels fronting their skirts. Over the top they
wore a short jacket, finished with trim and piping. Although there
would be few diamonds on display there was always an impressive
array of pearls and jades, cut and set into all shapes and sizes.

All the while my grandmother would still be reclining in her
apartment upstairs, away from the swamping crowds, receiving
only the select few. My father received close relatives and civic
dignitaries while my mother would be left to entertain the whole

phalanx of aunts, uncles and cousins. At less celebrated occasions the fare was seldom first-rate, but there was always a lot to eat and the appearance of each dish was as grand as the name it was given. No wonder many poorer friends and relatives gained the reputation of being 'professional eaters'. With a nose for the location of the next party they would move from one private celebration to another to keep their bellies filled, mingling with the guests, yet conspicuous in the same old robes that were stained and threadbare from their constant round of free-eating and socializing.

My mother was also the true centre of our little world. She provided us with all the love, affection and guidance that we needed. Being a typical member of the Wei family she took ease and pleasure in company. Whenever the opportunity presented itself she was always to be found gossiping freely. In the winter we would crowd around the fire and read the classics together, or she would tell us tales of her childhood on the banks of the Whampoa part of the Pearl River. She was undoubtedly the stronger and more quick witted of my parents, and coming from a large and distinguished naval family she had grown up amid the wealth and privilege that surrounded the Whampoa Naval College where Wei Han, her father, was Director. They had stables, boats and a firing range so that while other young ladies still had their feet bound she had managed to pick up some literary skills, could ride and swim and was a crack shot.

Whampoa Naval College, along with the famous Military Academy, was the training ground for China's brightest and most progressive young men.

Being well connected she could, and was more inclined to, pull strings. It was due to her that my father had landed the appointment of Commissioner of Foreign Affairs in Foochow and had graduated to any official status at all. After more of her manoeuvering he became the Commissioner of Foreign Affairs for the whole of the province and was responsible for liaising between the administration and the ever-changing military governors. Although he worked in a huge building and was in charge of twenty staff he never seemed to do much. We never thought of him as an important person, nor did he ever try to impress us with his status.

Perhaps because she was dissatisfied with my father's lack of inclination to get on in the public world, she often accused me of falling into the same indolent ways. It was not that she censured leisure pursuits. She always accompanied my father to his mahjong parties and herself led a busy social life during the day. Entertaining was her great love and she was quite accustomed to it. With numerous eligible sisters her own family had always been surrounded by a crowd of suitors. When her father had been Principal of the South-West Military Academy in Guilin my father had opened a riding school nearby and then followed the Wei family to the Whampoa River where, no doubt, he attracted her attention with his prowess at rowing.

Sometimes she would go home to her family in Shanghai, bringing back mountains of presents for us, and cautionary tales of the wild Mao cousins. But others in the Wei family had married well and, after her distinguished and exciting childhood in cosmopolitan Canton and Shanghai, it must have been frustrating to find herself stranded in medieval Foochow with six children and a husband who had virtually chosen an early part-time retirement.

Our parents sometimes had harsh words. We were, for the most part, sheltered from them, yet you could sense the tensions and sometimes hear my father shouting. As a consequence of her dissatisfaction with my father, Mother transferred all her hopes into us, and took great delight in our small successes. She was especially proud of Charles, who was both the first-born and the one who displayed the most aptitude, yet she never pushed us and was always scrupulously fair. Being in Britain must have allowed her to absorb new ways and she treated the girls with the same indulgence and respect as she did us, making sure that they were educated to the same standard.

'Identity crisis' was not an issue in the China of our youth. I was number two and Charles was number one. Every boy had a definite number in the family roll call. As gender equality did not stretch to this tradition the girls, who would probably be entering another family through marriage, had no number in the all-important family hierarchy. Just as they too were not to be graced with spirit tablets unless they had provided male heirs, they were known as first or second sister among their direct siblings or simply by their first names. The male roll call spanned the extended family to all the cousins of our generation. However, it excluded those born to our father's sisters. You might be the first son of your own father, but since within the extended family the counting started from the first of the male progeny of your father's eldest brother, if there were a dozen male cousins that preceded you by birth, you were only number thirteen. Henceforth you would be called the thirteenth brother. Although my father was the eldest son of my grandfather, my grandfather was one of thirty-one children, so on the larger family roll call my father was number nineteen. Since nearly all family events, whether birthdays or other celebrations, invariably involved the family at large, I heard him called nineteenth brother much more often than he was called number one.

A person's position on the family map was not only defined by latitude but also by longitude, and his position in the entire family chronology, stretching back generations, was defined by the 'family poem'. In the case of the Lo family the poem is eighty words long, and at Xiao we are the fortieth word, and therefore the fortieth generation since this poetic device was originated. If each generation represents twenty-five years, then one thousand years have gone by, and there will be one thousand years before the cycle begins again.

I often reflected on those one thousand years of family history. The Tang dynasty (AD 618–907) did not seem remote. In fact I imagined that little had changed in the humdrum world outside our garden railings. But as for a thousand years hence .. . that was another matter. Through the years that followed our return from Britain, I was vaguely aware of a world, somewhere, that was accelerating into the future at a much greater velocity than my immediate environment.

Lying on my parents' bed on the verandah I could see the white flagpole that shot proudly up from our neighbour's lawn. On top the red rising sun of the Imperial Japanese flag fluttered against the blue sky and the careering clouds. Was it heralding a new day through the thick foliage of the horsechestnut tree? And what of being Chinese in this new day – what did that mean?

But these were only idle reflections. In my little world goals were comparatively limited. These were still pre-school years. At ten I had no Creator to satisfy, just the people who surrounded me, or at the most my ancestors. And besides, I seemed to lead a charmed life with another bowl of chicken noodle soup always around the next corner. The sun was always shining, life was a 'team game' still played to prescribed patterns with little time to enquire into such lofty questions as 'the meaning of life'.

羅姓排行字

字			行		排			姓	羅
叔	公	伯	彦	成	經	用	十	應	咸
福	永	克	興	東	光	顯	茂	知	以
穆	昭	敦	嗣	賢	來	時	念	道	享
祿	常	食	業	德	新	日	本	貴	富
章	豫	振	名	芳	烈	鴻	前	孝	忠
裳	冠	萃	代	歷	第	甲	榮	朝	累
長	瑞	國	才	英	遠	聲	家	學	理
祥	麟	叢	衍	慶	實	秀	同	初	雲

CHAPTER THREE
Tigers in the Hills

The city is a seat of great trade and great manufactures. The people are Idolators and subject to the Great Kaan. And a large garrison is maintained there by that prince to keep the kingdom in peace and subjection. For the city is one which is apt to revolt on very slight provocation . . .

The Travels, Marco Polo. Foochow, 13th century

MY BROTHERS AND I soon followed my father's example and took to rambling. For a short walk we would go a couple of miles around to Lianghou (Behind the Hillock) and come back via a village named Dahu (The Large Lake) which was, in fact, no more than a polluted pond. For a four-hour ramble we'd go as far as Guojie Shan (High Ridge Mountain) which was the backbone of Nantai island, running east to west and following the course of the river. When we were feeling even more adventurous we would walk the whole way across the island to our aunt's house, taking a day to go there and back. The walks gave us a sense of sturdiness and independence. Although I did not have muscular legs, the excursions would never exhaust me and I took pleasure in the growing strength of my body.

We could have gone much further but the hinterland of the province had no roads and people never went there except in sedan chairs. The upper reaches of the Min in the sparsely populated northern highlands were blanketed with the only forests left in South China and it was from there that the country folk poled timber rafts all the way down the river to the town. In the remote hills the soil was so poor that farmers could only eke out a living planting tea and sweet potatoes. Tea had been planted for eleven centuries around Foochow and there were many kinds and qualities to be had. There was black tea and green tea. The most common was jasmine tea and when the bushes blossomed the girls would wear the flowers in their hair. One of the best teas was called the 'Iron Goddess of Mercy'.

The farmers never cut down trees for firewood and what coal there was was consumed by the Japanese electricity plant. Wood used for fuel could only be gathered from the forest floor on family 'wood gathering' expeditions. Because of this protection the hills around Foochow grew wild with shrubs and flowers. In spring time the slopes were aglow with the hues of wild azalea.

Gushan (Drum Mountain – 3,000 ft), towering to the east of Foo-chow, descends abruptly on the Min River. The path up the mountain travels through rugged and rocky ravines, barren in many places and in others covered in trees and brushwood. From there we could get a fine view of the Min valley, with its river winding through it, studded with junks and sampans and covered with green fields and canals.

On the summit was Yongquan (Boiling Spring) Monastery. Since the eighth century people had believed that the temple was protecting the town. It attracted many pilgrims on account of one of Buddha's teeth that was supposedly preserved there. One of the largest monasteries in China, Yongquan monastery was a sanctuary for some 3,000 Buddhist monks. But we used to go there to see the herds of pigs, goats and flocks of poultry that were allowed to live out their natural life span. It still stands there today, although somewhat reduced in size and circumstances since Liberation.

In the summer when the valleys became overbearingly hot the whole family would decamp to our villa on Drum Mountain. Often we would set out a month before our parents and lodge temporarily on the first floor of a shack belonging to a farming family. These farmers were not sophisticated cooks. We had a kind of veal and potato goulash for supper. It was very tasty at first but then was monotonously served up for several weeks. But it was nourishing food especially when taken between the tumblers of diluted condensed milk we drank for breakfast and tea. At night we listened to the grunts and squeaks of pigs and cows. They seemed very close through the cracked floorboards downstairs.

When our parents joined us we would move up to our own summer house amid the hill settlement of the foreign tea planters and missionaries on Drum Mountain Ridge. All the houses were built of granite with thick typhoon walls and long verandahs propped up with stout wooden pillars. There was a tennis club with six courts nearby, so life became a constant round of tennis matches, long hikes or swimming in deep pools made by damming the streams.

From the first floor window of Lo Lodge and over the tops of the trees we could see clearly the summit of Gu Shan (Drum Mountain). It was seldom shrouded in mist and cloud, so with Father's racing binoculars we could pick out the outline of the hamlets on the upper slopes. Most interesting of all we could see a sheet of white water cascading out of the mountainside. Drum Mountain was the furthest we would go on a day's ramble, and we would often go in search of that sheet of water. We never found it, despite tracing many streams to their source. We were repeatedly warned by villagers that if there was a cloudburst we should get out of the streams immediately. We were always waiting for a cloudburst, but it never came. It seemed a bit of a tall story. But the tell-tale flattened grass, ten feet up either bank of the stream, made us a little wary when a storm was threatening.

One day we decided to venture onto the north side of Drum Mountain. We had already made the three-hour hike up the mountain and arrived at 'Tipping Rock'. 'Tipping Rock' must have weighed some ten tons and was balanced precariously on another boulder which allowed it to be rocked back and forward with a touch of the hand. As we skirted the rock we all gave it a tip before we began our descent. The far side of the mountain took us five miles inland. Wild pigs, tigers and leopards inhabited the semi-tropical thickets that covered the slopes and valleys. We armed ourselves with sticks. It took an hour jumping from rock to rock, to the valley floor. Down at the bottom it was eerily quiet. We wandered through a couple of deserted hamlets, gripping our cudgels even more tightly.

Down in the fertile valleys 2,000 feet below the summit of the mountain the temperature was much higher and it was coming on to midday. The sun beat down, parching our throats. We followed the sound of water and, finding a stream, immersed ourselves, taking long, cool sips. It was a pleasant sensation. We were in a company of six, and one of the boys pulled out his harmonica, thinking to entertain us with a tune. As he put it to his lips he loosened his grasp and it fell into the water. I watched it shimmering as it rapidly sank with its silvery casing reflecting the noonday sun. In a moment it was gone – with its owner in hot pursuit. He soon re-surfaced, and two others dived in.

I felt more sure of myself. Grabbing a huge rock and cradling it in my lap, I took a deep breath and jumped in feet first. With the weight of the rock I could feel myself sinking quickly. The light began to fade and I could only see a tiny sparkle at the surface. Suddenly a new fear overtook me. Perhaps there was some unknown beast lurking in the deep! I let go of the rock and clawed my way upwards like a madman. It took a dozen strokes before I reached the surface. I'll never know what possessed me. Normally it was Charles that took risks. He would swim within a hair's breadth of swirling whirlpools in the Min River. But cold water terrified me. That day our roles reversed and I risked my life for the sake of an harmonica. Perhaps the heat had gone to my head and, in fever, I had lost my reason. We didn't recover the harmonica. Three hours later we signalled our return by tipping the 'Tipping Rock'.

Not more than a dozen miles from Foochow the range of mountains that stretch out to the north-west and east descended into wild gullies and ravines, still covered by thick semi-tropical shrub. Here the big cats roamed. Around our summer retreat I used to see local farmers ensnaring leopards in wooden-framed bamboo-and-wire cages. Because leopards were smaller than tigers the farmers seemed to regard them with scant respect, swinging the cage nonchalantly from a shoulder pole as if it were no more than a large basketful of live poultry. We used to listen with rapt attention to stories that our sedan-chair bearers told of their escapades with tigers. If there was a story to be told it had to be of proper tigers, despite the fact that leopards were supposed to be more dangerous.

Some of the tigers were man-eaters and the stories of victims, who escaped with their limbs half-chewed off, were riveting. When half-eaten animal carcasses were strewn around the village it attracted man-eaters. The villagers would suddenly be struck with a tangible fear, although they were no more stricken than if ghosts had been reported to be prowling about. The antidotes for tigers and ghosts appeared curiously similar: clashing gongs and flaming torches would certainly deter any approach, or at best even scare them away. No animal or ghost in its right mind would brave those huge gongs which boomed like cannon fire, or the large flaming torches wielded by those unlikely flame throwers. Most people in Fujian knew about ghosts and tigers. Guns and knives are no deterrent to a cat, no matter how small it might be, but the sight of fire and smoke and the clanging of gongs show off without a doubt the superior power of humanity!

But our poor family doctor, one Dr Moorhead and his Scottish wife, had neither a gong nor a flaming torch with them when they were carried up the mountainside. That summer morning they were bound for their mountain retreat, but had made the mistake of setting out too early in the season. Both of the two sedan chairs were carried by five bearers with two men behind and three in front.

At the side of the mountain path the face of a huge cat peeped out of the dense foliage. With only the mildest hint of a growl from the astonished tiger the ten sedan-chair carriers unceremoniously dumped the two sedan chairs and leaped down the mountainside at the speed of light. They knew the local saying, 'when running away from a tiger leap downhill'. Tigers, like cats, have long back legs and short front legs and therefore dislike leaping downhill. Similarly when running away from a huge snake always run zig-zag. It is very inconvenient for heavy snakes to work up the speed to pounce at rapidly changing angles! Once in the safety of the bushes below, the bearers lay low till they knew that they were not being pursued.

But what of the doctor and his poor wife? There was no sound of tearing limbs in the undergrowth. When they had plucked up enough courage to return to the scene of the inevitable carnage, they found the doctor and his wife still sitting there in the sedan chairs. Mrs Moorhead had taken the precaution of opening her parasol to protect her complexion from the fierce sun. Perhaps she also intended to use it to ward off the leap of the tiger.

Apparently the tiger was not a compulsive man-eater and, deciding that white flesh held little appeal to him, had simply stalked off in disgust. The incident made a deep impression on the Moorheads and they never again wandered up the mountains so early in the season, no matter how hot. The story also made a deep impression on me. I began to practise leaping downhill.

Marco Polo said that there were cannibals in the hills of Fujian. That was slanderous. There were no man-eaters except tigers, snakes and possibly a few ghosts with unsavoury habits. Much more likely to be a problem on a dark night were the bandits that roamed the hills. Townspeople reinforced the city walls and gates and houses were shut up as soon as dusk fell. People didn't travel at night and anyone who was lurking about was automatically assumed suspicious.

We could see the bandit regions from the top of Tiger Head Mountain which looked over the southern straits of Nantai island above my aunt's house. There were no bridges crossing the river at any point from here all the way to the sea, nor were there regular ferry services. The only way to cross was to hire a sampan or a motor launch. But city dwellers would not dream of going there, except in times of famine when the poor would take to the hills in droves to plunder neighbouring villages or imperial envoys. The best known bandit was Lou Xingpan. I knew little of him and could only refer to the famous bandits of the Ming dynasty novel *The Water Margin* to fill out the gaps in my fantasy. To keep command Lou Xingpan must have had some kind of understanding with the local security forces but later, when more organized troops arrived in the province, he simply melted away.

In fact the whole of South-West China was a wayward child to the central authorities in Peking. It was just too far from the heart of order and discipline. The government would be content if the major urban centres toed the line. The 1911 Republican Revolution had exacerbated the situation and policing fell more and more between a loose alliance of local élite, vigilantes and government units. Many of the élite had trained in military academies but, deprived of jobs in a stable civil service, fell easily into the hands of war-lords. It was also easy for the war-lords to enlist bandit gangs.

The war-lords were not all violent bully boys. Among them were even some progressive reformers. There was Wu Peifei, the Confucian war-lord, Feng Yu Xiang, the Christian and Chen Jiongming the Socialist. But without a viable political programme it was their military power by which they became known and they bled the people with exorbitant taxation.

Sometimes the local war-lord came to tea and brought an impressive battalion of bodyguards with him. They would be littered all around the well-kept lawn with their Mausers at the ready. Despite their intimidating appearance I would look forward with excitement to their visits. The bodyguards were always ready to show off and let me play with their guns.

My own political awareness began on such occasions and with the family stories that were told and retold, forming a deep impact on my young mind. The stories were always moulded by the teller of the tale and hence my first impression of the 1911 Revolution, two years before my birth, is flavoured with Earl Grey tea.

My father's ability to remain oblivious to political storm was demonstrated to me early on when I heard of how the first wave of revolution washed up against the Viceroy's yamen (office and residence) in Canton. He was taking afternoon tea with eldest maternal uncle, Uncle King (Wei Zijing). Uncle King, like my father, never did anything earth-shattering in his life. Although his official position was English secretary to the Viceroy, he had a dubious command of the language, having been educated largely in France and Belgium. But, like my father, Uncle King had style and it seemed fit and proper that these two gentlemen should be having an afternoon cuppa in a quiet corner of the yamen.

While the retainers served up toast and jam they were lamenting the difficulty of obtaining fruit cakes and cucumber sandwiches in South China, not to mention Cornish cream for their scones. These were the reforms that they would like to have seen. Suddenly people began yelling and rushing through the courtyards generally disturbing the peace. In the back courtyards there was more commotion and the sound of cannon fire. But there couldn't be cannon fire, not in the Viceroy's yamen. So they finished their tea and had the retainers clear it away.

Later that afternoon it transpired that there had been an attack on the yamen and that a considerable number of 'revolutionary ruffians' had been taken prisoner and were awaiting execution. Several days later seventy-two young men were beheaded. Several of them were relatives. The event is now commemorated as the 'Seventy-two Martyrs of Huang Hua Guang'.

According to my mother, who was more radical than her brother, Uncle King said, 'The government will be able to suppress all revolutionary outbreaks with one roll of the drums!' He was not only conservative, he was a royalist. My father said nothing. He was not given to making remarks on politics.

Then there was my grandmother's birthday. I have heard the events of that occasion recounted so many times that I feel I was an eye-witness to the event.

It was a cool October day in 1912 and my father had decided not to dine on the verandah, but to place a few additional round tables in the drawing-room. The drawing-room was not normally used for banqueting, but reserved for receiving special guests and dignitaries. Besides, it was difficult to move the grand piano. The guests had just arrived and most had been guided to their places where they stood awaiting the signal to sit down and commence banqueting. Suddenly there was a commotion at the front entrance and the wide glass-panelled door was thrown open by a dozen rough-looking men. The ladies, believing it to be a robbery, pulled off their jewellery. Some even threw their precious things into the piano.

Within a moment or two it became apparent that these rough men were after neither money or jewellery, they were hunting a man. After searching the three main banqueting halls, there was much shouting and they all converged on the dining-room. There, at one of the banqueting tables, a well-dressed young man leapt up from his seat and made quickly for the verandah through the French windows. He raced down the forty yards of the back garden with half a dozen men in hot pursuit. He was making for the lower kitchen where there was a window which opened out into the garden of the Japanese Consulate next door. We kept a ladder leaning up against the window for just such emergencies, but on that day the window was jammed.

The young man was Master Kong, a revolutionary involved in organizing the local insurgency against the war-lord Yuan Shikai, who, as the Second President of the Republic (after Dr Sun Yat Sen) had suddenly declared himself Emperor. Revolts against his dictatorial rule and unlawful assumption of the throne had first caught fire in the south-west and were beginning to sweep through the land. Our local war-lord in Fujian was under orders from Yuan Shikai to nip any organized rebellion in the bud. They stabbed Master Kong in the back and dragged him away bleeding profusely. My grandmother was flabbergasted: young Master Kong was her favourite young man. He was handsome, gallant and full of idealism. His hat and coat were left hanging in the hall. They were still there a month later when he was shot at dawn. My grandmother heard the gunfire, for she had moved to town to be nearer to him during custody. Unfortunately my grandfather had died just a decade earlier. As he and Yuan Shikai were blood brothers he might have been able to pull some strings.

Death by execution, revolution or simply disease was no stranger to us. Foochow was not a healthy place in which to live: one needed some measure of luck to survive into adulthood. Every summer there were regular bouts of cholera, typhoid, dysentery and the occasional bubonic plague. For several centuries the population had been increasing rapidly and there were many lives to claim. Although life seemed so cheap the constant presence of death made our own lives seem all the more precious.

Our house was on the way to the hillside burial ground and from our vantage point leaning over the railings in the front garden, Charles and I could watch the funeral processions. During the height of the epidemic season there would often be a traffic jam of coffins. The coffins of the rich were huge and imposing. They proceeded up the hill with awesome solemnity, borne by more than a dozen people. But the coffins of the poor were constructed from bare planks loosely nailed together. On hearing the crowds of wailers from afar we would rush to the railings and peer down, fascinated and yet gripped by fear. The limbs of corpses seemed to protrude from the gaps between planks. A whiff of decaying flesh was enough to send us retreating with screwed-up noses, but not without a certain satisfaction.

Sometimes we would follow the procession up the slope where, after centuries of burial, the coffins were buried one on top of another. Often they were inadequately covered. Where the storms had eroded away the soil, crumbling coffins projected out of the ground. Excited by the same morbid curiosity I would prod at them with a stick or jack open the lids. But the sudden dart of a lizard would have me fleeing for my very life down the hill.

In the hills four or five miles north of the city was a private plot, the family tomb garden where my grandparents were buried. It was not really grand but a good many times the size of an ordinary family grave. With the first flush of spring the weeds would creep all over the plot nearly concealing half the tomb. At the Qingming (gravesweeping) Festival in late spring, Qingqing prepared half a dozen dishes and, in the company of my uncles and their families, we would dress smartly and ride out in a fleet of sedan chairs or later in a horse-drawn carriage to spend the day gardening and tidying up the gravestones.

The greatest killer, especially of the young growing population, was not any of the diseases mentioned before – it was tuberculosis. Many of our schoolmates and cousins were killed before they had completed their teenage years. Although appearing to be quite robust, they would be suddenly struck down. It must have been a long process of weakening through undernourishment. A diet of soft rice was not enough to see my poorer schoolmates into adulthood. To go to a friend's household and to see him laid out in an open coffin clothed in a long shroud was awful. But, out of a mixture of affection and curiosity, we would go along anyway.

Illness rarely struck our house but there was one occasion which scarred my earlier years. My sister Mary fell ill with food-poisoning, probably from eating seafood. For two days she lay immobile on her bed. I remember her lying there – she had become so very thin. All through the night we could hear every breath that she heaved echoing throughout the house. We tried to get to sleep on the verandah but the haunting sound echoed through our fitful dreams. By the second morning the breathing had stopped, and Father came down to tell us that Mary had died. He said no more and it was impossible to know how he was feeling. Charles burst into tears and the whole house was racked with weeping. My mother mourned pitifully for months. Mary wasn't buried in the hills but in the foreign cemetery among the white marble crosses half a mile from Lo Lodge. It was cosier to have her nearer home where her grave could be tended regularly. I felt oppressed and unnerved by the atmosphere, and longed for laughter and sunnier days. In those months I took to fleeing into the hills.

CHAPTER FOUR

Heroes of the Min

The movement of Heaven is powerful,
the superior make themselves strong and untiring.

The Classic of Change (the concept behind the self-strengthening movement)

INNOVATION WAS TREATED with scant respect in the traditional education system. Each student had to have a good grounding in classical
literature so that he could emulate the great heroes of the Golden Ages.
The aim was to become a sage and a gentleman through strict imitation
and self-cultivation. Charles and I were initiated into this ritual the
moment that we returned from Britain, and with the onset of education
our responsibilities seemed to pile up daily. Every morning, at 9 a.m.,
our tutor arrived to drill us in the Classics. But first we had to master the
brush; so much of our school day was devoted to perfecting calligraphy.
Handwriting was not so much for communication, it was elevated to an
art form, and could expose any untidiness of mind or rebelliousness in
character. For a soldier or administrator, a perfect brush stroke and a
command of argument through classical allusion were mightier weapons than the sword. To us it was also 'piece work', for, at the end of the
day, if the tutor ringed a character in red or gave it a tick we could pick
up a cash reward from our parents.

In Britain Shakespeare was only to be read and understood, but
in China we had to learn our classics by heart from the first word
to the very last. We recited the texts in unison. And in the heat of

Foochow summers the rhythmic droning would mesmerize me so that I would slip into a half sleep, only to resurface later with the words still murmuring through my lips. In the meantime the moral messages of the Confucian classics, which often exceeded 10,000 words, had reached deep down inside my subconscious.

> Mencius went to see King Hui of Liang.
> The King said, 'You have come, not considering 1,000 li too far,
> and so must have the means of benefiting my country'
> He said 'My lord, why must you
> speak of benefit, speak only of benevolence and righteousness and that's all.'
>
> The Mencius, Book 1, Part 1, circa 3rd century BC

The first book on the agenda was the commentary to the *Spring and Autumn Annals*, which was supposedly annotated by Confucius in the fifth century BC. This was a blow by blow account of the history of the small state of Lü (modern Shandong) where he was an adviser. It described how the state struggled for survival as numerous kingdoms vied for supremacy around it. Written in a prose that thundered along like the hundreds of chariots that charged into all the battles that it recounted, it left you in no doubt about the courage of the charioteers and their hordes of foot soldiers. But the barbarity also rang through loud and clear. Confucius always held that ceremonial behaviour was the very essence of civilization. But even he barely avoided having his liver fried and eaten by the unscrupulous Bandit Zhi.

From Confucius we graduated to the *Book of Mencius*. Mencius was another roaming philosopher, who tried, mostly in vain, to convince the aggressive rulers of the Warring States period to behave with decorum. Mencius had set out the doctrine of the people's right to revolution, for, if the ruler's behaviour was not in harmony with the way of Heaven, Heaven would see and dethrone him through a mass uprising. I found Mencius more human than Confucius. He was also easier to memorize. After Mencius came *The Essays of the Warring Kingdoms*, and through them a familiarization with the subtleties of statecraft and diplomacy in those precarious times.

All these records and philosophers come from remote history in the centuries before the first unification of the Chinese Empire. But we recited our way through the records of the Han dynasty, and into the golden age of Chinese poetry. With their conciseness, their strict parallelism and metre, some of the Tang poems achieve an almost surreal abstraction. Without a ready command of Tang poetry no Chinese could be considered truly educated. We were to stop short at the Song dynasty (AD 960) and by-pass the Yuan, Ming and Qing on account of the pressing need to master more modern subjects.

Through my early education, through Qingqing's stories and family tales my childhood became populated with a pantheon of heroes. From the *Monkey King* to the paragons of Confucian virtue, legendary figures stepped forth from the pages of the classics. Hero worship was a long-standing tradition in China. Times of high culture and national success, or even periods of dynastic failure, had produced them in droves. They didn't even have to be real people, and many probably never were. The important thing was the way they gave us hope and courage.

Many of my childhood fantasies had come from Qingqing's rendering of the *Romance of the Three Kingdoms* and the battles therein, fought against the evil Caocao of Wei by the wise and brave defenders of the weaker Kingdom of Wu and Shuhan. Beneath the Red Cliff that rears precipitously above the Yangzi River, Zhou Yü, commander of the allied forces, fought a courageous naval battle against Caocao.

> The great river flows east,
> Sweeping away countless heroes.
> To the west of the old rampart people say,
> Is the Red Cliff of young Zhou of the Three Kingdoms.
> Wild rocks cleave the clouds,
> Rapid breakers split the shore,
> Rolling up a thousand drifts of snow.
> The rivers and mountains are as a picture.
> How many heroes were there at that time?
>
> *Reflections of the Red Cliff*, Su Shi. 1037–1101 BC

Another naval hero whose praise had been sung down the ages was the swashbuckling Moslem eunuch, Admiral Zheng He, who commanded seven great maritime expeditions (1405–33) reaching as far as the East coast of Africa. His fleet of junks was probably the largest fleet in the world but, unlike the aggressive European explorers, Zheng He was not charged with the task of expanding the Empire. He did it for fun! To prove the distance that he had covered and the wonders that he had seen, he brought home great trophies for the Emperor's pleasure gardens: giraffes, zebras, ostriches and other fascinating curios.

To my mind every sailor that plied the rivers and seas was a hero to be reckoned with. The boatmen on the sampans, the fishermen and the sailors who sold their labour to foreign merchants and navies, all provided rich entertainment. They were a breed that I could only watch from afar, having no point of contact with them in my own insular life. If we rose at dawn on the first day of the fishing season we could watch the vanguard of the fishing fleet making its lonely way out into the oceans, not to return for several weeks. Behind it was a great armada of some eight hundred boats, and the procession could take as long as eight hours to pass. This lengthy passage gave me plenty of time to wonder about the mysteries of seafaring life: how would they sleep, what provisions would they make to withstand the savage typhoons, why did they leave in such an enormous fleet and last, and by no means least, what and how would they cook?

I was growing up at a time when China had only recently emerged from three centuries of rule by an imperial family derived of Manchu Bannermen, who themselves had been threatened for decades with the aggressive technological superiority of the West. Even worse, the Republican revolution had degenerated into a brawl between local war-lords. So naturally the spirit of Chinese nationalism ran very high in us. We were especially proud of all the historic defenders of the Chinese realm. There was Zhu Yuanzhang, the first emperor of the Ming Dynasty, who had raised the banner of revolt against the harsh Mongol rule of the Yuan dynasty. To defeat the armies of the great Khans, Kubla and Genghis, was no easy task. But within a couple of years Zhu Yuanzhang had driven the Mongols out, routing them in one battle after another, proving himself not only a great administrator but also a great commander.

Towards the end of the Ming dynasty, around 1644, there was the hero of the Min River who was the last bastion of the Chinese ruling house. Threading your way through the offshore islands of Fujian, you can see a huge statue of him rising from a promontory on an island facing Amoy. This is Koxinga or Zheng Chenggong who, based in Amoy and with widespread support from the local population, held out for decades against the barbarian invasion by waging a guerrilla war with his large fleet of junks. Eventually the Qing forces had to evacuate the whole of the south-western coastal populace before they drove Koxinga out to sea. But he still didn't give up, and after beating off the Dutch and Portuguese colonials on Formosa (Taiwan), he remained there until 1683, a thorn in the flesh of the new government.

Unlike Koxinga, Chinese mandarins are generally no Samurai: they are not trained as fighters, but as scholars and administrators. Yet if you thought that the mandarin official was weak you would be thoroughly mistaken. There was a Confucian saying, 'Always treat another first with great courtesy, until you decide that he is a more suitable subject for the sword!' But when it came to laying down his life for a just cause or for the defence of the realm, the mandarin official proved as strong and brave as the Samurai. When the moment came for him to put his neck on the line, he almost invariably did, without hesitation, and as often as not his head was promptly chopped off.

And sometimes there was no call for such brutality, as the steely hero in question would, in protest, do himself in without further ado! Here we can recall Tan Sitong of the 'Revolt of the Five Gentlemen', who committed suicide in 1898 in protest at the Empress Dowager's betrayal of their reform programme. But even he was following on a long tradition that had begun in the mists of the fourth century BC with an honest minister of the Kingdom of Chu. Tradition has it that Qu Yuan was dismissed from court and sent to the southern wilderness on account of some intrigue at court. Burning with the injustice of his banishment and loyal to an emperor who, he felt, was irrevocably deluded by villainous ministers, he threw himself into the river – to become an eternal inspiration to later officials who remonstrated against corruption at court.

Of the renowned mandarins from Foochow, Lin Zexu (1785–1850), or Commissioner Lin, was perhaps the most famous. Commissioner Lin won a great reputation for honesty in his work within the judiciary system, and gained the nickname Lin Qingtian (Lin, Clear as the Heavens). To the British he was a scoundrel, for it was he who destroyed 20,000 cases of opium in Canton. But to the Chinese of the late Qing dynasty he was a patriot, and to the people of Foochow he was a great hero. In the mid nineteenth century huge amounts of silver were leaking out of China to pay for the rapid increase in opium addiction, and there was soaring inflation as a result. In 1838, riding on a wave of Chinese resentment against the annual importation of 30,000 chests of opium from British hands, Commissioner Lin, in his capacity as Governor-General of Hubei and Hunan, petitioned the emperor, remonstrating against the foreign economic invasion. He set out an overall programme for reform and, as a result, was sent to Canton to take charge of its implementation. He went to his task with great enthusiasm, humiliating the Chinese officials involved in the trade, blockading and starving out the foreign settlements in Canton and Macao, confiscating 20,000 chests of opium and ceremoniously mixing them with lime and saltwater before depositing them into the sea.

However, at the height of his glory Lin Zexu was betrayed by the Qing court. Not long after the stoppage of all trade with Britain,

British men-of-war assembled off the South China coast. After they had plastered Canton with gunfire and several forts had been stormed it seemed that the Chinese chips were down. To placate the invaders, the Imperial government in Peking, frightened to death that the British might launch a full-scale invasion, immediately disgraced and dismissed the Commissioner, exiling him to far-away Chinese Turkestan.

The image of the Commissioner, the upright mandarin, prepared to stand up to both the foreign invasion and the weak-kneed dynastic rulers, was an inspiration to me. We too could have the courage to brave the storms of change and bring back glory to our enfeebled country. The Commissioner took his place in a long line of enlightened mandarins who felt the sharp edge of western encroachment and yet demonstrated acute awareness of China's need to grow stronger from inside if she were to exist as a nation-state in the modern world.

Our own teacher, Chen Liji, was not much of an example. Although he had a fair command of the classics, he wasn't very bright. But he was a smooth operator, with his finger on the pulse of all the undercurrents in Foochow. When he wasn't tutoring us he was the warden of the YMCA, which, despite being an organization for disseminating the faith, was where you went to find out about the criminal elements of the town, about government intrigues and student riots. We listened for hours to their gossiping, and, notwithstanding his second-rate intellectual capacity, we were always better informed at the end of the day.

My early impressions of modern history took shape while listening to such conversations and as I came to understand more of the lives of the relatives and friends who milled around us, banqueting and playing mahjong. Lo Lodge was not so much a cultural centre as a cultural watershed. With my father's appointment as Commissioner of Foreign Affairs for the province, our home became a natural focus for all those who had an interest in the West and in developing our nation. There were those, like my father, who were not deliberately advancing the national cause, but who drew benefit obliquely through association with the West. Others, like the Wei family uncles, were involved in mining and therefore keeping closely abreast with technological advance. In Lo Lodge the old blended naturally with the new and we were not aware of any cultural conflict. It was all thanks to the shadow of my grandfathers and their achievements. They were the Min River heroes most vivid to me.

In a world that had been beleaguered by internal insurrection, population explosion and foreign invasion for many decades, my grandfathers were keenly aware of the urgency to reform, and their own efforts were part of a wider initiative called the 'self strengthening movement'. The reformers, spearheaded by those militarists who suppressed the Taiping rebellion, determined to find out the western technological secrets in order to prop up the Chinese empire.

Yet by the second half of the nineteenth century little progress had been made. The initiative swung back and forward between reformers and conservatives, always held back by the corrupt and reactionary court of the Empress Dowager. A common rallying cry was:

> Chinese learning for our foundation,
> Western learning for practical application.

Even the reformers mostly failed to understand the need for new methods of education and institutional reform.

It was within this world that my two grandfathers rose at the vanguard of a new generation, with a new education and vision. My mother and paternal aunts never failed to impress upon us that their own fathers had been infinitely greater than their grandfathers or their husbands. The women were frustrated by the lack of opportunity facing their generation, and worried about our futures. My father rarely spoke of family history, but our aunts and mother made up for his silence with many cautionary tales and eulogies. Bit by bit we became acquainted with the family origins.

Many centuries BC, during the period of the Warring States and the Eastern Zhou dynasty there was a tiny kingdom called Luo (Lo), nothing more than a large clan that occupied a few small counties. As the chariots of neighbouring kingdoms Ji, Jin Qu and Zheng swept across the featureless plains of central China, the Los were squeezed out and obliged to flee southwards, crossing the Yangzi river. Finally they gravitated to the mountain regions of the south-east, where the land was more rugged and broken by fast-flowing streams and ranges that offered protection to their small tribes. This sturdy breed of 'Chinese gypsies' came to be known as the 'Ke Jia' (guest families) or 'Hakka' in Cantonese – drifting settlers that spoke a hotch-potch of dialects, continuously moulded by their long migrations. When they settled they did so for lengthy periods, often many centuries, before they were up and off again, leaving behind a branch in each area. Famed for their hard work and fierce women, the Hakka people retained a resilience that had allowed them to survive as a distinct culture into this century.

Gradually the Hakka people moved through Jiangxi into the coastal province of Fujian, settling in each province as they went. From Fujian they struck out into the South seas, bound for Singapore, Malaysia, Burma and the Philippines in search of better pastures. It was from a branch of these people that settled in Fujian, lumbering and fishing for their living, that my family was derived.

The written record traces us back only to the forty-ninth year of the Emperor Qianlong (1784) when my great-great-grandfather Lo Bida was born. Our first-known ancestor was to make some headway in the military hierarchy, climbing on to the bottom rungs of the ladder and thus leaving some account of himself for posterity. He commanded troops stationed in Southern Fujian and held various ranks.

Lo Bida purchased the family home in Nanyang, the southern suburb of Foochow. It was the fifth year of the Daoguang reign period (1825). The compound was originally called the 'Mulberry garden' or the 'Southern Encampment', and the abundance of mulberry trees made it an ideal place to carry on a cottage industry, raising silkworms and weaving silk on looms. Ordinarily this would have been a peaceful enough occupation and for some decades it was, providing the women and the idlers with leisurely employment.

Lo Bida was eventually sent across the straits, to Fengshan, to put down an uprising, where he died of ill health on active service in Fengshan county in the thirteenth year of the reign period Daoguan (1853). The court conferred a posthumous rank upon him, allowing the first-born of the following two generations to take part directly in the Provincial examinations, by-passing the County exams.

It was, indeed, a privilege to be able to skip one level of the examinations. Because of the massive increase in population at every level of society, there was an enormous pressure to get on to the lower rungs of the civil service ladder. But the first son of the next generation proved unable to make any headway in the Provincial examinations. Despite having a competence in composing classical poetry and enjoying some recognition as a calligrapher, he did not distinguish himself. Crestfallen, he made up his mind to sell his soul to the foreign devil by learning the art of photography and how to administer the smallpox vaccination. The family always excused him for, as the product of a family who were engaged in the uncivilized military business that involved killing, he lacked the refinement necessary to become a Confucian scholar. Things looked pretty bleak for the family.

Our own great-grandfather, Lo Shaozong, the second son of Lo Bida, was something of a child prodigy and it is said he could recite the five classics by the age of seven. But he was not in good health.

Despite being dangerously thin and sickly, he abandoned his academic pursuits to follow his father into the army at sixteen. This was in the days of the Taiping rebellion. He excelled at marksmanship and riding. Eventually he rose to the position of Company Commander. When the Taiping rebellion was suppressed, disillusioned with the army, he left and led the whole family back to Foochow, advising his children to engage in agriculture. He was a modest man, which can be seen from the following few lines he wrote:

> I am but of mediocre ability.
> It is not that I dare to quit my official post to enjoy the
>   comfort of leisure.
> My intelligence is limited and I deeply regret that I am unable
>   to exercise self-restraint.

Lo Shaozong's lack of restraint led to his producing thirty children. They said that his obsession with reproduction was the result of the barrenness of his first wife née Jiang. Her father had come to be known as 'Jiang of the half-street' on account of his being the landlord of half a street of properties. Despite her good social standing and comely features, her inability to produce children led Lo Shaozong to consult a fortune-teller. On his advice he married one of his bond servants and, still not happy with the nine sons that she produced for him, he took three further concubines. They said that three of these ladies were quite charming but the fourth was ugly as sin, short, with no neck, and the waddling gait of a penguin. She is said to be our great-grandmother. With the burgeoning legion of offspring and every male descendant entitled to a room in the compound, the 'Mulberry Gardens' were soon transformed into a slum, which depended for its very survival on the cultivation of silkworms.

It was into this degenerating colony that my grandfather was born in 1850, the seventh son of Lo Shaozong. Denied the privileges of the first son, Lo Fenglu had no alternative but to enrol in the newly inaugurated Naval college at Pagoda Anchorage. The college and modern dockyard were the response of the court to the pressing call for military reform. It was charged with supplying the Chinese with a fleet of steamships suitable for maritime defence. To this end the court hired the team of eighty foreign technicians from France and Britain to supervise a programme of shipbuilding and education in navigation and navigational command.

Foochow was chosen for its plentiful natural resources. Firstly, it had a wealth of coal, scrap iron and ore readily available. Secondly, the port was easily defended. The entrance to the Min River, instead of forming an estuary of mudflats, was studded with small islands and narrow gorges, ideal for fortification, and the hills which lined the shore further inland led the channel in such a way that torpedoes could easily render its navigation impossible. Thirdly, the proximity of the city allowed easy access to high officials who could provide a direct line to the capital and authorize initiatives.

The project was begun in 1867 under the auspices of Shen Baozhen, the Viceroy of South China and first director of the dockyard. Conditions were medieval. They had to elevate the alluvial clay with firmer soil to provide a solid foundation and to guard against the regular floods that threatened to carry the whole operation downstream. The local work force had no experience of shipbuilding so tuition had to begin with the most basic skills. To add to this, among the foreign team there were those who considered the young Chinese inferior and were a great embarrassment to their French director, Prosper Giquel.

Eventually a primitive dockyard was thrown together and housed in a collection of untidy buildings on the river bank. To the credit of the French supervisors, in no time at all they had conjured up a rolling mill, a boiler ship and a fitting shop. By 1874 fifteen steamships and five gunboats had been built, albeit with wooden hulls, for the iron-clads specified by the court had proved too difficult an undertaking.

It was not considered a privilege for my grandfathers to attend such a technological school, for a military career had never been a time-honoured profession. As the popular saying went:

> Good irons are not used for making nails
> Nor good sons for enlisting as soldiers.

There was no obvious career ladder to climb. To attract applicants, grants were made available for cadets attending the naval college. To a semi-impoverished family that was the important thing.

Being the best student in the theory of navigation and the most competent linguist, Lo Fenglu led the first group of Chinese students who travelled west to study at Greenwich Naval College. Before leaving Foochow Prosper Giquel, in a progress report to the Emperor, had suggested that the students consolidate their study with trips to France and Britain. This was endorsed by Shen Baozhen and repeated in a memorial to the Emperor by Prime Minister Li Hongzhang. Li proposed that the brightest be allowed to study chemistry, law and diplomacy.

Lo Fenglu also understood that, in order to modernize China's archaic institutions, it would be necessary to get to the roots of western culture and philosophy. And so he majored in chemistry and politics at London University. He was also fascinated by western philosophy and studied Goethe, Voltaire, Rousseau and was especially intrigued by the British writers Locke, Hume and Adam Smith.

Not only was he an academic success, he also scaled the heights of society, both British and Chinese. By learning English and studying in the West my grandfather moved into a completely new social sphere. In those days few were versed in the languages and skills of international diplomacy and he was better qualified than most. From this point on, his technical training became redundant, for he was to by-pass the rigours of the Imperial Examination system and jump to the top of the civil service ladder.

In 1878, after only a year of study, he found himself attached to the mission of Guo Songdao, the first resident envoy from China to Great Britain. Guo was a leading proponent of academic reform, but a reluctant ambassador, always pleading ill health. He must have been glad to pass on his skills to a successor. In 1879 they were transferred together to Berlin before returning to China in 1881. On his return he was promoted to be personal aide to Li Hongzhang and Central Foreign Office translator.

Li Hongzhang was acutely aware of China's inadequate military capacity. In contrast, the programme of economic and political reconstruction under the Meiji Restoration had been successful and Japan was ready to wield her strength at an international level. When conflict broke out between Japan and China over Korea, China's weakness was exposed. Following a spate of local riots, Korea became an uneasy co-protectorate of both Japan and China. Japan then staged a successful coup, driving the Chinese back behind the Yalu river. On 17 September 1894 the two navies engaged in a battle at the estuary. While the Chinese had bigger guns, the Japanese ships were faster and their guns fired more quickly. Although they fought bravely, the Chinese fleet had fallen into disrepair and their leadership was ill-trained. One third of the first Chinese fleet was wiped out with one of our relatives, Lo Zhonglin, aboard. Japan moved into Manchuria, and captured Dalian and Port Arthur. A new invasion of the Shandong peninsula was launched and the Manchu forces were surrounded from land and sea. They surrendered without a fight and the Chinese admiral committed suicide, humiliated by the defeat.

It was not until March 1895 and after Japan clearly had the

upper hand that they agreed to negotiate. My grandfather had been assured of a place on the delegation. During his days at Greenwich Naval College, he had been a close friend of Prince Ito, now the all-powerful Prime Minister of Japan. During the negotiations, in an inexplicable act of violence, Li Hongzhang was shot in the face by an assassin. My grandfather took over.

Among the Japanese demands were the secession of Taiwan, the Pescadore Islands and the Liaodong peninsula, a new treaty granting Japan freedom to trade freely in China and a 200 million tael indemnity for the pleasure of being invaded! It is said that Fujian was originally included in their demands and that my grandfather, in personal loyalty to his ancestral home, fought for it, successfully salvaging a tiny bit of pride for the Chinese people. Otherwise I would have been born a Japanese subject!

He then followed Li Hongzhang to America, Europe and then Russia, where he attended the coronation of Tsar Nicholas. By November 1895 he was nominated Minister Plenipotentiary to the Court of St James. After attending Tsar Nicholas's coronation he returned to Britain to attend Queen Victoria's sixtieth jubilee. He and Li Hongzhang were invited to Windsor castle. Over tea Li Hongzhang was invited to sign the visitors' book. He pulled out his brush and promptly wrote a poem in Chinese. The Queen was intrigued and demanded an on-the-spot translation:

> To the west I gaze at our grandmother descending to the
>   Fairy Pool,
> To the east Master Lao passes through the Hangu frontier
>   gate surrounded with purple mists.

Delighted with Lo Fenglu's translation the Queen recommended to Lord Salisbury that he be conferred with the distinction of Honourable Knight Commander of the Victorian Order for his contribution to Anglo–Chinese relations.

Sir Lo Fenglu and Lady Lo made quite an impression on the late Victorian social circuit as they travelled up and down Britain. Among our memorabilia were two pantomime programmes printed on silk to commemorate their visit to Glasgow and Manchester, and cigarette cards with a picture portrait to record the same events. There was also the following news report from the *London News*:

> I believe a most interesting ceremony was observed when the body of
> Lady Lo, the wife of the Chinese Minister, was conveyed from their

official residence in Portland Place and placed on board the Japanese steamer Sanuki Maru. The coffin bore the quaint inscription on a silver breastplate in Chinese characters: Honoured by the Emperor of the Qing dynasty to be called a lady of the first rank, Lady Lo, of the family of Wei and beloved wife of Sir Chihchen Lo Fenglu, KCVO, died 10th Feb., 1899 in her forty-fourth year. The coffin was placed in the Reception Room of the Embassy; in accordance with the Chinese custom, on the head of the coffin was placed a cocamade of white cloth – the clarion of eternal mourning. Into this room, shortly before ten o'clock, the Ambassador with his children, six in number, entered, accompanied by all the official members of the staff, clad in white garments. The coffin, a handsome mahogany chest, with silver handles, was removed to an open four-horse hearse, and twelve men staggered under its burden. The Chinese Minister, following his wife's coffin, led the way, carrying a yellow staff tipped with red, attired completely in the most wonderful robes of pure white silk, exquisitely embroidered, also in white, with long drooping branches of the cypress tree.

While Lo Fenglu had flown the nest and not taken up the professorship offered him at the Foochow Naval School, Wei Han was still actively involved in the practicalities of shipbuilding. After his return from France he returned to Foochow. At that time the French were slowly moving up the coast from their colony in Vietnam. Li Hongzhang again pressed the government to negotiate. In 1884 they agreed to honour the treaties made by France with Vietnam. That summer there was an unexpected turn of events, a day that was to become enshrined in family history as a betrayal of outrageous proportion.

It was Bastille day (14 July) and Wei Han, on account of his command of French, was sailing down river to offer his congratulations to Admiral Gorbet. As his little steamer neared the French flagship he was greeted with a round of rapid firing artillery. Veering off course with the greatest of speed, he took cover in the weeds at the river bank and lay low for two full days. In a gratuitous show of violence the French ironclads plastered the Chinese wooden steamers with gunfire, reducing the whole fleet to a floating heap of matchsticks with considerable loss of life. The Anchorage was filled with mutilated corpses on a day which left a deep imprint on every native family. Foochow was in mourning.

Later that day it seems that there was, at least, some divine retribution, however small. As the French fleet steamed their way down river, they had to negotiate the narrow channels at the mouth of the Min where the Chinese hill forts were sited. As the vanguard of the fleet passed by, the Chinese opened fire from one of the forts that was equipped with a German-made gun. They reported a blinding flash and an explosion on the bridge. But the ship proceeded on its way out to sea. The French made no report. But fifty years later the Chinese stumbled upon the evidence to confirm the incident. When the Japanese surrendered to the Allies in 1946 and handed back the offshore islands of Fujian, the Chinese came across a number of Christian graves near to the estuary of the Min. Among them was one which bore the name of Admiral Gorbet.

Despite this incident, Wei Han's career had generally taken him on a quieter progress through life. He gradually bettered his position, first to become director of the Foochow dockyard for nine years from 1903, and then of the South-West Military Academy in Guilin before he settled in Canton, on the banks of the Pearl River, to enjoy the benefits of a prestigious navy position as president of the Whampoa Naval College. The college was associated with the world famous Whampoa Military Academy which was to produce such distinguished rivals as Chiang Kaishek and Zhou Enlai. Mother often recounted tales of these years and of her father's excitement every time he launched a new ship.

But it was my father's elder sister, Auntie Ying, and her husband, Uncle Chen, who spoke most often of Lo Fenglu and were to encourage us most in our studies. Auntie Ying took pity on us: Grandfather had passed away prematurely, and my father, in his dissolute, way was not equipped to offer us the guidance and support necessary for literary development and the strengthening of moral fibre. With her son Daisun already having flown the nest, she adopted us as if we were her very own, providing us with an environment where our academic potential could grow uninhibited by the clattering of mahjong and the constant round of socializing at home.

Although Uncle Chen didn't have an official post, he was the acknowledged Confucian scholar of the town and took his position very seriously. He was a kindly old man who would have found it demeaning to have to pull strings to find a job. Instead he spent his time buried in books, or reciting the classics. When China was in such turmoil the only option for such a man was to devote himself to nurturing his inner strength and practising self-cultivation, trusting that his beloved country would pull through in the long run. Besides, he didn't need a job, for his family had the weight of a scholarly tradition behind them which brought with it some degree of wealth.

His own uncle, also from Foochow, had gone north to be a tutor to the last Emperor, Puyi, and had been caught up in the desperate flight of the imperial family after the Revolution. He followed Puyi through the foreign concessions in Tianjin to Manchuria, where he took a post in the puppet government set up there by Japan.

The Chen family lived on the south side of Nantai island in a village called Louzhou, 'The Isle of Snails'. Travelling by sampan, it was a day's journey to Louzhou through a maze of tidal streams and canals with Charles, who had no fear of water, swimming along behind. Louzhou overlooked the Min River beneath the towering 'Tiger Head Mountain' that dominated the wide straits. The Chens lived in a mansion of interlinking courtyards at least half a dozen of which were occupied by Auntie and Uncle alone. Each branch of their family had its own courtyard. The atmosphere was rarefied by study. Many courtyards were devoted to storing books and one was converted into a two-storey library where books ran around at least three faces of the balconies. In others the ground was thick with bamboo that shot up thirty to forty feet into the air. Still others were intricately laid out with rock gardens arranged to recreate miniature mountain panoramas. A special ambience of meditation and tranquillity pervaded the whole household, nourishing the reflective mind and spirit.

Although such scenes were not so dear to my heart, they were much appreciated by Charles who already had the bearing of a fine scholar. I was more interested in the central courtyard where dinner was served each day on our return from playing on the river bank. During our sojourns in the Chen household, often three or four weeks at a time, our aunt's cook would provide us with the same fare as the adults, a far cry from the mundane food that was churned out in the schoolrooms in Lo Lodge. Every morning we would have three of the largest, freshest boiled eggs. I would wake to the sound of birds in the rafters, still dreaming of eggs that were so totally unlike the tasteless little ones available in the city. I was keen on building up my body and eating eggs, I was told, was the way to do it. And then there were the banquets at supper: dishes of meat, fish, tofu and vegetables washed down with soup. Often there were whole bushels of crab claws fresh from the river, to be dipped in ginger and vinegar with a touch of soy sauce. By the time we had cracked our way through the claws, and feasted on the tender flesh within, the whole of the banqueting table would be covered with huge mounds of glistening pink and red shell.

It was this kind of food that nurtured one of the brightest and certainly the biggest of my 'Heroes of the Min'. Chen Daisun stood an enormous six feet, towering over the rest of us diminutive Southern Chinese. While the first of the 'Heroes of the Min', Zheng Chenggong, stood as a granite statue at the entrance to Amoy harbour, the younger elements of this select band were just striding out towards the flickering mirage of a modern China. Daisun, like Zheng Chenggong, was a 'trail blazer', treading a new path across unknown territories that took him far away from the banks of the Min. His luminous career served as a beacon to light the way for us lesser mortals who followed in his wake.

When I was a toddler, Daisun had already left for the new Qinghua University. Qinghua was the top university for scientific research. It had been funded by the return of $320 million to China, originally confiscated by America as indemnities incurred during the Boxer Rebellion. This was part of an overall figure of $12 billion in returned monies that was invested in education. It was the beginning of the 'honeymoon' period in Sino–American relations which was to last right through the Second World War.

By any contemporary standard Qinghua University was lavishly equipped. There was a marble swimming pool and rubberized running track on the first floor of the gym. All undergraduates were required to be fit for the task of national salvation. Other universities were also established on overseas money: the Nankai University was established on money recruited from the YMCA, and Yanjing University, funded partly by the Rockefeller Foundation, was famous for its Department of Journalism and its innovative sociological studies. Harvard University had begun to fund the most accomplished students to travel abroad.

By my teenage years Daisun was already in Wisconsin, and he blazed on to Harvard where he spent four years working on a PhD in economics. Back in Foochow, with fawning adoration, we pored over the snapshots he sent home. They showed a life in the West of which we could only dream: the lakeside campus in Wisconsin, the glorious countryside, motor cars. News of success after success rang loud and clear in our ears.

On his return to Foochow there were no firecrackers or banqueting tables set up in the ancestral temple, such as one would expect on the return of a successful candidate from the Imperial Examinations. Nor did he perform the mandatory kowtow to his parents. But we could see his parents' pride from the faint but satisfied smile that became fixed on their faces. In their hermetic existence, their hopes for success, both personal and national, were all invested in this, their only son. I envied Daisun's command of functional language. Our own paucity of training in contemporary literature had left us with a Chinese that was somewhat lopsided. Our mother tongue was the local Foochow dialect, and it was in this soft, lyrical language that we communicated for most of our relationships and daily affairs. On the other hand, our own command of Mandarin came from the classics of antiquity and was hardly applicable for the tasks that lay ahead. I asked Daisun what he felt about his success. He answered that it was 'all a piece of (Moon) cake!'

Through repetition, the stories of illustrious ancestors, whether simply Chinese or those from our own Lo and Wei families, became forged into personal memories. Although he had died a decade before my birth, none was more vivid than my own grandfather. It was already clear that Confucius and Mencius were not going to take us very far. They had provided us with a moral foundation but, if we were to have any future in the modern world, we would have to follow in the footsteps of those heroes who had broken through to the West.

CHAPTER FIVE
Breaking Through

Bliss was it in that dawn to be alive,
But to be young was very heaven.

From *The French Revolution, as it Appeared to Enthusiasts*, Wordsworth

As DAISUN WAS blazing his trail in full view, the revolutionary history of China was also unfolding before our very eyes. Even as small children we had heard anti-Japanese slogans and witnessed the annual student demonstrations against the '21 Demands'. We had ducked as the occasional misdirected banner was hurled over the neighbouring consulate and came sailing into our garden.

One memorable day in 1926 Charles and I were sitting on top of our garden wall with our bare legs protruding through the railings. On the roadway below, the Eastern Route Army was flooding into the city on their advance north to crush the war-lords. The troops were an alliance of Nationalists and Communists under the overall command of He Yinjing and advised by Borodin, a Commissar sent by the Soviet Union to guide the 'novice' revolutionaries in this campaign. Most of the officers were trained at the Whampoa Military Academies, where only a couple of decades earlier my maternal grandfather, Wei Han, had been a principal. But the Whampoa Academy had become a hot bed of political dissent and revolution. They believed that the only way to bring China out of the backwood of feudalism was to smash the war-lords and set up a central government based on

Dr Sun Yatsen's 'Three People's Principles': Nationalism (fired by Anti Manchu sentiment), Democracy (a constitutional and republican government) and People's Livelihood (Socialism).

The ideologically-inspired revolutionary army was more than a match for the mercenary armies of the war-lords. They rolled up all opposition with minimal effort. There may have been some stout resistance from loyal units, but hardly any of the war-lord armies failed to buckle under after a few days' heavy engagement.

The revolutionary army also looked pretty bedraggled in their dirty grey-green uniforms. After all, they had been marching on foot for three or four hundred miles. Each one carried a rifle and the numerous heavy machine guns were carried by several men at a time. Charles and I were unimpressed and, yet to be inspired with ideas of democracy, were both very disappointed that the local war-lord, with his 200,000 mercenaries, did not stage a proper fight. We were hoping for a lot of cannon fire to stop them crossing the Min. As it was, in no time at all the war-lord army had melted away somewhere to the north-west of the city.

Besides, the war-lord mercenaries carried only large Mauser pistols with extended butts so that they could be fired from the shoulder like a rifle. They employed this technique when they fired into the back of their victims' heads – their normal method of execution. But would the pistols be of any use when faced with massed rifle fire interspersed with bursts of heavy machine gun attack? Suicide wasn't worth the money. No wonder they magically disappeared.

The only person to stand his ground was the war-lord's Security Chief, Zhang Guohua, and his bodyguard. They were a much hated pair in Foochow. Within a few years of rule they had exterminated many local youngsters suspected of having revolutionary leanings. Hated first and foremost because they were 'outsiders' from the north, they compounded it by being arrogant about local feelings. The Chief rode on a motorbike and carried two handguns. On his way home at night he would frequently open fire on dogs who dared to bark at him.

As soon as the Eastern Route Army had got the war-lord on the run the students saw their chance to settle old scores. From goodness knows where they had managed to obtain a stockpile of weaponry. Most of them had probably never handled firearms before, nor could they have had much last-minute practice. By the evening they had managed to trap the Security Chief and his bodyguard in a Japanese warehouse no more than a mile and a half from our house. Single shots and the sporadic exchange of two or three in succession were audible. It went on till past midnight, after which the sounds became scarcer and then died away. With the curfew and road blocks around the city there was no escape. The whole night we were up conjecturing about what might have happened. Our parents were no help at all and Father, as always, carried on sipping his tea and reading the British newspapers.

The next morning we were roused by the sound of our next door neighbour, the Japanese Consul General, who burst into our western dining-room demanding compensation for the damage done to the Osaka warehouse by the 'rioters'. Before long there was the sound of a crowd coming up the street. We ran to our positions on top of the wall. Forty or fifty people were surging towards us. Behind them were two bodies dragged along by ropes attached to their feet. They bumped woodenly along the ground. I averted my gaze but through the corners of my eyes I recognized some of our local basketball players and some of the students from Trinity College. They were heading for the hill-top basketball ground. We tagged on behind at a little distance. At the basketball ground they strung the body of the Security Chief upside down. He was dangling like a wind-dried duck from the basketball post, his face plastered with dirt and blackened with congealed blood. The burly bodyguard was sprawled out below on the ground, bespattered with blood. Fresh blood was still trickling from his body and it mixed with the earth to form a dark splodge growing slowly wider on the ground. I was frightened and impressed by the 'handiwork' of my contemporaries. They were probably no more than two or three years older than me.

When I returned home to resume my Chinese lessons the teacher did not seem to appreciate that I was preoccupied with the day's events, making it difficult for me, at least for that morning, to commit some of the passages to memory. That evening I was given some pocket money by Auntie Ying to partake of 'foreign fare' at the YMCA. There in the dining-room a few of the Russian Commissars were ordering my favourite dish, Chinese Peppered Steak with Chow Mien.

YMCA beefsteak ranks among the best I have ever tasted. It was not so much the quality of the meat, but the way it was pounded, brushed with soya sauce and flash fried. The end result, liberally coated with pepper, was thin and tender enough to cut easily, well scorched on the surface but rare and juicy inside. It was served up with lashings of noodles fried up with bean sprouts and thinly sliced onion and spring onion – a pasta delight that Marco Polo had overlooked on his trip to Foochow. If it had come to his attention he might have alerted the Italians to their eastern competition. This was followed by ice-cream and creme caramel. All in all, after a hard day's work, it must have been a rare treat to those Russians, whom I'm sure had never tasted the like of it!

The year that the Northern Expedition rolled through Foochow was the same year that we were enrolled in the Anglo–Chinese College. Despite its name, this institution was funded from America. It was a Methodist school situated on the incline near home and enjoyed the best reputation in the province, hardly rivalled by the Church of England Trinity School a mile away and on the other side of the hill. We could hear both the schools' chapel bells and college clocks booming through the horse chestnuts in our garden. The bells were always ringing; they rang to summon my 600 fellow students to hall in the morning, for the lusty round of mid-morning hymns and for prayer at dusk.

Missionary schools had made their appearance in China during the nineteenth century, and had enjoyed extra territorial status along with the westerners that taught in them. By the twentieth century they boasted 2,000 high schools and sixteen colleges and had turned out 36,000 graduates within three decades.

Our school was divided into primary, junior and high school grades. Notwithstanding that the school was fee-paying, the bulk of our classmates were from poverty-stricken families; they had scraped the bottom of the family barrels in order to improve their sons' prospects with an education at the best institution available to them. Most of the others had returned to their ancestral home from overseas. In such places as Sarawak, Manila and Singapore the emigrés from Fujian still considered Foochow to be a centre of excellence for education. The quality of their attire contrasted sharply with our local boys who often had just one pair of cloth shoes and a shabby pair of socks to get by with. Even though these country boys were so destitute that they had to wash and dry their socks overnight for the next day's wear, in other ways they were in better shape. They had sturdy physiques and the kind of legs that come only from bearing heavy weights uphill.

We, in comparison, were well-equipped, both financially and academically. There were a handful of others in a similar position. Some came from well-to-do manufacturing families. There was Ma Zhongyuan whose family owned the factory that produced fancy lacquer-coated paper parasols of the kind that were good for export to the European market. And there was the Shen family, also in lacquer, who exported vases, bowls, decorative boxes and cigarette cases to Shanghai and abroad.

As the time had approached for my brother and I to go to school, the emphasis of our study at home shifted from the classics to the more modern subjects, arithmetic, algebra, geometry, world geography and the ancient, medieval and modern history of the western world. With our command of English, we could make a flying start and were allowed to enter the last year of the Junior school and thereafter to graduate within half a year to the High school.

Most of the textbooks on modern subjects were written in English. I soon became acquainted with Alexander the Great, Richard the Lionheart and Napoleon Bonaparte. The exploits of Washington, Wilson and Lloyd George were all familiar to me. But I made most headway with geography. For a young Chinese who could recite the whole works of Mencius, to learn the size, position and name of every American state and its capital was as easy as pie. In the library at home I unearthed a huge postal atlas of China. Each province was depicted on a page the size of a tablecloth and when the twenty-two provinces were pieced together they covered the whole of the dining-room floor. It took me several weeks of poring over it with a magnifying glass, but in the end I knew the details of every province not to speak of the sixty-four districts of Fujian.

Although ours was a Methodist school the principal never attempted to ram the scriptures down our throats. Following the long tradition of the Jesuit Christians in China he believed in soft selling the Gospel. Scrupulously fair to all faiths, Mr Freeman Havinghurst was not obviously in the business of converting his heathen pupils. Anyway, religion was a way of life to us, a set of rituals that were dutifully adhered to, rather than a matter of faith. Of course there were the 'rice bowl converts' who, considering that their teachers were in a position to recommend them for jobs in the British-run postal or customs service, became suddenly and passionately aglow with the love of Jesus.

I regarded such jobs with disdain. However, I was quite taken with the textbooks by Dr Fosdick, *The Meaning of Prayer*, *The Meaning of Service* and *The Meaning of Faith*. And, determined to get to the bottom of this strangest of preoccupations, I set about studying Christian theology in earnest. 'Loving your neighbour' seemed fair enough and resonated with the ideas I had learned from the Mencius. But Christianity attempted to go further and to explain unknown matters in a manner that was at once both obscure and lacking in practical application. I concluded that the philosophers of Chinese antiquity were already far advanced, at least as far as morality was concerned.

Along with the hymns and prayers came a different kind of spiritual affirmation. The Chinese principal would read aloud the last

Will of Dr Sun Yatsen, and we would sing a rather dreary national anthem that loudly eulogized the 'Three People's Principles'.

> Our aim shall be,
> To found a free land,
> World peace be our stand.
> Onward and learn comrades,
> Vanguards you are.
> Hold fast your aim by
> Sun and star.
> Be earnest and brave
> Your country to save.
> One heart, one soul,
> One mind, one goal.

After passing through Foochow the Northern Expedition swept through to take Shanghai. But throughout this period the fissures between the Nationalist People's Party and the Communists were coming to a head. Undercover propaganda work carried out through the Communist Youth League and the trade unions was enlisting massive support in both urban and rural centres. Much of their propaganda in rural areas was founded on land reform and redistribution. But this success only served to aggravate the differences in the alliance, land reform being the lowest of the Three People's Principles on the Nationalists' agenda. Unlike the Communists, many of the Nationalist officers were from the landed gentry class and had no real intention of turning on their own. On the eve of the army's arrival in Shanghai, the heart of the labour movement, the workers had staged three separate uprisings and finally an armed insurrection, all masterminded by Zhou Enlai and other important Communist leaders. They succeeded in taking control of the City Council and were waiting in triumph for the allied army. But the army, waiting in the wings, did not move in. The alliance had been terminally strained. Chiang Kaishek, the right wing of the Nationalist People's Party, with the help of local bully boy organizations, brutally ousted the Communists in a massacre that claimed the lives of 5,000 people. Many of those lives were of women and children demonstrating against the vicious coup. The suppression of the Communists spread to many other cities along the Yangzi River until the Nationalists had wrested all control of the nerve centres of Southern China from their hands. Slowly the Three People's Principles, the rallying cry of the Nationalists, became part and parcel of life, the school's curriculum and examination system.

During my days at the Anglo–Chinese College, a whole bevy of new friends flooded into my life. Some of my compatriots were principally concerned with improving their status in the world and were frustrated at the lack of opportunity in Foochow. Others were beginning to line up with left-wing elements, and were finding their feet in a complex political environment. It was not at all clear to me what being 'left-wing' meant. But at least those on the left were not envious of wealth, and had the wherewithal to understand that the existing social and economic ladder was a transient affair. They were preparing themselves to take part in shaping a new world. As ever the YMCA was where the political debates of youth raged, and all the latest gossip about the national plight had its breeding ground. We were all growing up quickly and felt keen concern for the future of our country. I made friends with everyone irrespective of background or political persuasion, making a mark with my easy-going nature. I was genuinely happy and prepared to go along in my own way sharing everything I had.

There were other reasons that made the YMCA my natural habitat. The 'Y' represented all that modern life could offer. As well as serving up Peppered Steak and Chow Mien it also had a well-equipped swimming pool and an auditorium. When the restrictions on our nightlife began to relax, outings to the 'Y' were extended to include a film in the auditorium. We were treated to such epics as *Ben Hur*, the *Ten Commandments* and other Cecil B. De Mille extravaganzas. Images of Eddie Cantor, Harold Lloyd and Mary Pickford flickered before our eyes. Since most of the audience did not read or understand any English, a translator was mounted on the auditorium platform. He was often none other than Mr Chen Liji, our tutor. His presence made the 'Y' seem as cosy as if it were a natural extension of our home.

Back at school, leisure activities were to stand me in good stead. Personally I had been more taken with Freeman Havinghurst's muscles than his mild religious messages. He had once been the tennis champion of Kansas City and had the body to prove it. It was this principle that initiated me in the joys of tennis, and laid the foundation of my later success in the game. I was good at nearly all ball games although too thin to excel at soccer, too short to be the best basketball or volley ball player, but I was made for tennis. After three years of coaching from Mr Havinghurst my legs and my right arm were as sturdy as the country boys'.

The city sports ground was also the execution ground, the site of the death of my grandmother's favourite revolutionary, young Mr Kong. Sometimes our own games would also erupt into violence.

I would do everything to avoid being drawn into a brawl and by this time was expert at skirting around explosive situations. I was not afraid of pain, indeed, my pain threshold was high. When I had a bruise I would rub it hard with a piece of soap to show how much I didn't care. So on the rare occasions that my delicate manoeuvres failed and I did get involved in a rough house situation I usually came out on top. But more regularly we would feast on the wide variety of snacks, from sugar cane and water melon to the Guang Bing toasted buns stuffed with soya-braised pork and meat jelly, that were hawked around the sports ground.

My most memorable match on the city sports ground went to five sets and over three hours under the searing summer sun. I was thankful for having asbestos skin. All the same, the agony of serving into the fierce glare left me with dark crescents blinding my eyes for a whole week. Winning that first championship gave me the confidence that I had the stamina to fight the best of them.

I should have had a cool shower and drunk a few pints of cold water to replace the buckets of sweat that I had lost. But instead I decided to celebrate in one of the bathhouses of Huangcang Letian Quan (Fountain of Pleasure in the Yellow Store) to the south-east of the city where there was an abundance of hot springs. A trip to the bathhouse was the occasion for a private meal or joining the madding throng in the communal dip where hot snacks were laid at tables around the steaming cauldron. Light food was also served in the private rooms. After this exquisite indulgence you could relax on a wicker couch and sleep away the afternoon dreaming of nothing in particular. A range of teas would be provided – Jasmine, Dragon Well or even the superior brand called 'The Iron Goddess of Mercy'. Life was worth living when there was no need to see beyond the steam that rose from the surface of the bath.

The water in the bathhouse was brought fresh from the spring, boiling hot, by means of a well sweep. Notwithstanding the contraption was a primitive affair, it was effective. A wooden bucket loosely attached to a twenty-foot pole was balanced against a large stone at the opposite end. When the stone was manually raised the bucket was immersed in the boiling water and then, on letting go, shot to the surface and, hitting a wooden projection, tipped over, pouring its contents into a small pool. The water was then conducted away from the pool through numerous channels that fed the different baths. Most of the bathhouses drew water from several wells and as a result there was a continuous flow of hot water.

On that occasion I jumped into the first bath that I came across, without stopping to dip a cautious toe, and nearly killed myself in the process. It was not just due to the heat of the water, but also to the loss of salt that all my muscles went into cramp. It was all that I could do to drag myself to safety. Despite this uncomfortable incident the combined effect of sport and eating provided me with the resource never to be overburdened with my awareness of the political turmoil that was convulsing the land all around.

Two of my most vivid memories of childhood are associated with birds of prey: Charles and I were sitting on the south bank of Nantai island overlooking the Min River and trying to commit a tome of readings to memory. Distracted by the bustle of the busy river I lay back and, doing so, noticed a great bird encircling the two of us, way above in the sky. As I was lazily watching it, it suddenly swooped down, aiming at something behind us. But then it changed course, and levelling out and swooping towards us it clouted our heads with its heavy, outstretched wings. We both sustained a heavy blow and it was already twenty feet past before Charles and I came to our senses. Why had it marked us? Surely it hadn't mistaken us for mere rodents; besides, it hadn't even extended its claws. What was it trying to say?

A few weeks later I was still puzzling over this omen when an eagle flew into our chicken coop. One of our rickshaw boys raced in after it to prevent its escape and with the speed of light had twisted its wings backwards and trussed it up with wire. In his hands this noble creature was just another candidate for the pot, no more than a chicken or a duck. Then he flung it unceremoniously to the ground where it was left to the contempt of the chickens who eyed this most hated intruder with flustered suspicion. Moved to empathy with its desperate struggle I resolved to do the brave thing. I cautiously entered the coop to release it. Taking great care to avoid its beak and claws, I untrussed it, stood back quietly, and watched with joy as the eagle soared clear of the wire and sped away over the wall behind the lower kitchen making for the freedom of the skies.

I, too, felt cooped up and the route to freedom seemed beset by difficulties. Sport and eating were my greatest pleasures, but to get away meant graduating to university. I felt tied down by the rigours of examinations, and it was a struggle for me. Daisun had attended the Anglo–Chinese College and my brother, Charles, seemed to be following in his footsteps. Charles cleared academic hurdles with the greatest of ease – he seemed to be equipped with the same jet-propelled back burner as Daisun – once either of them neared a hurdle they would switch on and with an infallible swoosh they would land clear of the obstacle. Apparently I was not made of the same stuff. I was slapdash in my work and seldom prepared the ground with the same thoroughness as my elders and betters. When I neared a hurdle I would also switch on, but my back burner seemed to be faulty and instead of hearing the reassuring roar of an engine changing gear, it was always the gritting of teeth that accompanied my mad scramble to get over the top. But with Foochow still in the Dark Ages, with its ghosts and shabby coffins lying in wait for the failed examinee, I always managed to claw my way to safety. It was to the credit of the school that I, like Charles and Daisun, was ultimately instilled with some notion that we were still at the vanguard of a new generation of Chinese intelligentsia. We all had the confidence that if there were problems to be faced in catching up with the West, we would have the power of analysis to crack them.

It was on account of my tennis friendship with Freeman Havinghurst that I narrowly escaped expulsion. One of my young friends, Peter Chai, had copied my final examination submission and was foolish enough to have transcribed it word for word. When we were both hauled up before the Board of Directors, Peter, who was under the sponsorship of the mission, was looking very pale. Expulsion would have been most serious for him. But Mr Havinghurst came riding in to save our bacon. When asked for a reference he blithely replied, 'Kenneth has played tennis with me for some three years and has never once questioned a line call. He couldn't possibly have cheated in any examination.' With that the matter was dropped, and Peter and I both graduated.

By this time the motor car had made its mark on Foochow. In my eyes the soft-top Fords were the quintessence of modern romance. Like Toad of Toad Hall, the exhaust fumes were like perfume to me. With Charles already away in Peking and Mary's death still shedding gloom over my home, my smouldering ambition to leave had burned up into high fever and the glamorous worlds of Shanghai and Peking were beckoning. When the opportunity to leave appeared on the horizon I grabbed it with both hands, pulling up my roots and setting out on my very own 'long march'. I left Foochow without regrets, leaving behind family and a whole host of friends with seldom a backward glance.

CHAPTER SIX

Calm before the Storm

For life's fulfilment we should amuse ourselves to the full
and never let the golden wine-jar stand empty under the moon.
All of heaven's bounty must be enjoyed
If I squander a thousand pieces of gold – it will all come back
  to me!
Boil the lamb! Slaughter the ox! and so make merry,
and in one draught, drain three hundred cups!

Li Bo. AD701–762

IT WAS A cool dry September when I awoke on what seemed to me to be the brightest morning of my life. Lying on the couch in Daisun's living-room, I could hear bamboo rustling softly just outside the French windows. Sunshine streamed into the room, spreading the shadow of bamboo fronds in patterns over the floor. Life was pregnant with expectation. For a month I had been waiting in the oppressive southern heat. But finally I was in Peking and had caught up with Charles in the nick of time before the gap between us widened and he disappeared over the horizon.

Daisun's bungalow was in the professorial compound of Qinghua University, for he was already Dean of Humanities. I wished that he was awake early so that we could breakfast together. Daisun, who was not given to lying in, was up sooner than I had thought. Sure to be the gracious host, he was the first to welcome young relatives to the capital. Over breakfast he chatted with paternal concern without going so far as to offer advice. We had soft-rice congee with the Fujian dried 'meat wool', toasted peanuts, boiled eggs and toast. Soon Charles arrived with his bicycle.

In the western part of Peking, and especially where the suburban villages were more scattered, you had to have a bicycle to get around. There was no time for me to buy a bicycle, so I borrowed one and we rode to Yanjing university a mile away. We cycled past Yuan Ming Yuan (The Old Summer Palace), now a cluster of marble ruins amid derelict canals and lakes. We passed the large village of Haidian, the centre of this part of the suburbs. Our route took us along country lanes which, worn down by centuries of cartwheels, were several feet below the surrounding wheat fields. In autumn, when the summer rains cease, the yellow loess becomes loose and the slightest breeze or passing bicycle will throw up clouds of swirling dust into the air.

Yanjing campus was surrounded by a high grey wall through which we entered via the South Gate. Inside the grounds opened up into a landscaped garden, criss-crossed with paths and streams and dotted with pavilions. I felt as if I had just ventured into the Forbidden City itself. There was a large lake with a bridge connecting the east bank to an island in the middle. To the north of the lake stood four men's dormitories. The fourth dormitory was to be my home for the next few years. Each one was resplendent, with roofs that curved upwards at the corners, and was decorated with small stone statues of mythical creatures. Sturdy red columns supported the roofs, set off by classical patterns and pictures painted in deep blues and greens upon the wooden awnings. A verandah ran along the front of the buildings, and two dining-halls connected one dormitory to another.

The fifth men's dormitory, a two-storey pavilion, stood further to the east. The sixth dormitory was the most modern and where the radiators were reputed to be the warmest. I was told it was the exclusive domain of a gang of self-styled 'élite' students. Half-way around the lake was the men's gym. It stood just below a 100-foot water tower carefully constructed to resemble an ancient pagoda. We walked over to the presidential lodge where Dr Leighton-Stuart, founder of Yanjing University, was in residence.

Dr Leighton-Stuart was the best-known American missionary in China and had achieved a lot for Yanjing university. Yanjing was famous for its School of Journalism, where Edgar Snow was one of the senior lecturers. There were always one or two American lecturers staying on the campus. Behind the president's lodge was a small hillock. Following the ridge, we came across an open pavilion in the middle of which hung a huge ancient bell, ten feet tall and five feet across. Every hour the bell was struck with a wooden hammer and could be heard resounding around the campus. Behind the hill lay the women's dormitories, surrounded by thirty tennis courts. They even had their own gym. I imagined that, with tennis and the girls concentrated in one area, this would be my favourite haunt.

The main entrance to the campus was through the East Gate and over a stone bridge flanked by two enormous marble columns. A decade before, these columns had been dragged on timber rollers from one of the destroyed palaces, and it had taken fifty horses to complete the task. East campus was altogether a more serious affair. It had the administration building, library and some half dozen laboratories and lecture halls.

Most of the people I met that day were in my brother's immediate circle, and he had briefed me about them already. Some were fellow graduates from the Anglo–Chinese College: Harry, my old tennis partner, and George Gao. There was a new crop of friends: several stocky lads from Hawaii and a whole crowd of bright-eyed youngsters from Shanghai and Canton who seemed very well dressed. Charles had paved my way to the capital and, within a day, had already provided me with a new social life. I welcomed everybody with open arms and, with my gregarious nature, I soon felt at home. These were the young élite, and among us were many surely destined for fame and fortune. We were all aware how exclusive our environment was, but justified our privilege with the feeling that our role was to indicate how life could and should be lived in China.

With the pocket money that Auntie Ying had furnished me, as a parting present, my first adventure was to go into town to buy my very own bicycle. Charles and I took the university bus into Peking. As we trundled along I surveyed the landscape. It seemed rather barren and dusty after the fertile valleys of Foochow. The odd camel on the road enhanced my impression that the north was a dusty desert. The approach to the capital was traversed by numerous canals that, for 2,000 years, had been carrying provisions and troops to and from all parts of the Empire. From time to time, by the side of the canal, we could see men hard at work digging away at 'ice holes'. The holes were so deep that, right through the summer, blocks of ice could be dislodged from the bottom and taken to the town to cool the food and drinks. Soon we were through the city wall and travelling past the maze of alleys that spread for miles around the Forbidden City.

I bought a brand new BSA, good for five years' cycling. I wheeled it on to the cobbled street of Peking, mounted, and promptly fell over. The wheel had caught in the rut of a tramrail. That evening I rode every pathway within the campus. The 'harvest moon' was nearly full and the sky full of stars. Early in the autumn the northern skies were both cloudless and windless, which made me aware of the luminosity of the sky. In the south the weather was rarely so clear. As I sped round and round the lake the coolness of the air caressed my legs and body as it blew through the thin cotton trousers and shirt that I was wearing. I felt exhilarated. After padlocking my bicycle, I went into the fourth dormitory and took a drink from the water fountains that lined the corridors. The air felt dry and my lips were already beginning to parch. I sprayed my face, as I had noticed others do, and dried myself with a handkerchief. Everything dried so quickly here away from the southern humidity.

Before lights out at 11 p.m. I lay in the dorm next to Charles and reflected on the stupendous summer just past, now culminating in this new beginning. Although several thousand miles from home I felt secure and at ease. The years at university seemed to spread out smoothly in front of me. There were no hurdles which I couldn't leap with ease.

In the early days of winter when the surface of the lake first began to freeze, through the quiet of the night we could hear a sound of tinkling glass. If the progress of winter was interrupted by several warm days, then the ice would melt and it would take several freezing nights before it was firm enough for a person to stand on again. Huge buckets of water were thrown over the ice every afternoon so that the next day there would be a new shining surface. Once, knowing full well that the surface was still thin, I rode my bicycle at great speed over the lake. I thought that the momentum was enough to carry me over the hidden sections of thin ice without peril. To my amazement I found myself chest-deep in icy water. Having the confidence in my judgement shattered was almost as much of a shock as the icy water seeping through my clothes. I abandoned my new BSA to the depths of the lake and ploughed my way through nearly fifteen yards of ice before I came to a firm edge. After a rub down in the dorm my skin was tingling with warmth. That was the only time I could appreciate the wisdom of a cold shower first thing. I have never repeated the experience intentionally.

Because the skies were so clear our lake was flooded with moonshine at night. All the students could skate. Within a few days I, too, had my own pair of black leather skates and had picked up the knack. It was essential to do so. For this was our most important social activity. You could skate at any time of day, but at night, when classes were over, there was no better form of relaxation. The fourth dormitory was the closest to the lake. After donning my khaki overcoat lined with inside-out sheepskin, and pulling down the ear flaps of my furry mongolian hat, I would rush out to join my friends on the lake. By the side of the island was a marble boat, a miniature of the one the Empress Dowager had built at the Summer Palace. In our boat they served hot dogs, or weenies as the Americans called them, and hot coffee. Skimming over the shadows of branches and trees cast by the moonlight across the lake gave you a feeling that you were travelling at great speed, and intensified our mood of excitement.

After the Japanese invasion of Manchuria on 18 September 1931, the exuberance of college had largely been toned down. All the same, we still partied. In no time, with my more sociable nature, I had doubled Charles's circle of friends. Every month we were invited to stay at the house of one branch of the Wei family. They had a modern house built in the style of the traditional courtyard compound but with every modern convenience. They even had a sprung dance floor where, in the company of thirty or forty other young people, with exclusive family pedigrees, we pre-booked our partners on a printed list and danced the waltz and the quickstep to gramophone records. Double-breasted suits, light-coloured silk ties and black patent shoes were *de rigueur* on the dance floor.

Many of the parties were held in professorial residences on the renovated gardens of the old Manchu nobles, but our central venue was the old Peking hotel. At 2 or 3 a.m. we would return home by cab or rickshaw. Although the ladies had all gone home separately, the ride home by rickshaw was still romantic. The rickshaw-puller would take off his padded gown and tuck it around your knees before starting out on the two-mile jog home. Residual body heat from his gown warmed our knees and legs. Overhead the heavens would be filled with winking stars. Occasionally street vendors called out their wares from the hutong (alley) corners. Plodding at a steady pace, the rickshaw puller's soft-soled shoes made a muffled thud as his feet hit the dust-laden road, his breath billowing in the cold air. In the small hours of the morning complete peace reigned over Peking.

As we waited outside the girls' dormitories, ever hopeful to find a date, the moonlight always fell on clusters of white bloom, making them iridescent in the night. Our environment was a perfect setting for romance – but romance was not to be easily encountered. Despite our youth and the changing age in which we lived, we behaved with Confucian reticence. I have to blame Confucius. He said that in an orderly society 'men and women should not be intimate when handing objects to one another'. In the liberated atmosphere of a modern college we still could not go much further than holding hands while skating. I hardly got as far as holding hands with anyone.

Before long I had developed a fancy for two young ladies, both long-jump champions: one, Zheng Lihua, was the petite long-jump champion of Canton. Being from the deep south she was dark and had dimpled athletic legs. The other, Bian Zhunian, had longer legs and walked in quick, free strides. She had a pale face with an exquisite brow and a high-bridged, almost European, nose. Her mouth was small and tempting, but in all the five years at college I never kissed her once, although I dreamed of it many times. And many times I cursed Confucius for not providing instruction in the art of courtship. He had only suggested that it was a man's duty to produce record-breaking numbers of progeny, as effortlessly as possible and, seemingly, without resorting to the reproductive act.

Bian Zhunian always sat two rows in front of me in our French class. Twice a week I awaited her brisk arrival. I felt drawn to her long well-shaped neck and neat brushed-back hair, always hoping to exchange a few words before she sat down. The shape of her calves would set me fantasizing about the power she could release, and the leap that had won her the long-jump championship of North China. The hours would flit by and I would learn little French. After a year I knew little more than the 'du thé' or 'pig's trotters' that I had learned ordering tea on the *André Lebon* fourteen years before. But the trotters delighting me here were not 'pig's trotters' but the most magnificent, pale legs.

One winter's day I became so bold as to ask my goddess of the noble brow if she would care to have a wander over to the ruins of Yuan Ming yuan (The Old Summer Palace), no more than a couple of miles from our campus. The marble ruins were scattered along a string of pools and miniature lakes which, in winter, were frozen solid. With great joy I took the opportunity to hold on to her hand as she leapt cautiously from ice to marble and then to ice again. Once or twice she nearly missed her step and I nearly caught and embraced her, but I didn't. With Confucius whispering in my ear, I dared do no more. I could only appreciate the sun as it set, turning the ruins a luminescent orange, and imagine the sumptuous imperial parties and seasonal rites that, not so long before, had graced the palace.

After our cold excursion I felt deflated and could not muster the courage or energy to keep pursuing her. Eventually she drifted away and out of my life completely when she left for America a year later.

My interest in Zheng Lihua warmed up as winter loosened its

grip and spring broke through. The change of season was rapid in the north. No sooner had the sun's rays made it warm enough to shed our outer layer, than it was already hot, and on the banks of the canals the weeping willows turned bright green overnight. Zheng Lihua never shared a class with me. Our only chance of meeting was in the library where we would sit among our own clusters of friends. I didn't want to make my approach too conspicuously by barging into her circle.

Unlike Bian Zhunian, Zheng Lihua bounced around. I often dreamed of embracing her radiant body. But how could I get near to her? With such vivacity she must be a candidate for the tennis court.

One sunny afternoon I asked her to have a knock up with me. I brought out my best, new balls and hired Wudi (fifth brother), my favourite ball boy. As we sauntered towards the courts the spring gusts swept the yellow dust into the air. It seemed a fitting match, for I was tennis champion of Fujian and she, the long-jump champion of neighbouring Guangdong. We both intended to dominate the North in our own events. On the court she bounced around, but kept running into the ball. I wanted to sweep her away but Confucius only allowed me to hold her firmly by the wrist and place my hand on top of hers to demonstrate the proper way to grip the racket.

I had hoped that a series of tennis lessons might allow us to drift together through the summer. But Zheng Lihua was wrested from my grasp by a crowd of boys from Hawaii who sang all the romantic songs and played the guitar and ukulele. To her they were the quintessence of style. Not only had they never heard Confucius's maxims, they also had huge muscles, and thought nothing of pulling girls to sit on their laps. Within a few months I had lost all hope of my 'brown goddess'. Her swarthy skin had melted into that pack of brown-skinned boys from the Pacific.

Faced with these two 'romantic disasters', I reverted to activities more under my own control: eating and sport. With sufficient clothing and more than adequate hot food, the iciness of the northern winter was no deterrent to a hot-blooded southerner. The window from the first floor of the fourth dormitory looked east. From my bed I could see the red glow of the winter sun break the horizon. It rose rapidly, shedding a light over north-west Peking that turned the land a pure orange. Sitting up, still snug in the warmth of my bed, I could see over the frozen lake below the dorm. It was a fine view. After lying in bed for a while I would make a sudden dash for my clothing and, once properly dressed, would rush downstairs to the dining-halls.

We shared our dishes on a table of eight, but the tables were rarely full in the morning. Tianjin white cabbage in soup stock was served up for breakfast. For a few pennies you could have a fresh egg thrown into your own bowl, and that didn't have to be shared. It was hardly the most savoury of starts to the day, but a touch of soya made the fresh leaves palatable, and the stock always warmed you up and set you in good stead for the day. Following the soup came unlimited rice congee, and 'mantou' (steamed wheat buns), the staple diet of the north, were served at a fixed monthly rate. To finish off I would have 'you tiao' (deep fried fritter sticks) which, like the Spanish who dip their 'churros' in hot chocolate, I would moisten with soya milk.

Most of the dishes at our midday meal were flavourless, but there was a good variety. The pork was usually streaky, the fish too tasteless to be acceptable to someone from the south-east coast, but there was always a stir-fry with beef and tomatoes in the summer or steamed mince and cauliflower. And at every meal there was endless cabbage soup. Anyone could pay for an extra dish to supplement the four basics and often it was necessary for, if you arrived late, you would be faced with a table full of mantou and nothing else. For a treat there were plenty of enormous pears about the size of average grapefruit, and orange-red persimmons which we left outside the window overnight. In the morning we spooned out the flesh from under their thick, bitter skin as if they were ice cream.

If we ever felt starved of decent food there was always Haidian, not far beyond the East Gate. There, at café Tongshan, we could enjoy King Prawns in Reduced Sauce, Braised Garlic Lamb with Young Leeks or Sweet and Sour Chopped Spare Ribs. In late summer when the lakes were drained there would be carp, although if the carp hadn't been kept in clear water for a few days it had a muddy flavour.

When affluent we would take the bus into town and go sightseeing at the Temple of Heaven or to swim in the lake at Zhongnanhai, the only part of the Forbidden City open to the public. Afterwards we ate at one of the popular open-air Mongolian Hot-Pot restaurants in East Market. The market was a remarkable place where people had been plying their trade for centuries. It was a huge arcade and amusement centre where you could buy antiques, paintings, books, scrolls and calligraphy, cakes, sweetmeats, lanterns and kites while watching open-air theatre or listening to Peking opera.

The most enticing delicacy at the hot-pot stalls was Mongolian Barbecue of Lamb. Slices of lamb were dipped in egg before being grilled over a blazing fire and eaten with a spicy sauce. It was a feast fit for any Mongolian prince! Of course the Mongolian Hot-Pot itself is the very essence of northern celebration, far more so than Peking duck. Its secret is in communal effort: the diners roll up their sleeves and do the cooking themselves. Wafer thin slices of lamb are laid out on a mass of small plates that cover the whole table top. In the middle of the table a hot-pot full of broth is brought to a rolling boil. In the meantime the diners have each mixed themselves three or four savoury dips, some chilli hot, some spicy with ginger and garlic, and others with the nutty taste of sesame. Then, grasping a sliver of lamb with chopsticks, we would plunge the meat into the cauldron and hold it under for a couple of minutes. The hot, freshly cooked meat contrasts with the savoury sauce to produce a dish that is at once both simple and sophisticated. There is a flurry of activity around the table and in no time at all the little plates are empty. Once the meat is finished, a bowl full of noodles and a bowl of sliced cabbage are emptied into the broth and the pot is covered and allowed to simmer for five minutes. In the last rites of the ceremony each diner's bowl is filled with noodle, cabbage and broth for a final wash down. In the gloom of a winter's night, to sit around a blazing charcoal burner and a steaming hot-pot in the company of four or more good friends evokes the campfires and camaraderie of northern nomadic life.

On occasions when I felt inclined towards something more exotic, I would drop in at the foreigners' YMCA where they had a good range of ice cream and cake, hot coffee and fizzy drinks. On one memorable occasion I was sitting with some friends after a game of tennis. Suddenly there was a roar of cars and a half dozen bodyguards rushed in and lined up against the opposite wall, with guns cocked menacingly. When they saw that we were only armed with tennis rackets they relaxed a little. They heralded the arrival of the young marshal, Zhang Xueliang, then war-lord of Manchuria, who arrived amid a milling crowd of beautiful concubines.

A decade before my time at Yanjing University, China had won the tennis event at the Far Eastern Olympics for the first time, snatching the title away from Japan and the Philippines. The heroes of the tournament were two players, Gordon Lum and Koo Huhai. Gordon Lum had great style. He was already the junior champion of Australia and had come home to play for China. He had a well-refined service, a backhand slice and a forehand with an exaggerated top spin. Koo, returning from Malaysia, brought with him a steady game with a powerful lift forehand and lethal drop shot that was a challenge to Gordon. They were both an inspiration to me and although I never had the chance to go into battle with either, I felt honoured to play on the same courts.

When I first went north the two top players were the brothers Gao Huiming and Gao Ziming. They both stood over six feet tall and were the sons of the Principal of Hui Wen secondary school. In front of their house there was a hard court where we all had plenty of opportunity to play. Huiming, the elder, was a magician with the ball. Ziming belted it back like a bullet. He would run at the ball to put even greater speed into his forehand. They both had great potential, but their eventual undoing came from over-indulgence in their own particular talents. Ziming's drive was so fast it often went out and Huiming's 'magic' often backfired, especially when he undercut the ball so heavily that it would bounce back into his own court!

But even with all the stars of court and campus milling around, the person who had most bearing on my life was still Harry Li (Li Guofan). He had been my tennis partner in Fujian and we had won the provincial championship together. We complemented each other. He had a deep, bounding service and a smooth overhead volley while I was strong off the ground and played an industrious pounding game. Our game hardly ever went off the boil. When his service was wilting my forehand thundered, and when my forehand missed, his overhead cracked it down. We had great stamina, and if we could get through the first hour, our sheer resolve would always carry the day. Within two years our tennis ranking was third or fourth in the north, and by 1934 we had won the North China Championship in Tianjin.

Because Harry and I got on so well I rarely partnered Charles. When I did it was often disastrous. His game was too refined and he did not have the flexibility that I needed in a partner. I always played a rough and tumble game and needed someone who could bail me out. Nevertheless, when we played opposite each other we were well matched and he would win as often as I. I like to think that it was because Confucius always demanded respect for the elder brother that I let him get the better of me. Otherwise how could elegant swordplay ever be a match for the Monkey King's cudgel?

By summer the Japanese invasion had still not reached Peking or Tianjin. Although there had been some skirmishes along the Great Wall between the forces of the local security chief, Song Zheyuan, and the Japanese, as a university tennis team we still felt safe enough to accept an invitation to a jaunt to the seaside resort of Qingdao on the southern side of the Shandong peninsula. Qingdao had everything: warm sea, miles of white sand and a coastline of hazy purple hills laden with fruit trees. Pouring out of Lao Shan mountains came the renowned 'Qingdao Beer'. Qingdao also had four tennis clubs, two Chinese, one German and one Japanese. After the Boxer Rebellion

Qingdao had been under German occupation but had been returned to China at the end of the First World War. Since then it had become part of the Japanese sphere of influence.

In the tennis pecking order, the Chinese were kept in place by the Germans and the Germans by the Japanese. To keep up an appearance of cordiality between the communities in Qingdao, a friendly inter-club tennis match was organized with the blessing of the Mayor, Admiral Shen Honglie, a well-known character in northern Chinese naval circles.

Luckily our group of holiday-makers from Peking had brought rackets and tennis gear. After a short trial we were invited to play for the Chinese side. Our first encounter was with the Germans. They were flamboyant players but had no control off the ground. We wiped the floor with them. In the final encounter I was matched against the Japanese number one. He was steady and persistent. The sun was hot that afternoon and, coming from the southern tropics, I had a natural advantage. The match lasted into its third hour. My Japanese opponent was perspiring profusely and drinking gallons of iced water. I, unusually, had also broken into a sweat. On the rare times when I do sweat it has an intoxicating effect on me. As with the first swell of drunkenness, I am overwhelmed by a new confidence and feel I can run twice as fast. My Japanese opponent was unable to catch me out. He was panting for breath. All of a sudden he fell to the ground writhing. The Chinese crowd cheered loudly. I felt embarrassed. It was a true knock out, game, set and match.

That evening Admiral Shen gave a party to honour my personal defeat of Japan. We ate in a long sea-front restaurant, festooned with orange lanterns, and I got up and sang the song 'Blue Hawaii'. I must have been drunk on my sweat and the local beer!

After winning the North China Championship in Tianjin, I was elected to captain the Peking team to the National Olympics in Shanghai the following year. The Shanghai tournament was held in the brand new civic centre stadium which, built to scale with the stadium planned for the 1936 Berlin Olympics, had a seating capacity of 100,000. Teams from all over China, Xinjiang, Yenan and Heilongjiang were converging on Shanghai for the biggest ever Olympics. We must have had ten teams travelling from Peking, including the fastest sprinter in China, Liu Changqun. Liu Changqun ran a record 100 metres in 10.6 seconds. All the way from Peking I remained stretched out horizontal on the luggage rack until we crossed the Yangzi River at Nanjing. It was a wonderful ride and I arrived in peak condition, both mentally and physically. We all felt as if we were riding the crest of a wave.

To be part of this national sports meeting gave us all a great sense of strength in number and unity. Surely we could not be pushed around indefinitely by Japan.

That first evening in Shanghai I slept in a dormitory with a sloping roof directly below the stadium seats. With no carpet on the concrete floor to insulate against noise, the snoring of hundreds of travel-weary athletes seemed to reverberate rhythmically around the cavernous room. The next day Charles and I moved to Uncle King's lavish, modern house in west Shanghai where we could be sure to get a good sleep.

It was a bright sunny morning when we jumped in a taxi and sped down to the first morning of the games. Our first thought was to get in a good breakfast and we descended upon a shop built into the galleries around the stadium and had a breakfast of congee with salted egg, pickles and cold savouries. As an official member of the Peking team I should have participated in the march around the stadium, but I must have been late. All I remember was a flight of doves which swept up into the sky as we entered the stadium.

The first event was a volley ball match between a North China team and the Air Force. The Air Force team wore smart, well-cut leather jackets and looked very sleek. This was a new generation of Chinese warriors and I felt proud of them. I clenched my fists and felt a new strength welling up inside. Perhaps at last China would come into her own!

On our return to Peking the feeling had mounted that we were living in a 'fool's paradise'. With a background of conflict between the Nationalists [under Chiang Kaishek] and the Communists and massive Japanese encroachment into Chinese soil, students were clamouring for the government to make a committed stand against the invasion.

Chiang Kaishek with his Nationalist army, at the head of a war-lord coalition was being cautious. He had even gone so far as to say 'We shall not forsake peace until there is no hope for peace. We shall not talk lightly of sacrifice until we are driven to the last extremity'. I suppose that, having been trained in Japan, he had a healthy respect for the Japanese army and was more aware of its real menace than even the western leaders. While using the war-lord forces as a buffer between the Japanese and the cream of his own fighting troops, he was building his military strength with the military adviser General Faulkenhauser. Numerous young officers were even sent to train in Nazi Germany. His air force was being strengthened by Mussolini through the help of Count Ciano, then Italian Consul-General in Shanghai.

Towards the mid 1930s neither the Japanese nor the Chinese were faced with easy options. On the surface it seemed as if the Japanese Army held all the cards, but we felt China had size, numbers and talent and should be arriving on to the international scene. She also had plentiful automatic weapons, land mines and mortars. The war-lord armies numbered at least three million and Chiang's crack units no less than one and a quarter million men.

Nevertheless, the winter of 1934–35 was our 'winter of discontent'. Student activists were vociferous in denouncing both local and central government for not defending our homeland. This was an issue that both left and right agreed upon, and by 13 December 1934 the 'Qinghua critic' had pre-empted the Communist call for a United Front against the Japanese. But despite Chiang's clarion call to all youngsters who wished to enlist, there were few student volunteers. Although small detachments were putting up resistance to the Japanese, it was many hundreds of miles away in Manchuria and in a terrain and temperature where students would hardly survive.

Three days later, at 6.30 a.m. on 16 December, a freezing morning, we were all up and standing around the national flag which had just been hoisted to the top of the pole. Against the clear blue sky the flag, lit up with the rays of the morning sunshine, was a great inspiration. We saluted before commencing our twelve-mile hike to town. Only a few hundred of us set out from Yanjing University but the Qinghua contingent would make us a substantial part of the demonstration. By the time we entered the city walls all the schools, teacher colleges and universities of Peking would make up thousands of demonstrators.

I wasn't entirely clear what the student demands were and felt nervousness at the pit of my stomach as we marched along shouting slogans. During previous student demonstrations against war-lord rule, the gendarmes guarding government offices had opened fire. But after four or five miles' march, warmed and excited, we reached the city's West Gate. It was locked. At the vanguard of the demonstration the students picked up a telegraph pole, lying conveniently at the side of the road, and rammed the gate as if storming some medieval castle. The huge door put up little resistance and we swarmed in. The few gendarmes, in their padded military coats, merely stood aside and watched us. I had brought my bicycle along and rode through the gate as part of a flying cavalry unit protecting the flanks. Once inside the city I was able to move unchecked through the maze of hutongs (alleys). I headed east where I was familiar with the lay of the land.

When I had put two miles between myself and the main contingent of demonstrators, an even better thought crossed my mind. I had just read Hemingway's *A Farewell to Arms* and remembered the hero who, disillusioned with the First World War, rowed across Lake Constance and eloped with an English nurse. Since love wasn't an option I decided to do the next best thing. Why besiege the foreign ministry when I could just stop where I was and have a good meal? Just at that moment I passed the 'lü ming qun' (The Deer Call out the Spring), where I was joined by several other outriders and sat down to a good feast of mutton hot-pot.

Down at the foreign ministry 7,775 students had congregated to protest. The police, unnerved by the biggest demonstration they had ever witnessed, turned ice water on to the crowd. But although wet and cold, the students' spirits remained undampened and they could claim at least partial success. Song Zheyuan, using the possibility of further unrest as a negotiating point, managed to get the Japanese to release their 'five province autonomy' demand. The movement spread through the rest of China, with telegrams flying back and forward between student organizations and a total of sixty-five demonstrations staged around the country. But in spring Song Zheyuan redoubled his efforts to suppress student unrest, and the Communist sympathizers were forced further underground.

No doubt the demonstrations were the effective result of the work of Communist party members who were circulating all around. Chiang Kaishek had set up his capital in Nanjing, which left a power vacuum in Peking. Under the umbrella of extra-territorial status in the university campus, communism could flourish in relative safety. Many students saw the Communists as having a clearer policy against the invasion, and many of the western teachers were also left wing in orientation. In particular Edgar and Helen Snow were holding student meetings, urging on a mass movement among the students. Although I never attended the meetings I had a general awareness of the debate. Students were organized to go out into the country. A campaign was mounted in Hubei bringing songs, plays and speeches intended to elevate the country people's political consciousness. It was not an overwhelming success, and the students probably learned far more about life from the peasants. Country people were only moved by the prospect of tax reduction and talk of land redistribution.

Mao Zedong and Zhu De, having survived the arduous Long March, were re-grouping in Yenan in the north-western mountain stronghold on the borders of the Gobi desert. They had learned a lot on their journey and, by treating local people well and carrying out social and land reform, had left a trail of support behind them. Backwards into China, right down into the Yangzi valley, across the plains of North China and into Manchuria, there were Communist detachments waging a guerrilla war and spreading propaganda. Students, both male and female, were slipping away in droves to fight for the cause.

To dissuade China's youth from drifting towards Yenan and Communism or joining up with the now famous 8th Route and 4th Route armies, Chiang was attempting to weed out all those who had sympathies with the left. I first came across the Nationalist secret service while taking an afternoon siesta. So that I would not be easily disturbed, I had chosen to take my nap in the room of an old friend from Foochow. Finding myself without a light for my cigarette, I pulled open one of his drawers and, to my surprise, found that he had a Mauser pistol and Mills bomb hand-grenade. When he returned I cross-questioned him about his artillery and he replied casually that he was in the pay of the 'Special Service' [De Wu Dui]. He told me that he was paid very little and pledged me to secrecy. I was alarmed at the nonchalant way with which he stored his weapons, but wanted to try out the Mauser all the same. The Mills bomb grenade seemed a pretty useless weapon for catching 'red agents' but he insisted that he was going to throw it at the Japanese when the time came. At the back of the sixth dormitory I fired two shots at a brick no more than four or five yards away and missed, blaming the Mauser. It kicked too much to be accurate. I wondered how long the Secret Service would keep such a lackadaisical *agent provocateur* on the payroll.

It was a relief that intelligence under Chiang's regime was so ineffective. If you were fast on your feet you could run rings around the cloth-soled *agents provocateurs* and their security systems and still get away with murder. Many did get away to join the 8th and 4th Route armies or slipped away to Yenan. Some were caught, but mainly because they had regarded Chiang's security with a little too much contempt.

I saw little of the real world from my ivory tower on the Yanjing campus. Life went on as usual, oblivious to the distant thunder of war. After 11 p.m. the electric lights were turned off, and through the night the windows flickered with the candle-light of students burning the midnight oil. In the afternoon and evenings the lake was still full of skaters skimming over the lake in pairs.

I had begun by majoring in physics with a view to transferring to Qinghua University to study a technological subject. I sat half-a-dozen papers. Ironically I scored highly in Bible studies and came top in photography. Dr Fosdick's books on 'faith', 'prayer' and 'service' had set me in good stead. But I failed to transfer and, after a while, abandoned theoretical physics to major in English literature where I had a natural advantage.

My love for English literature was in no way diminished when I found that Gong Busheng, the elder of two attractive sisters, was studying in the same department. She was an unorthodox, jade-like beauty and, although I had no hope of a romantic engagement, it was a pleasure to sit side by side on the steps of the women's study, revising together and offering her advice on translation. We ploughed our way through *Clarissa*, the eighteenth-century epistolary novel, in eight volumes, by Samuel Richardson and then became completely immersed in John Galsworthy's *Forsyte Saga*. In poetry I was chewing over the poems of Keats, Shelley, Coleridge and Wordsworth with the same slow deliberation with which I had consumed the Confucian classics. Others were more inclined to mathematics but, despite the personal tutelage of Hua Luogeng, a renowned mathematician, I concluded that my strength was with fellow human beings and not figures.

After five years people began to accuse me of being a 'perpetual student'. More of my determined contemporaries were joining up with the Communist troops, some detachments of which had already penetrated into the hills in underground burrows not many miles from Peking. I didn't know exactly when Edgar Snow went to Yenan to interview Mao or when he wrote *Red Star over China*, nor when Lord Lindsay joined the 8th Route army as a wireless operator, nor when the Gong sisters melted away to become assistants to Zhou Enlai or when Han Suyin became converted to the cause, but I skated with them all on the frozen lake in Yanjing.

During the spring months of 1936 I was becoming accustomed to the thought of leaving China. A distance was growing up between myself and my peers. When the crunch came I knew I wasn't going to be with them. Sometimes I felt like a rat leaving a sinking ship. A second cousin from the Chen family, a bosom friend from Foochow days, wrote me a thirty-five-page epistle to remind me that, although I was planning to leave China, I must not forget my responsibility as a member of our generation. China might become further and further away, but her resurgence was dependent upon the liberation of the common people, their appreciation of the issues at stake, their preparedness to seize the power within their grasp. I kept his letter. He was already a member of the Communist party. During the last years in Peking, between the *agent provocateur* and my communist cousin, I had had two old friends who were underground operators. Still, China was large and had room for all sorts, but for how long?

I decided to leave politics to other more radical fellow students. Perhaps the lack of political discussion at home had left me unprepared for it and, more personally, as political affiliation served to alienate people, it offended my gregarious nature. With my memories of London the allure of the West became irresistible. It had been settled that Europe was to be my destination and I was praying that I might be able to slip away before the jaws of the Japanese closed. I explored the cheapest ways of travelling to Europe: the Trans-Siberian railway was expensive. My cheapest option was to cadge a lift with the 142-strong Chinese Olympic team on its way to the Berlin Olympics. They had been in training for three months on the Qinghua campus. I was friendly with the organizers, and it was not difficult to persuade them that if they were making a block-booking one extra should make no difference. I could act as an interpreter since there was no-one fluent in English on the whole team. For three weeks on an Italian liner, then by railway to Berlin and four days in a Venice hotel, the total was £41, less than half the rate of going it alone. To travel with the Olympic team was altogether more exciting. And as one of China's rising sportsmen I didn't feel a total impostor.

Since I wasn't an official member I had to obtain a German visa independently. I was concerned that Nazi Germany might have some reservations about admitting an unofficial element of the yellow horde. But with General Faulkenhauser as an adviser, Chiang was forging increasingly closer links with Germany and sending many of his young officers to be trained there. Not only had they returned with military expertise but some even had German wives in tow. It transpired that I didn't have to pay. The consular officer handed back my passport the very same day with the black German eagle stamp sprawled across it. I shook his hand and said 'Danke schön' in my best German accent.

By summer I was all set for Europe. Although I was not given an Olympic uniform, they furnished me with a wad of Olympic labels to stick on my luggage. I was taking a trunk and two suitcases: one, that heavy leather suitcase of my father's, had seen better days before the First World War and the other, a small magenta-coloured one, I had purchased in the East Market. They both looked resplendent with the stickers and I surveyed my luggage with pride.

The weather became warm as my departure approached and everything about Peking began to look transient. The willow trees by the lake were heavy with foliage and tomatoes were served with every meal. My Chen cousins gave me a farewell dinner attended by twenty friends and family. Even Dr Leighton-Stuart entertained me to a private dinner in his lodge. I remember saying to him that my life abroad was likely to move my career on to a more specific plane – perhaps the diplomatic world. I knew I could do nothing for the 85 per cent of the Chinese people who were peasants.

After stowing away my luggage, I sat on the steps of the train as it pulled out of Peking station. There were a dozen friends to see me off. I would miss all the boys I had studied and played with in the south and the north but I would miss Charles most. I had shared almost every experience I had ever had with him. He was racing along the platform keeping up with the moving train. I waved and waved. It was a great wrench. I felt rivers of hot tears running down my cheeks. I wiped them dry as I turned and climbed into the train to take up my seat. The athletes, laughing and chatting away, didn't have a care in the world. They were merely going for a couple of months, but how could I know how long I was going to be away?

CHAPTER SEVEN

Second Journey to the West

送　友　人

李　白

青山橫北郭　白水繞東城

此地一為別．孤蓬萬里征

浮雲遊子意　落日故人情

揮手自茲去　蕭蕭班馬鳴

Green hills overlook the north wall,
White water swirls around the east city,
This is where we must part –
a lone puff of thistledown on a thousand mile campaign.
The thoughts of a wanderer in the drifting clouds,
The sentiment of old friends in the setting sun,
The horses whinny
and with the wave of a hand you are gone.

Li Bo. AD 701–762

MY DEPARTURE FROM Shanghai was less emotional. It became merged into the departure of the Olympic team, a national event that was emblazoned across every daily paper. China was still able to present a united front at something and sending us off was guaranteed to whip up a wave of nationalism. There was a great uproar on the dock. Flags and streamers, like ribbons of multi-coloured spaghetti, cascaded over the side of the Italian liner, the MV *Conte Verde*. Over 10,000 well-wishers gathered on the dock to cheer the team on.

My parents, in the company of a dozen aunts, uncles and cousins, came aboard. Harry Li, who had been in Shanghai for over a year, was there too, beaming reassuringly in his carefree way. It made our parting seem a celebration. We drank soft drinks in the bar until the siren hooted and I shook hands with my parents for the last time. The siren hooted again, a band struck up a tune from the dock, streamers billowed like clouds and everyone cheered. I did not shed any tears.

Soon the ship was in the estuary of the Huangpu River. Gazing back at the featureless mudflats of the coastline I whispered 'My country 'tis of thee!' and then again, as the liner began to gain speed, 'My country 'tis of thee' came murmuring through my lips.

It wasn't that any psychological problem was assailing me at this critical juncture in my life. Unlike the western youth that I was soon to come to know, we Chinese had had no private world to grow in, no secret garden within which life can all too easily become dreamlike and surreal. I was 'number two', neatly indexed and tabulated, and any private garden that I might have nurtured had long been trampled by hordes of concerned relatives.

With such a sturdy 'anchorage' I could venture, with confidence, into the world. But I was very worried about China. Once there was a solution to our national crisis all personal problems would surely, simultaneously, dissolve. I kept telling myself that China's size and numbers would pull her through. Even with the worst of luck there would always be people left to rise, like the phoenix, from the ashes. But what could the worst of luck be and how long would it be before she rose again?

My solemnity, as ever, was short-lived, and in a moment the words murmuring through my lips had transformed themselves to 'What a great country, so many good things to eat!' Turning away from the sea, I shifted my attention to making better acquaintance with my friends on the team, the various decks where we could promenade and jog, and to savouring the wafts of spaghetti bolognese rising from the Italian kitchens. Our team had brought five Chinese cooks, but they had been barred from the galley and, besides, all the essential ingredients were locked in the hold.

As soon as the ship passed the Wusong forts at the junction of the Huangpu and the Yangzi Rivers, I went below to unpack. The forts would be useless to deter the Japanese. My four brand new racquets were more reassuring. They had been made by Yang Zitian, a private racquet maker who visited Yanjing campus once a month. For not more than £2 he would have a racquet made within two days, hand strung to the right tension and colour co-ordinated to order. These were the weapons with which I would take on Europe. Although not as perfectly crafted as their western counterparts, they had served me well to date, and I was impatient to cross swords with the best of my generation in Europe. I also had a brand new, handmade tuxedo. Although not of the latest style and fashion, it sat well on my shoulders and gave me the confidence to anticipate the whirl of social life at the Chinese legation in Copenhagen.

Days passed quickly. When I became bored with jogging and promenading I practised clay pigeon shooting with our German lady interpreters or grappled with a girl from the martial arts team who was constantly taunting me. It was quite impossible to hold her down. She was a great wriggler! The martial arts team were just there for show as no opponents could be found in other countries. Our greatest hope was Liu Changqun who, although short, could run 100 metres in 10.6 seconds, only 0.4 seconds slower than the great Jesse Owens. Our strongest man, Hu Baolu, hailed from Harbin, near the Manchurian border, and had some Russian blood in his veins. Our shot-putters couldn't outdo me in arm-wrestling. I was sadly disappointed and could only conclude that they should have stayed at home. Our best-known footballers were Li Weitong, the centre half of South China, and Little Black Charcoal (Xiao Heitan) who was to share my cabin.

After ten days' sailing we arrived in Colombo and it was high time for a haircut. I followed my nose to the Metropole Hotel.

Passing under the huge, black head of an elephant that straddled the hotel lounge, I began to have the strangest feeling of *déjà vu*. It was not until the revolving brush was whirring over my head that it began to dawn upon me that I had been here before: seventeen years before, in the same barber's chair! I peered at myself in the mirror, eager to detect the changes that seventeen years had wrought. Finding little deterioration I returned, satisfied and well groomed, to the ship.

For youngsters from the Far East, the East and Middle East held little appeal. Like the Monkey King, our quest was for the secrets of the Western Heaven (even though West for the Monkey was India!). Whatever adventures that were to be had in between would certainly be distractions and probably lead to some kind of devilish trouble or other. Consequently when the ship docked in Bombay, I remained aboard, mindless that the steel became so hot that it had been transformed into a metal oven. Shaded by the promenade of the top deck, I stretched out on a deck chair and absorbed myself in *Lady Chatterley's Lover*. Finding it disappointingly light on pornography, not at all what it was cracked up to be, I sped my way through it and returned to Goethe's *The Sorrow of Young Werther*. I found the latter was more to my taste. It didn't seem to aspire to be anything more than a sentimental piece of writing. Perhaps I missed Goethe's point, but I enjoyed it all the same!

Before long we had sailed the Red Sea and were breezing through the Mediterranean. Venice did not leave me with a favourable impression. We stayed four long days while waiting for the Italian and Austrian teams to assemble themselves for the onward trip together. The old city did not live up to our expectation of a developed western city. We were put out by the familiar stench of humanity, and failed to admire the classical architecture. We had also imagined that mosquitoes were a preserve of China's paddy fields, but Venetian mosquitoes needed to learn nothing from the Chinese.

As we steamed through the Alps via Innsbruck and passed through Bavaria and Munich, on our way to Berlin, people recognized the respective national colours and flags that bedecked each carriage and came along to cheer us on our way. Early the next morning we pulled into Berlin station. No sooner had we disembarked than we were all lined up on the platform to sing our national anthems. But we were altogether drowned out by 'Deutschland Über Alles!' which swelled up on all sides. This did nothing to alleviate the apprehension that had crept up on me as we had neared Berlin. I was not a member of the Olympic team and I was to be in a strange city.

In my uncertainty I followed the road of least resistance and tagged on behind the team as they piled into the khaki-camouflaged military coaches, which were drawn up alongside the platform. We were on our way to the Olympic Village. The village area assigned to the Chinese team had a beautifully designed common room and dining hall at its centre, with dormitories radiating out in four directions. Within moments our cooks were despatched to the kitchens so we could christen the new home Chinese style. I was sharing a room with Little Black Charcoal again and, after settling in, we went out on to the sports ground to greet the team members from other countries.

Liu Changqun looked puny against the American giants, Jesse Owens and Metcalf. I tried running beside them but, after twenty yards, just felt silly. As I had never been much of a spectator, I felt out of place in the village and decided to get on with my own life. Little Black Charcoal gave me a ticket for the Games and, the next morning, I went to town to prospect for a place to stay. Feeling a little lost, I instinctively made my way to the nearest Chinese restaurant in Kant Strasse, called the Nanking, where I found a flat to let for £3 a week. I moved in the next day.

The highlight of my few days in Berlin was not attending the opening ceremony of the Games, but buying two German tennis racquets. My handmade racquets had warped during their passage through the Red Sea. And then there was the afternoon that I spent in the Tiergarten telephoning the Fraüleins on another table. Sadly my German was not fluent enough to invite a girl to waltz, and the girls, who seemed intimidatingly large at close quarters, all declined to take up my offer.

Although midsummer, it was cool and easy to sleep in my room, which was decorated with heavy drapes and furniture. I reminded myself that this was Northern Europe and once the door was closed everything became private. No friends or relatives were likely to come barging into my life. I was a little nostalgic, but still could banish these thoughts and concentrate on life ahead of me, in Copenhagen and Britain. Rather than hang around Berlin feeling rejected, I determined to speed up my passage to Copenhagen. I went back to bid farewell to our Olympic team and was surprised to see that Hu Baolu had reached the semi-finals of the pole vaulting. After a goodbye tussle with the girl on the martial arts team, I left.

The Chinese Legation was situated by a wooded beach in one of Copenhagen's better suburbs, called Helzupp. As Chinese ambassador to Denmark, my uncle always lived in some style and they knew how to make me feel at home. My aunt was a great socialite. It was the same

aunt and uncle who had been with us in London before, and baby
Becee, whom we had pushed around Hampstead Heath in a pram, was
now a junior tennis champion. Her mother was very proud of her and
with her Danish education she had everything she could ever want.
Even Qingqing had left Foochow to join them. With his familiar care
and cooking there was no one better suited to settle me into life
in the West. They also had another Chinese servant and a Packard
limousine with red wheelhubs.

Uncle Yi was on very good terms with the British diplomats
in Copenhagen, and often went out with the military and naval
attachés. He had been up at Jesus College, Cambridge, and was very
much at home with the English language and culture. He also saw
a good deal of Nielsen, the Danish consul to China, and Ossing and
Lange, who were wealthy importers of duck down. These connections
were most important: money was remitted irregularly under war-lord
rule, so Uncle Yi often had to rely on sympathetic Danish merchants.

Apart from these distinguished work associates there was even one
family from the Danish royalty on their social circuit. I never saw
much of Prince Eric but I saw a good deal of his wife. In fact she was
not Danish at all, but a Canadian timber millionairess, who was keen
to live it up like a natural-born princess, probably even more than a
natural-born princess. When I stayed the weekend in her castle, the
Bierbygaard, we were served by several liveried footmen and dined
on gold-tinted plates.

With my tuxedo, my English and a fair command of English
literature I took to this life like a duck to water. And it took to me.
It transpired that the Princess had a friend, an engineer at the Tuborg
breweries but, more significantly, a ranking tennis player. When he
discovered that I was keen to play and even had numerous tennis shirts
and some very, very white trousers, he was already excited. When he
found that I could challenge him on the tennis court he was overjoyed.
I began to receive more invites to the castle than my aunt and uncle.
As a comparatively young man, he needed more than a middle-aged
princess and a host of livery men to keep him entertained for a long
weekend in a cold Danish castle with an unheated swimming pool.
Before he drove me back to the Chinese legation in Copenhagen,
we would go and visit the vast breweries and dine at the old Vivex
restaurant, next to the Tivoli.

As tennis was clearly my passport to the Princess's castle, it
didn't take my uncle long to realize that there was more to the
sport than might at first meet the eye. He immediately engaged a
famous Czech tennis coach to give me a half dozen lessons. I was

thrilled. I had already heard of Kozeluh as the greatest tennis player that Czechoslovakia had ever produced. After six lessons I was playing with much more assurance. As he spoke little English, we would spend the second half of the session playing an all out set. I had to work hard to catch him, although I did once reach ten games all in one set! Those were the days of pounding forehand drives, rallied back and forth interminably from the baseline of red shale courts. Unconsciously I was being moulded into this sturdy, dogged type of player, having no experience of the 'high speed, sudden death' type of game.

It was early September and high time that I went on to Britain. I talked it over with my uncle. It was the first time I had had such a long and animated conversation with him. I dearly wanted to represent the third generation of the Lo family to study in Britain and be the second generation to go up to Cambridge. The subject provoked Uncle Yi into reviewing his career in some detail. We snuggled into easy chairs placed opposite each other and barely noticed the arrival of dawn and then broad daylight. We concluded that I had better go over to Britain as soon as possible to catch the start of the autumn term.

My first application to St Catherine's College, where my father had been an undergraduate, elicited a lukewarm reply. It simply instructed me to apply again the following year as it was already far too late to consider starting that autumn. It had been thirty years since my father had been at Cambridge and nobody remembered him. Back to square one. Uncle Yi advised me to try Fitzwilliam House, where several uncles had studied. Fitzwilliam House was still a non-collegiate body with over 90 per cent of its members residing outside the college. It was likely to have less of a restriction on quotas than the old colleges whose halls were bursting at the seams. Uncle Yi also cautioned me to play down my academic qualifications, which in any case were not very brilliant, in favour of basking in the glory of my grandfather's more impressive achievements. As for my own talents, it would make more of an impression to mention that I was tennis captain for Peking and champion of North China. I added ambitiously that I aimed to have a Cambridge Blue in the first year. This time the reply from the Registrar was warm and he invited me to see him for an interview.

A couple of days later I left Copenhagen with Peter (the second son of my eldest maternal uncle). Peter was more westernized than me. He seemed distanced, almost disinterested in China past, present or future. I excused him, for he hadn't spent the last decades in China. He hadn't studied the Chinese classics, witnessed the great northern expeditions or marched on the student demonstrations in Peking. They had been formative years which had made me proud of my country. Even if the dormitories and sanitation of our Shanghai Civic Sports Stadium couldn't compare with the Olympic village in Berlin, it was at least as big!

After Esbjerg, Harwich and Liverpool Street station we emerged from the dingy London underground at Tottenham Court Road. Buses swung with a grinding of gears into Oxford Street. The buses had roofs now and the taxis had balloon tyres instead of hard wheels. Otherwise, I noted with satisfaction, little had changed in seventeen years. Buses 73, 8 and 25 even travelled the same routes that I had known when I was five. I felt I was an 'Old London Hand'. It was 12 September 1936, my twenty-fourth birthday. Having in mind the cream teas of old with my mother at Lyon's Corner House, I suggested to Peter that we might celebrate, before taking leave of each other. Peter favoured Frascati's, an Italian restaurant near at hand. Nearly a month on an Italian liner from Shanghai had not endeared me to spaghetti bolognese, but out of respect to Peter, who didn't understand the joys of Lyon's Corner House and felt that I was a newcomer to the West, I consented.

After dinner I made my solitary way to Roy (Peng Shuling) and Sylvia's flat in St John's Wood. Roy was originally from Sichuan, and Sylvia from Tianjin. He was reading a PhD at Imperial College, while she was studying sociology at the London School of Economics. They were just married and had a small, modern flat where I could stay while in London. As old college friends I knew for certain that their welcome was genuine and, even though they were newly wed, I had no sense that I was intruding. Chinese people do not mind having crowds milling around – it suggests prosperity. Once I had been in Britain a little longer I was to realize how quickly you could overstay your welcome with the natives, but here in a little oasis of China I felt very much at home. With Roy and Sylvia attending to their studies during the day, I was left to my own devices, which was just as well, as I needed time to reflect on how I was to map out my immediate future.

There were two things that preoccupied me that first evening in Britain, two things that were entwined together in my mind. My future studies did not perturb me. Even if I were unable to do justice to my grandfather's academic eminence, I was already light years ahead of my father. Second-hand memories of their time in Britain flitted before my eyes: my grandfather's private Landau, his knighting at the palace, his career in diplomacy – then that of my father, those Edwardian ladies in their elegant long dresses who smiled out of the sepia photographs in

Lo Lodge, his Savile Row suits. If one was all brilliance and dignity, the other made up for his shortfall in style. But times had changed. How was I going to be brilliant or stylish with just £4 10s a week on which to live?

As I stretched out on Roy and Sylvia's couch, pondering how I would work my passage and perhaps even be able to make an impression upon my own time, in my own way, there were other images that distracted my attention. Images of all the European girls that I had met since leaving China kept invading my plans. In Venice the Italian girls were plump, like overripe tomatoes. The girls in the Olympic village and the Tiergarten had solid frameworks as heavy as the German furniture in my hotel room. The Danish girls were like the Germans, but they had lovely light down on their sun-tanned arms. At that moment the British girls seemed the most outstanding. I loved seeing them wearing college blazers with their matching neck ties, and their glorious waves of silken hair. It was a triumph in restraint. They were slim, yet had firm, voluptuous limbs, quite unlike Chinese girls who, when slim, were slim all over, like skinny boys. To exude the all-British sex-appeal, like Deborah Kerr did, was to be able to stun an audience with hardly a hint of flirtation or flaunting.

As Anglo-Saxons are drawn to the mysteries of dusky East Asian beauties, among boys from the Far East there is an equally strong yen for shapely western maidens, whose golden suntans are covered by a light fluffy layer of down. It was all a great torment to me. When should I have my first proper encounter?

Next day I was off to Cambridge where, at the station, I recognized the longest railway platform in the world from my father's tales. A little later Mr W. S. Thatcher gave me a warm welcome to Fitzwilliam House. Half of his face had been blown off during the First World War, but he was still able to raise a trace of a smile that confirmed his interest in you. He was especially good at settling overseas students. Mr Thatcher recommended that I spend two years getting a broad grounding in English literature and language before devoting myself to specialized research. At the time I did not appreciate his wisdom, believing that he was undervaluing my degree from Peking. But I accepted his argument, only too glad to have enrolled anywhere successfully.

I breathed a sigh of relief as I left Fitzwilliam House. There had been nothing imposing about the place, for which I was glad. In fact, it was little more than a red brick house with a dining-room for forty. Opposite was the more imposing Fitzwilliam Museum. I was only a little disappointed that the museum was not the college and vice versa. After all, I was only likely to visit the museum once or twice during my stay, and if it had been the college it would have been a wonderful venue for all the grand meals and balls that I had been led to expect were the mainstay of life at Cambridge. Fitzwilliam wasn't King's, Queen's or Trinity, but at least I had a home for the time being.

During that first year at Cambridge, my most memorable time was not spent at my studies or enjoying the long promised college social life. The dreary winter that followed the autumn registration, when I spent all my time wrapped up in a college scarf or huddled up to my little coal fire reading Tennyson and Jane Austen, was not likely to be stored in the treasure chest of life's golden memories. My digs, although well-carpeted, seemed to have nooks and crannies wherein demons of the cold and dark were lurking, and I didn't venture far from the safety of the stove. These hard times were to ferment over a number of years, along with other, more comfortable memories, into a more all-round feel for 'Cambridge life'.

No, it was that unforgettable Easter of 1937 that was recorded for posterity, and was to settle once and for all that it was to be tennis, more than any other skill, that would work my true passage and my passport to Britain. It was not so much that I became an outstanding success in the course of a few weeks, but the feeling that a new world was opening up before me.

The spring of every succeeding year serves to remind me of that time. Being short of money, I had spent the Christmas holidays in my primitive accommodation in Cambridge. When I went down to London in April the weather was still quite cold, colder than I had anticipated. Fortunately, in the late 1930s almost every fourth house in the Metropolis was a boarding house, and at least a quarter of the female population of London seemed engaged as full- or part-time landladies. Even in the more salubrious districts such as St John's Wood or Hampstead there were rooms to let in impressive residences. In those days the sharp edge of racism was not obviously directed towards people from the East. There were very few Chinese or Japanese people around and those that were were just viewed as oddities, on display in musicals or in operas like *Madam Butterfly*.

So it was that I found a comfortable room on the first floor of a house in Notting Hill Gate. It was a tall room with French windows, heated by a meter-fed gas fire in the shape of two four-foot high drainpipes that were lit from the bottom. After ten minutes the pipes warmed up the whole room. Over a breakfast of a small pot of tea, cereal, toast and marmalade, I could sit at my French window and watch the people going by and listen to the lilting strains of Easter music . . . *'your Easter bonnet with all those frills upon it.'* . . . London fascinated me. Knowing it both through a child's eyes and through literature made me feel as if I belonged. And my new place in Notting Hill was comfortable enough for me to sally forth and set about my purpose; to make an impression on the London tennis scene.

The majority of my Chinese friends were members of the Paddington Bowling and Tennis Club and stayed nearby at the Lauderdale Residential Club. As students from Hong Kong or Singapore, money was no problem to them. I went to practise tennis with them daily at the club, but couldn't join them for card games. That was no great loss for me as I associated mahjong with my father's inability to make any headway in life. On the odd occasion I would join my friends at dog racing at the White City Stadium, and although I won far more than I lost, it never awakened in me the desire to gamble. I knew that the only game of any value to me was to be tennis.

The earliest tournament of the season was held at West Twickenham. It was a total wash-out: it rained, it drizzled, it snowed and it hailed. We sat in the very cramped clubhouse and watched the depressing weather change from hour to hour, always for the worse. Nobody made an impression on the court that week, least of all myself!

The second tournament I entered was held at the Herga Club in Harrow-on-the-Hill, where I was told that Fred Perry, the world champion, was a regular and that the current Junior Champion of Britain, Bob Nichol, was also a member. It was obviously the place to be seen. Competing in the tournament was Dan Prenn, a member of the German Davis Cup team and one-time partner of Von Cram. Among the superstars playing on the British side was Bunny Austin, Fred Perry's partner on the winning Davis Cup team. The previous year Austin had achieved the remarkable feat of beating Ellsworth Vines in straight sets, despite the American's great serve and powerful drive.

The weather was almost as depressing as it had been at West Twickenham. The courts were damp but, from time to time, the drizzle lifted long enough to enable play to commence. Between showers the competitors would rush out on to the courts with their racquets wrapped up in their mackintoshes.

I saw from the programme that I was on the same side of the draw as Bunny Austin, although I'd have to win through three rounds before I could meet him in the quarter or semi-finals. I had no impression of the form of the other players who barred my way to the top and could only pray to be allowed to taste what it was like to trade blows on an international level.

It was an easy passage through the first round. The second round was quite 'sticky'. I was playing against a man called Stroud, reported to have been the champion of Burma. He played a little like Freeman Havinghurst, the head of the Anglo–Chinese College, and perhaps like all colonial players play, lacking the all-round opposition that forces you to polish your game on all fronts. Stroud's game relied, almost entirely, on a big forehand drive. Being young and fairly fleet of foot, I could run rings round him and eventually beat him in three sets. In the third round I came up against Bob Nichol, the Junior Champion, who was reputed to be another hard-hitting player like Fred Perry. He always took the ball early, but unless his play got off to a good gearing I reckoned he could easily overshoot the baseline or have his flat shots land in the net. If I could move fast, catching him out first before he began to slam home winning shots, his errors would pile up. The match soon fell into this pattern and by the end of the first set I knew that I'd got him. He was losing heart. I won by a decisive score of 6–4, 6–1.

In the next round, my match against Bunny Austin was bound to be a different story. As a world-class player he would have his 'safety nets' in place and would only attack from prepared positions where the success of his shots was assured. But I had not anticipated that he would be prepared to go to lengthy rallies in order to wait for such an assured position before mounting his attack. There were always plenty of balls to put away, before he had established control of the rally and would attempt an outright winner. I attempted to break his pattern by going all out for early winning shots. Occasionally they made a dent in his style, but more often than not they went astray and my errors began to pile up. However, I did not consign my game to the rubbish heap before seeing that he also made very ordinary mistakes. I had taken the lead in both sets before he came sailing past me to win 2–6, 4–6. Despite my failure, I, arrogantly, concluded that a world-class player could be beaten.

The next tournament was back at the Paddington Club. It was primarily a bowling club, but had eight well-kept courts, enclosed on all four sides by four-storey flats, the kitchens of which looked out over the courts. When a match lasted into the late afternoon under a darkening sky, the lights from the kitchens would illuminate the court and the players could see silhouettes of housewives setting about the evening meals. Later on, when beyond this pool of light everything was shrouded by darkness, the kitchen lights would glare into the players' eyes and the ball would get lost en route between light and shadow. It had never been my practice to glue my eyes to the ball. I half closed my eyes, estimated the height of the ball and whacked it back instinctively into the gloaming. More often than not the ball seemed to find its mark. In this manner I ploughed through three rounds to reach the semi-finals, beating an ex-Cambridge Blue and a strong tournament player from Queen's Club. In the semi-final I came up against Littleton Rogers, an Irish giant who stood 6ft 7in. Although little known to me he had, for many years, been the champion of Ireland. His main artillery was a cannon-ball first service and a sweeping backhand drive. However, his forehand drive was quite weak and his second service could be easily dismissed. In the first set I put away many of his second services and in the second set I led by 5–2, but faltered at the kill. The final score was 6–4, 5–7, 2–6, an ignominious exit.

To compete at Paddington I moved to Maida Vale, two to three minutes from the club as well as close to most of my friends. The basement room I found in Sutherland Avenue was even cheaper than Notting Hill Gate, no more than twenty-five shillings a week. The price included the usual breakfast with some canned mandarins thrown in as well. Even if I didn't get another meal that day, I wouldn't exactly starve. When I had the chance of eating out with my better-off friends in a Chinese restaurant, it was a great bonus. With Chinese meals, five or six dishes could just as well feed six people as five, so mostly I was not required to make a contribution. Everyone knew I was short. I was also learning the rudiments of urban survival.

By the middle of the month the greyness hadn't lifted, but by the third week there was a slight suggestion of spring in the air. These suggestions of sunshine were never robust enough to be reliable. Perhaps the interminable drizzle had finally dampened my cheerfulness. There was no exuberance left in my game for the next tournament. I went down without a struggle to an ex-Cambridge Blue called Dickie. Dickie played a 'useful game'. He relied on frustrating his opponents rather than hitting them off the courts. The encounter illustrated how vulnerable my own game was, how easily it could still be frustrated by mediocre players and how far I still had to go before I could feel that I had matured on court.

Spring came suddenly and triumphantly. One day the hazy morning light, which normally would fade and become a cloudy drizzle by afternoon, blazed into that sunshine, not only bright but unexpectedly hot. I was taking a taxi to the Melbury Club with my good friend W. C. Choy. Sunshine streamed through the thick foliage that grew in profusion along the avenues of this residential district. Not a gust of wind disturbed the air. W. C. Choy was sprawled out over the back seat with his feet up on the opposite seat and he urged me to do the same.

In fact, I was in a far less confident mood than our posturing would suggest. I was heading for my second encounter in less than a month with Bunny Austin. Bunny was a gentleman of a player, who commanded some of the finest, smoothest ground strokes in tennis history, and I was an upstart from the East who only wanted to show that there was still something in the chip-off-the-old-block of China. I had hardly slept at all the night before. Austin's bare legs, in impeccable shorts, were running backwards and forwards at the end of my bed, as if at the opposite end of the court. At dawn, exhausted, I had managed to snatch a few moments' sleep, but it was hardly enough preparation for a crucial match. Sleep or no sleep ultimately would not make any difference. The forthcoming encounter felt like a continuation of my dream: a dream battle.

I had no clear plan. I would run and hit as it came to me. After all, the tennis court was not such a large patch of ground and if you stood on the baseline, every ball would be in front of you at least. Austin didn't have a punishing serve so I always had a chance to return to the wings.

In the first set, in the time it took for him to get his service into gear, I had landed a number of big shots just inside the tramlines. Emboldened by my small victories, I began to swell with pride and, all of a sudden, from some far distant source, classical verses began to echo through my mind and I began to chant softly. First the 'Romance of the Three Kingdoms', then the 'Mencius'. The crowd began to think that a new tennis star had risen in the East. The Movietone News camera began to whirr on the court side. Time passed in a flash and I had won the first set by 6–2!

A feeling of satisfaction began to settle into my stomach. I even felt that it didn't matter what happened now. I was young and had a lot of time to learn. While preoccupied with these thoughts I failed to see the determination rise in Austin's face. He swept through the next two sets and I won only one more game!

After five eventful weeks in London I was told by Freddie Knott, the secretary of the University team, that I was required to play for Cambridge in the forthcoming match against Oxford. In other words I had won my Blue in the first season! Although we'd one or two international players on the Cambridge side, most of the British men were flailing around in the backwaters of county tennis ranks while

I'd created a slight ripple on the international pool. But it was the end of me. In the intervarsity match I lost both games against Oxford. Then followed a series of disasters when I lost every other match I played.

Most of the 'nuts and bolts' of my game were still loose and required serious tightening. But Freddie still had faith in my game. He put me to play first string for Cambridge in a match against Chiswick Park. My opponent was a national player called John Comery. I beat him in three long sets, 8–6 in the final set.

Freddie was so pleased that his judgement had been vindicated that he took me out to dinner in the West End that evening. It was a rare treat for me. Few undergraduates ever invited one another out. They invariably went Dutch. But that evening Freddie insisted on treating me. That evening he looked dashing in his grey and white pin-stripe suit with his shock of blond hair.

I knew that Freddie had some gift for writing. He was always keen to take the tennis club minutes. But it wasn't until some time later that I realized that he was, at that time, absorbed in writing *Dial M for Murder*. I was belatedly sorry I had underestimated his off-court talents when he had been so supportive of me.

CHAPTER EIGHT

The Cambridge Years

Say is there Beauty yet to find?
And Certainty? and Quiet kind?
deep meadows yet, for to forget
The lies, and truths, and pain? . . . oh! yet
Stands the Church clock at ten to three?
And is there honey still for tea?

from *The Old Vicarage, Grantchester*, Rupert Brooke. 1887–1915

MY DIGS WERE about half way to Girton, half an hour's plod along Bridge Street, up Castle Hill and all the while gradually crossing the great class divide. The scale of the buildings became smaller and smaller until I arrived at a house about the size of a birdcage, a semi–detached bird cage. My landlord, a retired porter from Trinity College, resembled a bird himself. And it was his elderly, less bird–like wife who looked after me when I arrived. I was shown a tiny upstairs bedroom coop, but the front room of the house was also for exclusive use as my study and dining-room.

I was mildly surprised how medieval Britain could be. Few of these early Victorian semis had bathrooms and most people still washed at the public washhouse. WCs were outdoors at the end of the garden. But in my case I had the luxury of a WC next to my bedroom. My landlady proudly demonstrated how efficiently it could flush. The cost of the accommodation, breakfast, daily lunch and hot bath on Thursdays was £3 10s a week. With a total budget of £4 10s, I took it straight away, feeling I wouldn't find anything better.

Life up Castle Hill was not without its joys. My landlord and lady were extremely polite and keen to show me the delights of British working-class life. I discovered how to derive fortitude from hot tea and biscuits, served beside a small, but well-stoked coal fire. And on Thursdays my landlady would build a blazing fire in the front room and position the tin hip-bath in front, drawing the curtains. I would be provided with two large metal jugs of hot water and a large crisp sheet of towelling. I undressed in front of the blazing fire and exposed my naked body to the radiant heat. It was a treat unequalled anywhere on the Mediterranean coast, and with a weekly shower at the university tennis club, I managed to keep myself comparatively clean during my first two years in Britain.

Another luxury of those early years in Cambridge was the 'Blue Barn'. The Blue Barn was a tiny Chinese restaurant, no more than a bar, where a dozen people sat along the length of the counter. It was run by some friendly Cantonese who chatted with me in a distorted Mandarin. I was brought up to believe that all Chinese should speak Mandarin, but in practice many overseas Chinese have a very poor command of the language. And I never made an attempt to learn any of the regional languages of China apart from my mother tongue. The 'restaurant' served only three dishes: Chop Suey, Chow Mein and Fried Rice, but being just opposite the students' union, in a narrow passage that ran down to Midsummer Common, it was packed nearly every evening. Clearly, if properly situated, a restaurant need only serve three to four dishes to exist and perhaps half-a-dozen to prosper.

The Chop Suey at the Blue Barn was a dish of stewed meat and cabbage, awash in tomato sauce; the Chow Mein was topped with a fried egg and the Fried Rice was equally substantial, stir fried with an abundance of goodies, onion, peas, chopped meat and tiny spoons of shrimps. Any of the three dishes would have been adequate to appease an ordinary appetite, but being young and vigorous, I needed two dishes to satisfy myself. Such a meal was something to look forward to once a week and would make my day, especially when the second dish was shared with a good friend. The cost of a meal at the Blue Barn was about 3s 6d, the same as dining in Hall, which I was obliged to do only twice a week.

Otherwise I was dependent on the breakfast and luncheon provided by my landlady. Undoubtedly she tried her best, but with her husband's meagre appetite and requirements as her only guide, she could not know what good, substantial food really was. He was a walking skeleton and I feared that I might go the same way. Even propped up by a dinner or two at the Blue Barn I was barely able to keep my weight over 9 stone.

In China, in the old days, nobody milked cows and cheese-making was totally unheard of. It usually takes twenty years for a Chinese to appreciate cheese. But I was so ravenous in those days that it took me just two. I found it quite incredible that when I was invited to lunch with English friends in their college rooms, they would almost invariably serve up this rancid, formless mass, to be eaten with dry bread, and raw or pickled onion, and finally washed down with cold beer. As I didn't drink beer I was left to wash the whole lot down with water. Like the nostalgia that I imagine is finally engendered by years of public school privation, endless repetition of this nauseating ritual allowed me to appreciate the sophisticated distinction between various gradations of rancid and sour. More than anything I did appreciate the way it sat in the stomach like a dead weight, making you feel as if you really had feasted to the fill.

In comparison, learning to savour the flavour of Cambridge life was not difficult. That flavour was not so much revealed in boating on the river or the college balls, but in listening to the tolling of bells at dusk as one donned a black gown and rushed to hall through the college gates and quadrangles under the evening lamplight and over wet, cobbled stones. Perhaps youth kept out the cold as my un-buttoned gown fluttered in the wind, with just a college scarf wound casually around my neck. All else melted into the greying yellow dusk, but the pealing bells seemed to drown the colleges and all the life within them, as if time had stopped to herald supper every day.

I would be transported back to the wooded slopes of Drum Mountain where the monks of Bubbling Spring monastery began counting their beads and chanting sutras before day-break in the dimly lit and cavernous temple halls. Or perhaps it was the bells of the Anglo–Chinese College summoning us to daily prayer or to sing the Nationalist Party's anthem? And then back I would be, running along the banks of the slow-flowing Cam. Listening to the tolling bells reminded me that I now belonged to an exclusive band who were also bound by semi-feudal codes of public school and, like the monks, moved round to bells and some seemingly aimless, prescribed pattern. Sometimes the students would also make a quantum leap in their own understanding, even if this was not toward enlightenment but to the glory and advancement of their special field. Sometimes, by reflection, I too could feel a hint of that 'nascent flavour' when someone, by opportunity or design, happened to turn over a stone to reveal something which had never before been discerned by human eyes in that particular light. I was fortunate that through a juxtaposition of circumstance, both mundane and unusual, I had been plunged into this world, where I could observe history at the crossroads of the 1930s in this university town.

Most memorable, too, were the distinctive smells of Cambridge. The first was the smell of accumulated layers of summers past, like one long summer, that came in wafts of newly-mown lawn cuttings. Yet Cambridge summer was like no other summer. It came like a dream to break the spell of rain, mist and half-light that was cast upon the town from break of autumn right through to midsummer day. The other, equally distinctive smell, was more acrid. It was the smell of unwashed tennis socks hung up to dry and air in the men's dressing room at Fenner's. After many weeks the socks began to stiffen, until by the end of term, some could stand up by themselves!

Life began slowly in Cambridge. Nothing urgent ever happened in the morning. There was little or no café life, and at the very most one might put the finishing touches to an essay in advance of the next tutorial. Writing a presentable essay was one of the bug-bears of undergraduate life. It always required greater effort and more energy than most of us would admit to. How to pull the wool over the eyes of one's tutor? After all, it was his subject and he had chosen the topic. To go to a tutorial and not to have made any preparation was to admit that you were not interested in the subject, and created an embarrassing situation. If it happened more than a couple of times, the tutor would have no alternative but to recommend that you changed your subject. I never allowed my academic relationships to drop to quite such depressing levels, if only because I was genuinely interested in what my tutor had to say. By reading the set books with care and underlining the crucial passages in heavy pencil, as I had done with classical Chinese texts, I was always able to conduct a lively conversation with my tutor, even if I had not completed the essay which I had been assigned. Above all one had to show interest.

My favourite and the least draconian of all my tutors was the renowned critic I. A. Richards. He didn't wish to encumber himself with correcting too many essays each week, so he never encouraged us to work hard. He had also just spent a few years as Professor of English at Peking University so I tracked him down as soon as he made an appearance at Cambridge. Although a fellow at Magdalene college, he was only a visiting tutor, yet some people considered him one of the greatest literary critics of the century. He had already written the *Meaning of Meaning* and *Practical Criticism*, two books which were required reading for anyone who was studying English Literature. One or two lectures, which he gave in Mill Lane with T. S. Eliot, were packed out and ranked amongst the few I ever attended during the many years I spent around the university. Normally I simply read books, and concentrated on those written by the lecturer.

Dr Richards and I would meet in his room overlooking the Cam at Magdalene. He would simply pull a book of poetry at random from the shelf and we would read a poem or two together. As we went along he made comments, and to establish my curiosity I always asked respectful and inquisitive questions. My relationship with him was not unlike that I had enjoyed with cousin Daisun's father, who had all the literary quintessence of his uncle, the Emperor's tutor. I thoroughly enjoyed our tutorials because Richards, seemingly, made no demands on me at all and I could immerse myself in his company.

It was as if I had been invited to dine at the table of a master gourmet. Progressing from one famous dish to another, chewing over morsels which had been prepared by great exponents of the past, I was being asked to comment on their flavour, texture, aroma and the methods adopted in their preparation. We explored all the options open to the chef at each stage of the preparation. I felt it a great honour to have the great critic all to myself. Slowly I gained more confidence in my own opinions. I felt I could reserve literary judgement until the material had been tested with the methodical and leisurely approach with which Dr Richards savoured his 'dishes'.

The first job I assigned myself was to read Wordsworth's poems. After the classical Chinese tradition, I began to memorize them all from beginning to end. But I didn't get very far. As a now critical adult I found myself less tolerant of rote-learning. Besides, I discovered that the great poet did not always write with inspiration. The bulk of Wordsworth's writing seemed repetitive and clichéd. Even his arrival at Trinity College was recorded in the most mundane piece of narrative poetry. Indeed, I discovered that the great nineteenth-century poets were not superhuman and only on rare occasions wrote poems like 'Westminster Bridge' or Keats's 'Ode to a Nightingale'. The rest of their work seemed designed to plaster up the yawning gaps between inspiration. Yet I marvelled at the best of modern English poetry. It was an intellectual exploration, which compressed many more ideas than ever were contained in the stylized and restricted forms of classical Chinese poetry.

Chinese literary figures, especially contemporary ones, fared even worse under my new-found critical scrutiny. Hu Shi, who inspired the May 4th Movement of 1919 and helped to invent the 'vernacular literature', wrote poetry which was not even good prose. I was, however, struck by the young romantic, Xu Zhimuo, an elegant writer of the early 1930s. In his essay on Cambridge, 'The Cambridge I knew', he described careering down the hill on his bicycle with fine rain beating on his face. I was so impressed with how accurately he managed to convey both the romance and the hardship of Cambridge that I translated it. In Cambridge I did one better, cycling down the full length of Castle Hill, 'no hands' and in the drizzle!

It seemed to me that Chinese were more talented and had more opportunity in science than in literature. To write good critical essays in English was a hard task for any foreigner. But studying literature was a wonderful way to try to understand what made the British tick. The key to all their loves, hates and passions was there, hidden within the pages. And it seemed a privilege, handed to me firstly by my early visit to Britain and thereafter by my exposure to English culture during my growing years, that I had begun to major in English literature and could end up spending several years just lost in books. W. Thatcher's wisdom in making me go back over a basic training in English Literature began to dawn on me. It was a real preparation for my new life.

During my time at Cambridge I was joined by half-a-dozen scientists from Peking, including Hua Luogeng, my old tutor in Peking, now a mathematician of world standing. Then there was Wang Zhuqi, Zhang Wenyu and Shen Shizhang, all physicists working at the forefront of science. There was also a handful of Chinese students destined for fame in the arts such as the talented film director Huang Zhuoling. I was glad I hadn't stayed in science to tangle with them. I was content to be a sportsman, part-time student of English literature, human nature, East-West politics, social history and whatever other subjects did not require full-time application.

In the aftermath of the Spanish Civil War, undergraduates at Cambridge spent a lot of time debating the merits of right- and left-wing forces in the world arena. Some contemporaries were just back from fighting with the International Brigade and had had harrowing experiences at the hands of the French as they fled the battle arena in Spain. As I was fresh from the front-line of student demonstrations in Peking, my fellow students were curious about my views on the clash in the East and the declining grip of the Imperial powers. Many of my friends were from India, others from the West

Indies and Africa. They were inclined to become impatient with me when they found that anti-imperialism was less virulent in my blood than in theirs. After all, China had not been colonized and although she had been economically exploited and politically bullied she had, ultimately, retained her political independence. Japan's colonialism was more brutal, more akin to naked militarism, and simpler to hate than the insidious cultural domination of the Western powers. Of course I found colonialism basically abhorrent, but my own experience had taught me that a home-brew of feudal-militarism could be worse for the population at large than old-fashioned imperialism.

My natural agreement could only be with the Left as I found it in Cambridge. Even the top-grade students seemed to lean Left. Among my close European friends I numbered Ian Watts and Victor Kiernan, both talented and vociferous advocates of left-wing politics. On the other hand the right wing, whom I tended to come across in the sporting world, were not natural allies. They were mostly the cream of top public schools, who easily excelled at sport and tended to be bound for the army. In those days Asians were still barred from the Hawks Club, the main sporting centre. Fortunately for me, tennis players were more civilized. For my own part, I joined protracted political discussions which progressed from the tea-rooms to individual digs and rooms in various colleges, where we would read poems like Auden's 'Guernica' and 'Spain' to fortify our morale. I enjoyed the spirit and camaraderie of being left wing and was overtaken by the sheer romance of the common struggle for a better world. I even learned to hum the 'Internationale' which, like the 'Marseillaise', I found very stirring.

When Isherwood and Auden returned from a tour of wartime China they wrote *Journey to a War* to document their impressions. Fascinated by what they might have to say we, the Chinese Society, invited them to come and give a talk. I was excited to meet such eminent defenders of the cause, whose works had already provided me with food for thought. I was detailed to entertain them, and we gave them luncheon in the Students' Union dining-room. For some reason I did not find the occasion memorable: neither the food, nor the conversation, nor the lecture that followed was illuminating. Without the necessary literary vehicle, their politics seemed naive and uninteresting. With my own family leaning every which way, the problem could never seem so simple to me.

Towards the end of 1936 I heard Edward VIII's abdication speech over the wireless. On the same wireless, a year later, I heard of the Japanese army's occupation, first of Peking and then Chiang Kaishek's seat of government at Nanjing, and of the terrible massacre that took place there. Letters from home arrived regularly, despite the national upheaval. Charles wrote once a month and my mother wrote from time to time. My own family were beginning to scatter in all directions. Walter had arrived in Peking before I had left and had been staying with the Wei family, trying to enter the Catholic University. My mother and father had been in Shanghai since my departure. They felt that being nearer to Nanjing their chances of employment were better. Michael and Anna were back at the Anglo–Chinese College finishing their middle school education.

It was during this time that my mother was rumoured to be carrying out intelligence work. All her life she was in close association with the officers who became the leaders of the 19th Route army. They had all been trained in the South West Military Academy of Guilin, where she had grown up and where her father, Wei Han, had been principal. It was an easy alliance of old friends. The 19th Route army did not have a strong political alliance in the civil war, but were united in their commitment to the war of resistance. It was they who put up the strongest fight during the invasion of Shanghai. And they had bitter criticism for Chiang Kaishek when he failed to support them. It is said that my mother carried messages back and forth over the battle lines, concealed within her plaits. This came as no surprise to me. I never doubted her courage.

Charles himself had left Peking for Shanghai and was making the difficult decision of where to go next and how to contribute towards the war effort. During this period, most of the universities were moving southwards and setting up in Kunming. Cousin Daisun had been evacuated there and his presence was a natural attraction for Charles. But it was not possible to go direct through the war zones. He had to take a circuitous route by boat to Vietnam and then back up overland through the tropical rain forests. When he eventually arrived he wrote to say that he had easily found a teaching job. From the relative safety of Cambridge, the scenes of war and massacre seemed quite remote during the day. But my fears for Charles were very real in the loneliness of the dark winter nights, when I carried my candle up the stairs to bed. I would think fondly of those 'moonlit nights in the old capital' and worry about what would happen to him and all my loved ones if the Japanese won the war.

I stayed in my first lodging for nearly two years before I moved on to the Manor House in a village called Coton. It was a far cry from the highly respectable dolls' house I had been used to. The landlady was taking in a few lodgers out of either loneliness or philanthropy.

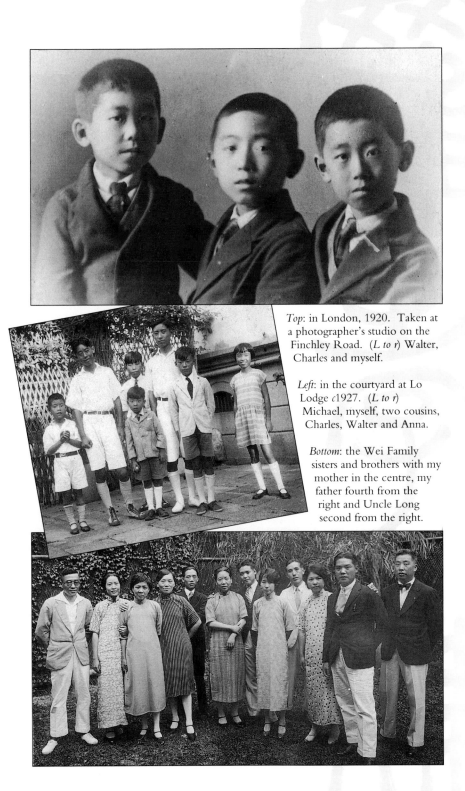

Top: in London, 1920. Taken at a photographer's studio on the Finchley Road. (*L to r*) Walter, Charles and myself.

Left: in the courtyard at Lo Lodge *c*1927. (*L to r*) Michael, myself, two cousins, Charles, Walter and Anna.

Bottom: the Wei Family sisters and brothers with my mother in the centre, my father fourth from the right and Uncle Long second from the right.

Top left: myself, Charles and Mother on her visit to Peking, 1934.

Top right: on the same visit at Uncle Wei Zitong's house.

Left: my father in the 1960s.

Bottom: the Chinese Davis Cup Team in Copenhagen after defeating Denmark in 1946. (*L to r*) Kho Sinkie, W.C. Choy, myself and Edward Li (manager).

My paternal grandfather, Sir Lo Fenglu (1850-1901).

My maternal grandfather, Wei Han (1850-1929).

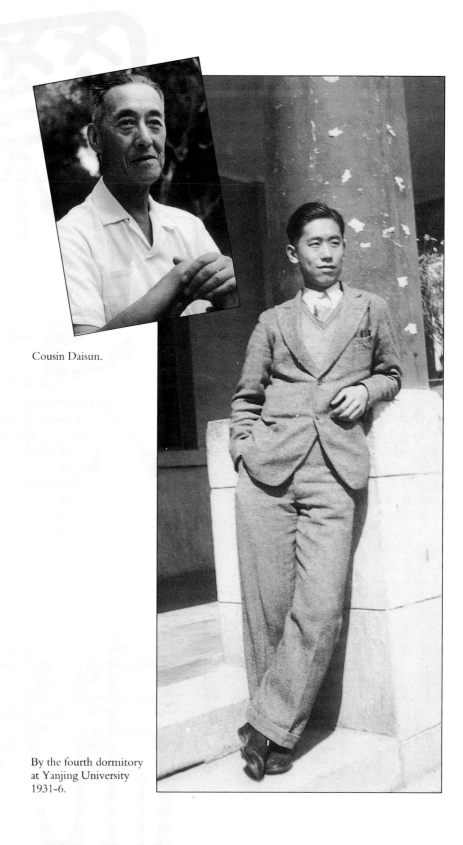

Cousin Daisun.

By the fourth dormitory
at Yanjing University
1931-6.

Skating at Yanjing 1931–6.

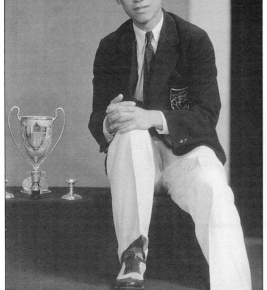

Winner of Men's Singles Championship – Yanjing University 1931–6.

Yanjing University grounds 1931–6.

The Student March on Peking.
16 December 1934.

My BA Graduation certificate in English Literature. 30 June 1936.

The combined Qinghua and Yanjing tennis team *v*. Nanjing, summer 1934, with myself in the top row, centre and Charles bottom row second from the left.

My year at Yanjing taken in 1935, with me, the only student carrying books!

Cambridge 1936–41.

Taken aboard the *Conte Verde* on the way to Berlin, 1936.

On the Cam with Robert Yafu Li and Una Tan.

A little unsure – with the Cambridge local ladies before a party.

Anne aged about seventeen or eighteen.

St Martin-in-the-Field, 16 May 1954.

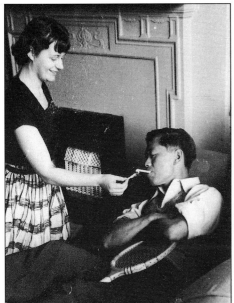

Top left: newly married at the Empsons' house, No. 1 Hampstead Hill Gardens.

Top right: Anne with the twins, 1955.

Right: Vivienne and Jennifer in Trafalgar Square, 1965.

Bottom: myself with the boys in the garden at 11 Perceval Avenue, 1958.

'The colt', by Xu Bihong, the prize of Cathay Arts, my first business in the 1950s.

Bottom left: my first cookbook published in 1954.

Bottom right: experiments for my first cookbook in the 1950s.

EGON RONAY finds: a chef who outshone the French, chopsticks are "easy," a former diplomat whose hobby is cooking, no birds' nests or gastronomic nightmares, and decides that

Chinese Food Is Exciting, But Not Exotic

Mr. Kenneth H. Lo, author and expert on Chinese cooking, demonstrating the art of holding chopsticks to Mr. Ronay at the Great Wall Restaurant.

L UDWIG BEMELMANS, American author-gourmet, told me that Chinese cooking in London is disappointing. In spite of his criticism, I have since found Chinese restaurants with many delicacies and at least one great Chinese chef who outshone the French.

Kenneth Lo, retired diplomat, whose hobby is cooking, challenged me after I had quoted Bemelmans in this feature, to see for myself. I accepted reluctantly, fearing to be fed with bird's nest and other gastronomic nightmares.

At the **Great Wall Restaurant**, Oxford Street, my apologies for lateness were waved aside by Mr. Lo, and I felt a breath of the timeless East: "There is no hurry, you have to take your time anyway over Chinese food."

Confronted with the choice of fork or chopsticks, Mr. Lo made it seem so easy—as these pictures show—that I chose chopsticks, and got on famously. Chinese dishes consist of small bits for which forks are too big.

The meals are rather like a buffet. We were served with four dishes, each delicate and tasty. Even the pork was light, small pieces fried into crisp little balls (5s). The excellent Pacific prawns (7s 6d) were done in Chinese soya-sauce and the transparent, spaghetti-like, Chinese vermicelli was the star of the mixed fried vegetable dish (4s). The prices apply to a dish enough for three or four people.

We took our time over a tiny cup of green tea. "Bemelmans had more chance in New York, of course," said Mr. Lo, "there are over 2,000 Chinese restaurants there, as against London's 25."

I tried to make use of my little knowledge, mentioning chop-suey.

"That is the American idea of a Chinese dish," said my friend. "Less discerning people like it, but it is only an inferior kind of hash."

Next I visited Mrs. Hsu, whose many international friends enjoyed her home-cooking so much that they persuaded her to open this place, and who showed me a Chinese mandarin

HOW TO USE CHOPSTICKS

Chopsticks must project three times as far forward as they do behind the hand as seen above. Grip lower stick firmly between base of thumb and second and third fingers. Hold upper stick lightly between thumb and forefinger.

To eat rice, scoop it up with sticks held in same way but with the bottom points kept close together and parallel.

coat. You write your measurements on a printed pattern and choose one of the gorgeous brocades. The order is flown to Hong Kong and the made-to-measure garment is sent in two weeks, all for 8gns.

ARTIST WITH A CHICKEN

The highlight of my Chinese week was the **Restaurant Asiatique** Irving Street, off Leicester Square, owned and managed by retired diplomats. The number of Chinese diners in that ornately Eastern décor was a good omen for delights to come. Mr. Hwang, former chef to the Chinese Embassy, is truly an artist. His deliciously light egg-and-cream soup (1s 6d) was followed by dishes I shall always remember.

Any French chef would have been proud of the sweet-and-sour sauce in which the sole-slices were cooked (8s). The pièce de résistance was a chicken speciality; the extraordinarily tender

texture of the chicken (like sweetbread) is achieved by multiple cooking in oils of varying temperatures.

It is served in a delicately flavoured sauce with slices of apple-like water-chestnuts and half walnuts, the last an unexpected ingredient (10s 6d the dish). Lychees in light syrup were a fitting finish to this poem of a dinner.

FOR THE HURRIED LUNCHER

Even after all these wonders, the **Hong Kong Restaurant** in Shaftesbury Avenue, held its own. Here the gastronomic art is translated for London's hustling lunch-crowds who contrast vividly with the efficiently quiet and placidly smiling Chinese waiters. Fried crispy noodles with bean-sprouts and sweet-and-sour pork made an ideal lunch (7s 6d for two) and Mr. Young, the proprietor, assures women that the exquisite after-lunch jasmine tea (1s for two) will help them to slim.

"Delicate but, alas, impractical at home," I told my cicerone after these feasts. Mr. Lo promptly invited my wife and me to his Hampstead home.

He cooks most evening meals himself for his pretty young English wife and their twin boys. Not for nothing is he the author of "Cooking the Chinese way."

The dinner, with Chinese pork-casserole, was excellent. Over-publicising fantastic dishes, exotic even in China, does a disservice. Chinese food is not exotic, only deliciously different and —Mr. Bemelmans—even in London genuinely Chinese.

1956. Even Egon Ronay needed instruction in the art of holding chopsticks. (*Daily Telegraph*)

An amusing cartoon from a 1950s edition of *Punch* taken from an article written by Miles Kingston and myself showing how the English were still wrestling with chopsticks. (*The Punch Library*)

Playing in Monte Carlo with Rosco Tanner and Roger Taylor.

In Pimlico with my grandchildren: *(L to r)* Pearl, Ria-may, Kelly, Louise with Gary and Aaron on the floor. (*David Steen*)

Jean Borotra, Vivienne and Jenny at Hurlingham *c*1974.

With a couple of customers in front of our Chelsea Harbour restaurant.

Peking, Autumn 1986. Playing with Wan Li, one of the deputy Prime Ministers of China.

At the cookery school, Memories of China, the culmination of my life's work.
(*Paul Mellor*)

She only charged £1 15s for full board. For our £1 15s our young landlady would invariably roast a huge joint for Sunday dinner. She would always put me at the head of the table while she carved the joint at the opposite end. The other lodgers and all the friends that we invited would line the two sides of the table. We lived in great style! She was then just thirty-eight years old but her husband, who was bedridden, was eighty-four.

Coton was four miles outside Cambridge by the signposts. At a steady pace it took twenty minutes to cycle there, less at night when I was encouraged to cycle faster by the rustling hedgerows. Although I knew there were no lurking tigers and despite the five battery lamps I had fixed to the front of my bicycle, I would arrive at the village in a sweat. Darkness was never a comfort to me. But the welcome and the fare once I had reached the Manor House made me feel as if it were my second home.

No sooner was I established in Britain than I was cut off from my source of income. With the whole of the eastern coast under Japanese occupation, Uncle Yi had been recalled to China and I had been left high and dry. I spoke of my financial embarrassment to the Master of my College, Mr W. S. Thatcher. To my great surprise he said that the College would be able to help. First of all he could waive my college fee – not an inconsiderable sum. That left my living expenses. He said that there was an interest-free Loan Fund in the College from which students in dire need could borrow. I had to sign that I would repay as soon as possible. I borrowed £50 and came out of Fitzwilliam House feeling a rich man.

With my new-found wealth I explored the Cambridge social circuit. Life seemed to warm up in the afternoon. As 4 p.m. approached the tea houses began to fill up. If I was not immediately engaged in sports, then my natural drift was towards the Whim in Trinity Street, the Copper Kettle in King's Parade or Tullivers further down in Trumpington Street. To meet up with local Cambridge ladies meant a trip to the Dorothy Café at the centre of town, because only at the Dorothy Café did the barriers between Town and Gown become flimsy.

The majority of the undergraduates, having barely emerged from the single-sex background of public school, were yearning for any kind of contact with girls. When the time came it was within a fairly unrestrained environment; the boys were so full of excitement that they could hardly refrain from fits of giggling. It must have been because they were in such a giggly state that they would invariably describe the girls as giggly! This did not appear to me to be the case.

The girls conducted themselves with more decorum. Catapulted into such a different social and sexual climate, I was often quite embarrassed and unnerved to find myself in the midst of so much alien giggling. Twenty centuries of Confucian teaching gave me no clue as to how to behave under such circumstances. I felt disadvantaged. To fondle the voluptuous bodies that were certainly within reach would be to behave like an animal in the eyes of the Master.

I soon withdrew from having to face up to such embarrassing dilemmas and turned my attention to more restrained and intellectual exchanges with women undergraduates. However, such a shift of target had its own innate danger. The object of desire might easily drift imperceptibly away, along the road of one unending debating society, where any future change in tempo would become quite impossible. Confucius said nothing. It was a wonder to me that since I had moved West, Confucius had made no pronouncements on how I should face up to the most basic issues of life.

Although the Master had not provided rules of conduct for this liberated young society, I found that I could still enjoy the other tea houses. I was a great conversationalist and even though English was not my mother tongue, I could hold forth on practically any subject on earth, except sex. My Indian friends, far and away the most intellectual folk around, were much more adept at waltzing down the risqué road in their conversation. Apparently the Buddha had a different approach from Confucius. Indeed, when the Indians were around our tea-time sessions became very lively.

Emboldened at my success in borrowing, I decided to throw caution to the wind. I found two Tan cousins from Singapore at Queen's College. Wasn't it their father who gave us £3 each for Christmas in 1920, and didn't he come to Shanghai in his own chartered vessel in 1933? Didn't their mothers wear diamonds between their toes? Surely the man reputed to be one of the richest in the colony could spare a few coppers for a poor relative, down and out in Cambridge. The younger brother conveyed my plight to his father and, sure enough, back came a remittance of £100. This prompt response gave me heart to go on a spree to Paris, if only for a last fling. It was not that I had planned to go, but when invited to join my good friend Robert Yafu Li and a group of his cronies I said a hearty 'yes'.

Robert was the typical offspring of a long-established feudal family and had the confidence to prove it. His family had monopolized the salt trade in North China for more than 300 years. His elder brother had married the daughter of Cao Kun, the northern Chinese war-lord and fourth president of the Republic, so they were well connected, even amid the turmoil of the preceding decade. They were not short of money. Unlike the nouveau riche or the war-lord/bandits they were never vulgar, but a proud sort with a good classical education and a little training in Chinese martial arts, always learned from the best private instructor.

I was convinced by Robert that an essential element of a cultivated lifestyle was associating with 'singsong girls'. He said that it was as much a part of a good Chinese upbringing as the 'Grand Tour' or the debutantes' ball would be to British aristocratic youth of the same period. So when we arrived in Paris, the first thing on our agenda was a visit to a brothel. I was not a little apprehensive. My own family were not given to such indulgences. But the Madame soon put all of us at ease. Instead of providing titillating foreplay, she merely paraded her girls as if displaying cuts of meat with varying degrees of succulence. It was all very matter of fact. Since the different meats were much of a muchness, it didn't seem to matter which cut the Madame had selected. Once paired, each couple would disappear into a cubicle where they did what was to be expected. This didn't seem to match with the image that I had of the 'courtesan' who would be trained in the arts and well educated so that she could entertain young scholars. On the way out, I noticed that the place was strewn with whips and other instruments of brutality and torture. I was saddened by the sight and couldn't quite imagine how these things were meant to be employed in the pursuit of pleasure. Robert pronounced that the visit was a necessary ritual for every young 'soldier' before he was let loose on Paris without a chaperone. I did not feel that the experience had allowed me to graduate to any status at all. Confucius refrained from commenting.

During the rest of our stay in Paris we were joined by Zhang Xueming, Mayor of Tianjin and a brother of the Young Marshall, the war-lord of Manchuria, whose bodyguards had given me a fright in the ice cream parlour in Peking. The Young Marshall's sons Raymond and Martin were also there. They had all belonged to the same clique before the war. With barely a dozen pounds left in my pocket, how I ever got mixed up with this crowd, whose style and opulence reflected fabulous wealth, was a mystery. They would begin every evening in a Pigalle night club by opening a dozen bottles of champagne, to create the right impression. Thereafter, at regular intervals, bottles were opened, half-a-dozen at a time. Millionaires who have to make their money are always somewhat calculating in their expenditure, but this lot collected their money in taxes and were prepared to spend as if there were no tomorrow.

When the Tianjin crowd disappeared, I was left to fend for myself. But I was quite content with cracking open single bottles of Coca-cola instead of champagne! Besides, although I had been abandoned by all the other hostesses in the Caprice Viennois, there was one left who had taken a shine to me. Her name was Tina Seibert, a Viennese beauty who, although unable to speak a word of English, was so gracious that she made me feel we were having cultured exchanges. I must have fallen quite in love and went to meet her every night for the ten days I had left in Paris. Each night, after kissing her goodbye, I walked happy and entranced through the streets of Montmartre on the long trek back to my hotel in the Latin quarter.

Back in Britain I returned to the dark wintry countryside of Coton. Before long our elderly landlord caught a cold which turned into pneumonia. For a few days he seemed better, but then relapsed. I had spoken to him that very morning when he was still quite chatty. But by early afternoon the landlady came downstairs crying. I did what I could to console her while calling the doctor to come and certify the death. The three of us took tea in the basement kitchen. The doctor had left his stethoscope upstairs and I was asked to fetch it. From the doorway the dead man's face was the colour of ivory. I snatched the stethoscope from his bed and practically jumped the stairwell in one leap. I wanted to leave straight away for London, but felt I should stay to keep the landlady company. I stayed one more week in the Manor House, which had transformed overnight from a warm social centre to a dank morgue. I wished I was back in Paris with my Tina: I began to equate sex with life!

My financial resources had run to their lowest ebb. I was no longer on the undergraduate course and couldn't borrow any more from the college's Loan Fund. Nor was my skin thick enough to keep asking for loans from wealthier contemporaries. It was quite obvious I was not spending my time improving my scholarship or erudition. All I was doing was reading the books which I'd always wanted to read. I felt that such pastimes were, in fact, the ultimate in education, but I was at a loss to encourage others to dive deep into their pockets to help someone who seemed to want to idle away his life. No shadow of 'Protestant work ethic' hung over me to spoil my fun. For hadn't most of my own adult family been so fully engaged in self-cultivation and leisure pursuits that they had no time for work? My time would come. But in the meantime I had nowhere to go, nothing important to do and, accustomed to Cambridge life, I was loath to leave for another town where, without family or connections, I would feel at sea.

It was not only my own personal finances that had taken a battering, but the fortune of the whole Lo family. Letters from home began to come less frequently, but those which did arrive spelled out a grim picture. With massive inflation during the war years my grandmother's pawn shop and tea houses had suffered great losses. Distraught by what she perceived to be her own personal failure, she had passed away. Charles had moved on to Chongqing and entered the foreign service there. The town was being heavily bombed, and I was acutely aware of the danger that he was in. He was also in love.

I moved again, to a lively house in Harvey Road, opposite the Catholic church. The landlord was Decio Petoello, a Reader in Italian; his wife, Madame Petoello, was a handsome middle-aged Italian, bounding with life and energy. She was an excellent cook and the life and soul of the household. They had two teenage children. Laura was a blue-stocking intellectual with a taste for classical music and opera. Her bespectacled elder brother, Lorenzo, already had firm opinions on specific masterpieces of European literature. Being properly brought up, they both deferred to their father for the final pronouncement on the quality of a given piece of music or literature. Madame P knew that her husband was a literary buffoon, but would never raise any dissent, for in politics they were allied against Mussolini and disinclined to attack each other in any area. I heard a great deal about Garibaldi, the 'Risorgimento', and heated arguments over Il Duce and his son-in-law, Ciano. Political refugees from Spain and Italy would use their home as a 'transit camp'. Madame Petoello treated them all with great sympathy and cooked delicious Italian meals.

For a year or two, apart from the two windfalls that I have described, I had been living through a period of great privation and only eating bread and butter, eggs, apples and tea. I was not suffering from under-nourishment but I was desperate for a good 'nosh'. So when I was invited to join them at dinner, it was a great treat. I was not given a permanent seat at Madame Petoello's excellent table, because, being a confirmed socialist, she had a deep prejudice about work: work was sacred, and there was I not working out of choice! Perhaps she felt that if she fed me more frequently I might become permanently unemployed. I was mainly browsing through such writers as Damon Runyon, Hemingway, Steinbeck and P. G. Wodehouse – nothing which could be classified as serious study.

In order to justify my staying in such a household for what might turn out to be an indefinite period of time, I moved from the large, luxury front room to the fourth-floor landing, where Madame curtained off a storage area and made up a bed for me. There she would charge me no more than 5s a week rent. My upward move suited both of us. I liked life in this tiny garret, and the aroma of Madame P's wonderful food and her guests' international cuisine came spiralling up the stairwell to where I lay stretched out, appreciative, on my bed.

After they had all done with cooking I would drift downstairs to the basement kitchen to boil my two eggs, make my toast and tea and eat my apple. Madame regarded my 'lean cuisine' as a self-imposed privation for which she had little sympathy. I could almost hear her muttering that no-one unprepared to do physical work should live off the fat of the land. Every now and then she relented and passed on some large and tasty morsels which I wolfed down like a half-starved mongrel.

By this time the 'Phoney War' in Europe had entered a more serious phase. German bombers, returning from bombarding Coventry and Birmingham, would occasionally unload their left-over incendiary bombs over East Anglia and Cambridge. If left unattended the incendiary bombs could cause greater damage than the much heavier explosive types. From our back garden lawn, we watched a huge conflagration next door when a school burned down in under an hour. On other nights we heard the thud of heavier bombs landing around Cambridge. A direct hit on the Blue Barn snuffed out a good friend, Ram Nahum, in the middle of his Chow Mein. The closest cluster of three bombs straddled Fenner's with a final hit right on the base line of number 1 grass court. Excited by the inaccuracy of the German bombing, the Petoello household thought it high time to build some defences. Decio P decided to dig a trench which could protect us. They set to work on the design: the trench would be covered, with a strong timber frame, plastered a foot deep with concrete and finished off with three feet of packed earth. Although the construction bore no comparison to Hitler's own redoubt, it probably could have withstood anything but a direct hit. It took just ten days. On our next visitation of German bombers I was quite nervously awaiting the direct hit, but less so than if I had been in my extremely exposed garret wardrobe.

Digging the trench and building the garden shelter served another purpose: it gave me the opportunity to demonstrate to Madame Petoello that I could be useful, and if so moved could apply myself longer and with greater vigour than any one else in the household.

Even though I fell a little short of her true socialist hero, I reminded her that nearly a quarter of a million Chinese labourers helped to dig trenches in the First World War and that their work was universally praised. Anyway digging holes, itself, seemed an aimless exercise strangely akin to my mood at the time. With my continuous application, the trench was built in four days under the projected fortnight. Thereafter Madame Petoello increased her invitations, and to my great delight I was allowed to sit at her table once or twice a week.

As the war on the Western Front intensified, fortune turned rapidly in my favour. Having witnessed that I could apply myself with vigour, Madame Petoello was not ashamed to give me an introduction for the job of fire watchman at the University Library. As the bombers only passed over at night the job began in the evening and went on through the night. It paid just £2 10s a week but there were some good perks. We eight fire watchmen were free to consume whatever perishables might be left over in the canteen from the day's consumption. There was no rule to prevent us from inviting friends in to help us polish off the surplus cakes, biscuits, sandwiches, tea and coffee. We were all graduates or undergraduates, and so had a party in the library canteen almost every night. It was a pleasant gathering and all we needed to do was to keep our buckets of sand within easy reach, ready to dump on top of any incendiary device that happened to fall in the library building. I don't remember any real-life fire drills. We just had instructions to use the bucket of sand and never to pour on water. Not one of us had any experience in putting out fires, but we all seemed quite confident of the theory. Night after night the German bombers came over, but hardly anything dropped within a mile of us. We wished that some of the drops were nearer so that we could go into action, instead of just sitting around eating cakes!

A Scottish girl called Betty from St Andrews University moved into the large attic bedroom right opposite to my landing. She had come to Cambridge to do postgraduate work in English. It was ideal. No-one would come up to the third floor where the two of us were co-incidentally quartered together, and disturb our literary conversations. For once Mencius had something relevant to say on the subject, 'The advantages of time and season cannot be compared with the physical advantage of position and proximity; and physical advantage cannot be compared with the advantage of human accord and alliance.' Human accord and alliance did not take long to develop. One evening when we were strolling back from the University Library where I had been at work, and she hard at research, her hand slipped naturally into mine and I squeezed it firmly. Our relationship had passed an important threshold. As if in celebration, we began to swing our arms in unison and our feet began to move in dancing steps. Before crossing the Cam at Silver Street I diverted our walk towards Grantchester Meadows, crossing the iron bridge instead. There on the bridge I hugged her and held her by the upper arms. I could feel the firmness of her limbs and the fullness of her body underneath her dress. Although she was not a ravishing beauty, her youth and energy was intoxicating. Hope and expectation surged through me, and the stroll home was one of the most beautiful moments I had known in Cambridge. From that moment our fourth floor attic became a love nest, a joyous interlude that I had never dared to dream could be mine.

Soon it was winter and one evening while fire-watching in the library the news of Pearl Harbor was broadcast over the radio. I knew at once that we were now all in it together. So long as the European war against Hitler and the Pacific war against Japan were perceived as separate, we Chinese had no place in the European theatre. Now those wars were one I knew that very soon I must participate. I wrote to the Chinese Ambassador immediately to offer my services. I emphasized that I was able bodied and willing to do anything. Before he replied I was asked by Stuart House (the Cambridge University extra-Mural Board) to go and lecture to the Eastern Command Army who were bored stiff and waiting by their coastal guns to repel 'the Jerries'. Their education officer thought a lecture on the current affairs of China and the Far East would do the troops good. The Army had also undertaken to train some 800 officers to speak Chinese. In case of a conjunction of British and Chinese forces, they would have some rudimentary communication. Very optimistic! I was first to lecture in a land-based naval establishment in Yarmouth. As I walked from the railway station towards the Navy compound, I noticed that many cadets were eying me with more than a little suspicion. It took me some time to realize that, to them, I was indistinguishable from a Japanese Kamikaze pilot, and that it was not many days before that the pride of the British Navy, the *Repulse* and the *Prince of Wales*, had been sunk by Japanese bombers off the east coast of Malaysia.

When I reached the gates I was abruptly challenged by a cadet with a fixed bayonet, demanding to know my business. He showed visible relief when I explained that I'd come for lunch with the CO and afterwards to give a lecture to the men. News soon got around that I was able to give an illuminating talk about the Far East and I was inundated with invitations. I enjoyed being driven around the bleak, flat countryside in an army jeep and giving two lectures a day.

Even more of a surprise was that so many of my contemporaries at Cambridge had become lieutenants or COs, and I enjoyed many a lunch with them in between lectures. The sergeants would march the men into the Nissen huts and make them stand to attention before barking at them to salute and sit down when I entered. At two and a half guineas a time and half a dozen times a week, within a couple of weeks I was a rich man and able to pay my debt to Madame P.

'Fortune seldom comes in single spies, but in battalions.' Before a couple of weeks was out I was solvent! Not only had Pearl Harbor brought me money, but I was asked by the BBC in Portland Place to give at least one Mandarin broadcast a week – a weekly news summary and commentary. I was to write the news summary and commentary in English first and then have the pieces translated into Chinese and taken over to Broadcasting House where, after approval by a censor, I would read it live over the air. As an alien, I had to have a 'switch-censor' supervising in case I interrupted the broadcast with a hearty 'Heil Hitler!' For the complete job it was thirteen and a half guineas, which I thought a tidy sum. I would invariably bring my booty back to Cambridge to show Madame, who by now was really quite proud of me. And that was not all!

Within a month of my new-found affluence, a telephone call summoned me to an audience with the Ambassador at the Chinese Embassy. Brimful of confidence and enthusiasm, I went to see him straight away. The Ambassador, a neatly dressed little man, received me in his private office. As he had been a Prime Minister before he had reached thirty, I held him in great respect. He said he wanted me to go to Liverpool and join the Consulate as a 'Student Consul'. My special task would be to organize the Chinese Seamen's Union so that they might best continue to assist the Allies in their war effort. I should persuade the men that it was in their interest to give of their best to the common war effort. At the same time, I should see that their legitimate rights and welfare were well protected. Because of the danger that they, too, would be in on the front line of the war, new terms of employment would have to be negotiated for them, both with the British government and the individual shipping companies. We, as the Chinese government, could not do all the negotiation for the men, but we should act as their guides in official and legal matters.

This kind of work was a great challenge to me and I accepted it without hesitation. I was to start as soon as possible. But I needed a couple of days to settle my affairs. I returned to Cambridge to say goodbye to Betty. My departure was a natural conclusion to our relationship. After the first flush of romance, ours had quickly become

a 'marriage of (fourth floor) convenience' and wasn't going anywhere. We parted affably. I bid farewell to the Petoellos and, with
excited visions of a new life, set off for the north.

CHAPTER NINE

The Forgotten Wave

Just now I drank the waters of Changsha
And ate a fish from Wuchang.
I swim across the endless Yangzi
and see to the end of the sky of Chu.
I don't mind the blowing wind or the battering waves,
it's better than strolling in the courtyard.
Today I have leisure.
On the river you said that –
Passing away flows just like this.

Swimming Song, Mao Zedong, 1956

THE TRAIN WAS already moving when I arrived at Euston and I just managed to jump the tail end of it. The way to the sleepers, at the front end, was blocked by a locked coach in the centre of the train. I had to sit all night with the ticket redundant in my pocket. Trains going north were often unheated, whether deliberate, as an economy, or because of blocked pipes was a mystery to me. All I knew was that when I arrived in Liverpool I was in extreme discomfort.

The port had recently been heavily bombarded. In fact the 'India Building' in which our office was situated had been hit by a 500 lb bomb. The building, with all the solidity of any Victorian edifice, would have required a dozen such direct hits to level it. But we did have to vacate temporarily to Sefton Park, a stone's throw from the residence of the Holts, the proprietors of the Blue Funnel Line.

This was a matter of convenience. The Blue Funnel Line fleet were all manned by Chinese seamen – my charges to be. Along with the Anglo-Saxon (Shell) fleet, with its tiny 11,000 ton tankers and crews of forty, there were well over 100 ships mainly manned by Chinese. In addition there were Chinese on the Ben, Glen and some Dutch, Norwegian and Greek lines, as well as a few Panamanian ships. The great passenger liners, the troop-carrying Empresses of Britain, of Russia, of Japan, and of Canada all had complements of 450 Chinese to a ship.

Altogether, at a conservative estimate, some 10,000 Chinese seamen, with hip pockets bulging with money, could be released into the smoking port at any one time. And they all made for the same district. Chinatown was concentrated within a few grubby hilltop streets beneath the towering Anglican Cathedral. Being close to the docks, it was a natural dormitory for the sailors. From Pitt Street through Nelson and George Street to St George Square, the area was teeming with sleazy boarding houses where the sailors were put up in multi-tier bunks, a dozen to a room.

The area had suffered numerous bombardments during the war. But Chinese losses on land were nothing when compared to their losses at sea, where inadequately defended convoys were ambushed by U-boats as they moved in and out of the western approaches. Not knowing whether they would survive from one day to another, many would throw caution to the wind when in port and, having just picked up their wages after several months or, in some cases, years, they had the money to do so in style. But once they were down to the last few notes depression would set in. It was not uncommon for a sailor to take to his bunk and remain there all day, save for the evening meal.

Their meals were paid for by the Ministry of Transport or the shipping companies in subsidies which were made over to the avaricious proprietors of the boarding houses. If they weren't up in time they could always get a better meal at the restaurant next door. There they would have to pay, even though the meals would have been prepared from the same ration cards issued to the boarding house masters. But nobody cared who grew fat in the process, so long as there was good fare on demand.

Some more enterprising souls would band together and set up restaurants specializing in dishes of their own regions, often as part of a provincial club such as the Ningbo, Foochow, Hainan, Swatow or Shanghai. These were probably the earliest regional Chinese restaurants in Britain. The food was invariably authentic, for it was produced with local pride, from the 'distilled memory' of several homesick chefs.

I began to eat well, for I often found myself elected Patron or President of such associations, and was always given preferential treatment, if not, simply, free food. What a change from the crumbs of Madame Petoello's table!

Within a few weeks my academic life in Cambridge seemed remote and I was completely immersed in life in this war-embattled port. Everyone moved about with a sense of purpose. It was hard not to be caught up in their sense of urgency. People beetled back and forth, by train to board a ship, to catch a convoy, already waiting on one of the sea roads and from there to heaven knows where. In convoy there was at least a modicum of protection from the escort warships. Rank didn't seem to matter. To minister or kitchen hand, the war made every moment of your life seem precious. As I shook hands with departing friends, we both knew that many would never return. Yet most were cheerful, even stoical, determined to take every new day as it came. Having been brought up within a nautical tradition there was no wonder I was drawn to the saltiness of life in Liverpool. Cambridge seemed lukewarm by comparison. With daily tides of new people arriving and the recently met departing, maybe for good, life was more spontaneous. How could you plan weeks or months? Everyone lived for the day and most were prepared to be generous with one another.

On my very first day I was given a taste of things to come. As I went to take up my office I stumbled over thirty-five Chinese sitting on the floor in the hall. They were waiting for me to arrive! My Cambridge training had not prepared me for this. Our initial introduction was awkward, but I hoped that by listening to them some vague picture might emerge. It seemed that they were from the port of Ningbo (about 150 miles south east of Shanghai) where they had been recruited by agents of the Blue Funnel Line, and it was with a Blue Funnel ship that they had been serving. Having completed their contract, they were on strike, refusing to sign for another term of service without some improvement in pay for hardship and danger. Indeed they had just sailed from South Africa, where the climate did not suit the Chinese. Many were suffering from dysentery. Opium smoking, to ease pain and depression, was widespread. The Ningbo dialect seemed part-Mandarin, part-Shanghai and I could only just glean a part of the story. I sensed their fear of going back to sea. At a time like this, who could blame them? It wasn't even their war. But they were here for the money, and the best I could do was to offer them my English and negotiate the best terms.

It soon became apparent that my role was to ease negotiations between the Chinese seamen, the shipping lines and the Ministry of Transport, so that the Chinese manpower could be dove-tailed into the Allied war effort without any unnecessary hitches. Chinese participation was crucial to sustain life-lines from the New World to Britain and any part of unoccupied Europe. To the Allies, at this vital and highly sensitive period of war, Chinese participation in Europe was even more crucial than the expeditionary force which Chiang Kaishek had sent to re-enter Burma with the British 14th Army. Without them the German U-boats, E-boats and battleships such as the *Bismarck* and *Scharnhörst* might easily have cut the jugular, long before Roosevelt's frigates or the American liberty ships arrived in sufficient numbers to save the day.

And then there was the *Jarvis Bay*. She was a merchant ship that opened up her pea-shooters on a German battleship at close range. In the few minutes' grace before the Germans recovered from their shock and unleashed the might of Teutonic technology, the rest of the convoy had the chance to flee. There were Chinese seamen on the *Jarvis Bay* when she made that last dash from certain extinction. It was a brave act, but there were almost no survivors.

Bureaucratic rigidity seemed part of the British plot to keep aliens in their place. And strikes were a foreign response to injustice, originally introduced to China by the Communist Party, only a decade or two earlier. But with their exposure to foreign working practices, the seamen were the quickest to catch on, and by the 1940s would strike at the drop of a hat. Both sides clashed with the arrogance of august imperial traditions behind them and an ocean of language between them. What could I offer the situation?

The advantage of being a young educated Chinese was that I was accorded the respect traditionally due to a young 'mandarin' and my words were weighed carefully. I learned to listen patiently to the men's complaints, to speak clearly when I spoke and always to stick to the point. Before long I gained considerable respect from them, even graduating from young 'mandarin' to 'parent of the people', a designation for senior officials and sometimes even the Emperor! With this came considerable influence and a way through threatened intransigence.

I worked hard. I have never worked harder in my life, long beyond office hours, making interminable telephone calls, visiting the Walton prison to bail out errant seamen. I had to be seen to be effective if I were to keep my influence. If I managed to claim back any sizeable sums due to the men, I would make a great show of distributing it personally in front of the largest group of people possible. This was primitive public relations. Their appreciation of me was all the more when they learned that my pay as 'Student Consul' was a mere £6 15s a week, considerably less than I had earned in my brief career as a lecturer and broadcaster.

But I hadn't come to Britain to make money. I had come to learn, and Liverpool was teaching me a lot about life. Ironically I had to come all this way to understand the character and style of the people I had grown up among, but with whom I had never had a chance of rubbing shoulders.

The natural unit that the seamen fell into was a loosely aligned, regional group with a gang leader who called the tune. Bullying and coercion enforced compliance. Bearing a new standard of democracy, I had to try to galvanize these men into some form of organization that resembled a union. Fresh from university, I was enthused with the power of the democratic principle and keen to graft it upon their primitive social organization. In any meeting I encouraged everyone to speak by asking lots of questions. I found that people liked the sound of their own voices. To encourage them to express their views was the first step towards a solution. Above all it was essential to prompt the gang leaders to air their views publicly. Once they had committed themselves to a policy, then it was easy to encourage them to abide by it. Their word was their bond, and public declaration made the issues clear. The gang leaders would not lord it over the others when speaking in public; they would all feign humility in their speeches and ultimately be prepared to abide by majority decision.

When the Ningbo seamen left the office on that first day, another dozen men appeared from the Anglo-Saxon tankers. There was something familiar about their faces. As soon as they opened their mouths I recognized from their heavily accented and broken Mandarin that they would naturally speak a dialect from the Min River. For a while I let them struggle on speaking the unfamiliar, official language of China, for of course they assumed me to be from the north. Then, in the very best Foochow, with all the polish I could muster, I replied to them in my mother tongue. They nearly fell head over heels. What a pleasure it was to meet strangers that spoke our native tongue in such an alien environment! For our language was peculiar to a small area of the Min River around Foochow, and anyone else would find it impossible to understand. They immediately forgot what they had come to see me about and insisted that we should all go out and celebrate.

To commemorate the occasion I composed the following poem, to bring Foochow, Cambridge and Liverpool a little closer.

For the Men from the Min River

They come in, beaming with the glow of dawn in the Eastern sea,
wreathed in smiles like so many songs of sheer delight,
the imprint of centuries' etiquette,
they come forward and speak,
rough wrinkled hands telling of a storm battered past,
of gales weathered over life's tempestuous ocean,
their stories run a course as
strange and tragic as the Yellow river.

Behind, the tall steel ships have aged them
for years of sailing the memory soaked seas and, perhaps,
to sink in a moment like a stone or explode as a bomb
disappearing with the sorrow of vanished love,
spraying clouds with stars and fireworks,
or raising enormous ghosts to lick the sky with fantastic, fiery tongues.

Far away, between the steady command of the megaphone and
the noise of dim port over dark waters, they hear the sounds of
    summer's drought,
the all night grinding of the wooden pump in the creek, and then
the incessant report of New Year firecrackers
crackles through the churning propellers,
and like a dream between the cranking of cranes and the unexpected
    sirens
comes the interminable drone sound of cicadas.
While the ships' bells toll,
marking with their silver tone, the ethereal movement of
what has passed, is passing, or might have been.

(The foreigners do not understand at all, or do not bother,
their women largely amused,
all sharks ashore fattened on their toil, remorseless as the sharks at sea.)
The sailors smile again and suddenly grow taller, stronger than
    their ill-cared for bodies.
Their faces and words glow afresh with deeper meaning . . .
till they almost resemble their own familiar heroes.
They nod, withdraw, half bowing,
leaving behind a trail of modern history,
boiling and foaming
in the wake of a great ship passing.

                                                                K. Lo

One of my biggest cases concerned 450 seamen on strike from

a Canadian Pacific Empress liner which was due to carry troops to the front line in North Africa. The shipping company and port authorities threatened to sack them and thereby make it possible to withdraw the men's right to set foot on British soil. News of the strike got through to Chiang Kaishek, who had appointed himself Foreign Minister as well as Commander-in-Chief in China. He replied with the instruction to withdraw the total force of Chinese from the Allied Fleet if the British employers were to continue coercing Chinese with such brutality.

The British bluff was called. Minor bureaucrats, including myself, scurried around ironing out differences in order to avert this threatened disaster. If any one of the larger liners were to fail to sail on account of the intransigence of a couple of clerks in the Ministry of Transport, a division or more of troops could go missing on a vital front. Knowing the importance of the Empress's cargo, my flurry took on an even greater urgency, although, from time to time, I did reflect upon the logistics of arresting 450 Chinese seamen with what amounted to no more than the dozen CID officers left in the whole of Liverpool.

On another occasion I found myself making an overnight dash 150 miles to Milford Haven. We had begun late. Every now and then the two searching headlights of the coach flashed upon the bobtails of hares fleeing from our hasty progress. I reflected upon our mission. Thirty ships were impatiently awaiting a last straggler to join them out on the sea roads, but the last straggler was manned by Chinese. As I surveyed my twenty sleepy fellow travellers, it dawned on me that when the situation became heated all these people were bystanders, minor bureaucrats from the Ministry and shipping lines. If the strike were to be diverted I was the only person to do it. No-one else spoke Chinese, and a decisive breakthrough had to be made by late morning or the seamen were to be taken into custody. A sweat broke out over my brow.

On arrival at the port we freshened up at a boarding house. I drank a huge jug of strong, sweet tea to give me Dutch courage. From there we ferried across a choppy sea to the rogue ship which was rolling on the high seas. There was no wooden gangway to cross from launch to ship and the only way to board was to scramble up a rope net which was unfurled like a carpet over the side of the ship. The informality of this arrival broke the ice for me and I simply swung myself up like a monkey. On entering the mess the men were already gathered to meet our deputation.

At one glance I knew that I was home and dry. They were from one of the villages that dotted the lower reaches of the Min

River, where I used to sit for hours, from morning till late afternoon, watching fleet after fleet of fishing boats head out towards the sea. I waited until everyone was well settled and then tried the opening gambit, 'Might you be from the riverside village of "Zhang lou (Eternal Happiness)?"' The Bosun, with wind taken out of his sails, spluttered, 'How the devil . . . ?' I answered, 'I guessed . . . !' A broad smile spread across the face of every man. We immediately settled down to a cosy two-hour chat without a trace of confrontation. Of course the Anglo-Saxons were at sea, thinking it all serious negotiation, but when bowls of noodles appeared around the conference table they knew that the wind was blowing in the right direction.

Another time that I was called out to a straggling Canadian boat that was holding up a convoy, I ended up on the Manchester Ship Canal. Problems had arisen over money. The crew were refusing to use British banking facilities. They would not accept a receipt they could not read as guarantee that they could reclaim their money later. Who could blame them? But the men could also not sign on for another tour of duty if all the past accounts had not been settled.

When I was shown into the mess thirty pairs of eyes turned to scrutinize me closely. I asked them if they were enjoying their dinner. Of course they invited me to join them. But this was not the time to party. I had one piece of essential information to convey to them: the Bank of China had just opened a new branch in Liverpool. If I could take their cash to Liverpool that night, bank it in the morning, thirty bank drafts and receipts could be drawn up in Chinese in time for them to catch up with the convoy. The receipts could be in individual names and stamped and sealed with the official stamp.

A medium-sized suitcase was produced and the counting started, supervised by one officer and two men. £10,000 in £1 and 10s notes had to be put into about thirty packages and marked clearly with the seamen's names. At midnight the ship was nearing Warrington where I could catch a train to Liverpool. I suggested that the men might like to send a couple of their boys to accompany me, but I seemed to have inspired total confidence in them. I also had sufficient faith in my own honesty, but I was not so confident about being able to guard my 'cash haul' safely to the bank.

I was lowered over the side of the ship and rowed to a point near the railway station. In the train compartment I stowed my suitcase on the top luggage shelf and covered it with my grubby mackintosh. Once in Liverpool I thought it would be safer to walk up the middle of the street rather than to hug the sidewalks where any attacker would be invisible in the dim light. I had never carried so much money and deeply regretted not having insisted on a chaperone. By the time I was climbing the hill to Upper Parliament Street I was sweating profusely. But I arrived home safely and threw the suitcase under the bed before falling into a relieved sleep.

The next morning the banking of the notes and issuing of drafts proved more expeditious than I'd thought. Two men and an officer had come to meet me at the bank. It seemed strange that they should be so suspicious of banks when they had entrusted their entire savings overnight to me, a total stranger!

Those Chinese seamen who didn't show when the ship set sail were arrested later and put on the next ship whether they had their worldly possessions with them or not. Hearing the heavy institutional doors clang shut behind me soon became a familiar routine. It was my job to make sure that the men had not been locked up without good reason and that they had adequate defence in court. Many excuses were offered for being late back to the ship. There were those who refused to leave until the laundry had finished pressing their clothes! The British authorities could be equally arbitrary and were in the habit of withdrawing landing permission, leaving sailors with no pass to be in this country at all. Then there was no protection. Chinese were not covered by the current British National Service Act and there was no separate agreement with China.

I met some interesting characters in the local prison. One of them, Lo Ping, was a respected gang leader from Shanghai. With his sunken cheekbones he looked the part, except he was rather small. But he made up for his slight stature with eloquence and putting around the rumour that he carried guns. One day Lo marched into my office and slammed a revolver down on my desk.

'What's this for?' I asked with all the severity I could muster.

'Since I'm not planning to use it again, I thought you would be the best person to keep it for me,' he answered wryly.

'Give it to the police,' I said.

He shrugged off my comment and smiled. That was the last time I saw him. A little while later I heard that he had died, ironically of a burst ulcer. His funeral was the largest held for a Chinese in those war years. All the taxis in the whole port were commandeered for his cortège. As the procession snaked around the streets of Liverpool, the Liverpudlians watched and wondered whether Royalty had passed away.

As a consular official I was often called upon to interpret. Once ten seamen were on trial for having caused 'an affray', which I was led to believe could be a serious charge. I was called on to interpret the words of the judge, the police, the prosecution as well as for the numerous witnesses, the defendants and the defence barrister. In that hot stuffy courtroom in midsummer I became the traffic lights in a six-lane verbal traffic jam! After three hours of it I began to wilt and was glad to have a break for lunch. The only thing that kept me alert through the haze of the afternoon was the performance of our lady barrister, who had been engaged for us by a well-known firm of solicitors called Silverman and Livermore. She stood erect and smart in her gown and did not mind delaying the court until she was quite sure that everything was crystal clear. She was young too, not more than in her late twenties, and as she stood there in court she appeared like a vision of a modern Portia. I wanted to tell her so, but at the end of the session she slipped away.

Nevertheless, tomorrow was another day and the judge had yet to sum up and brief the jury. There was ample time for me to make 'gallant' remarks. But when the next day arrived the only remarks I had to make were to interpret the sentences the judge meted out to each one of the seamen. That did not put me in a good mood at all and I stalked out of the court in a huff without even a 'goodbye' to my Portia. I even told the court they could stuff their fee.

When I visited our solicitors to tie up the loose ends, I discovered that Portia's name was Rose Heilbron and that the court was paying her no more than they were meant to pay me. At three and a half guineas I felt she had been poorly rewarded and that I should invite her to dinner to thank her personally for being so thorough. When I rang the call was answered by a male doctor. I gave up. He was probably her husband. The next day I took her secretary out instead. She was a lively young woman with whom I had become acquainted while 'stitching' together the seamen's case.

Liverpool produced many visions of womanhood to tantalize me. I was always in love. I would become totally transfixed by a tiny waist here, a shock of glorious red hair there, endless permutations of loveliness. But the women were as fickle as we men would have liked to have been. There was a miner's daughter who would look me up whenever she came to town. Then there was a nurse from Liverpool General Hospital. That summer our hideaway was on the banks of the Dee, as it meandered through such towns as Parkgate, Kirby and Hoylake. The grass was so long that if you lay down nobody could ever see you and anyway you could walk for miles without seeing a soul. It was idyllic. The riverside seemed to become our very own and the moments in which the riverside existed were forever. That summer initiated and bound me to the 'good earth' of Britain.

My other hideout during those post-Dunkirk summers was Southport. I was advised to move to this satellite town in case the Germans resumed their bombing. I felt they were probably too preoccupied on the Eastern Front. All the same I went there to join a friend who had found inexpensive accommodation on the promenade. The landlady of the Queen's Hotel, a glorified boarding house, was friendly and a sound cook. We commuted to Liverpool on the 8.10 a.m., the latest of the cheap-rate runs, meant for the labourers who worked on the dockside in Liverpool. We returned by the 7 p.m. Stepping off the train, the freshness of the sea-breeze washed away all the cares of the city.

Southport seemed a place of some splendour. The broad Lord Street was not only fashionable, but it was dotted with cafés and seemed to have the colour and character of a Parisian boulevard. We occasionally sat out in one of the cafés to sip at coffee, pretending that we were garret-dwelling artists on the Left Bank of the Seine. Indeed the leisure to be found at Southport was a great antidote to the daily pressure of Chinese labour problems.

For junior consular officials there were not just labour problems to attend to but also urgent community problems. Once there was an unusual clash between the Chinese and the West Indians. I say unusual, for the two ethnic groups normally live together in peace, not only in Liverpool, but in most parts of the world that they cohabit. It was a squabble over women that sparked the friction: probably who was organizing prostitution and where. With both groups of men away from home, any question of territorial rights over women was bound to be charged. The Liverpool girls certainly held sway.

It was reported to us that the West Indians were brandishing knives and coshes and that the Chinese were armed with choppers. The police warned that the CID were down to a dozen men and they feared the worst. If the confrontation continued it would undoubtedly result in fatalities. As 'parents of the people' we had to step in quickly.

But we were a rum bunch. There were four of us at the consulate. At the apex of our operation was the bespectacled Consul, slightly slow in speech, meticulous in everything, a perfect bureaucrat who would have made a very good sub-postmaster. He always annoyed me by daring to correct my English drafts. He, who had never heard of E. M. Forster or T. S. Eliot! Then there was the Vice-Consul, Zheng, who claimed to be a distant relative of mine. On the face of it he was a traditional careerist whose sights were on the diplomatic service, but underneath he was a total physical and mental wreck who often got down on his hands and knees to kowtow to our visitors! The fourth member of staff was my friend Christopher Chen, a law graduate from LSE, whom I had brought up to Liverpool to help with the contracts of employment. He was acquainted with all the fashionable society gossip as well as the notable names in the worlds of contemporary literature, history and music. He would have been more at home reading a copy of the *Tatler* than faced with a chopper. Could this unlikely team steel itself for action and quell the threatened racial riot?

As we set about planning our mode of operation I couldn't help feeling as if we were about to ride out on the 'Charge of the Light Brigade'. Not one of us had the remotest experience of the West Indian community. So first we summoned the Chinese gang leaders, making sure to round up representatives of all the provincial groups. There were the elders of Shanghai, Ningbo, Foochow, Hainan and all the acknowledged leaders of the local Chinese community. We tried to impress upon them that a clash between Chinese and West Indians would not only be futile but extremely dangerous. The chopsticks might yet prove mightier than the sword. To defuse the situation, as responsible elders of the Chinese community we should invite the West Indian leaders to a sumptuous meal at the brand new seamen's club.

The West Indian leaders were overjoyed. They loved Chinese food! The next evening we played host to over forty men and no women. After the first half dozen courses had settled everyone down, we allowed drink to flow freely. We even invited a few members of the local constabulary to come along and do some low-profile community policing! We drank to our eternal friendship and by the end the incident that had ignited the brawl had been completely forgotten. Relations were normalized immediately and the two peoples never smiled more broadly at each other.

After nearly a year in secluded Southport I moved back to the scrum in Liverpool. This time I lodged in Upper Parliament Street. I had been joined by Christopher Chen and Teddy Teh, another law student from Cambridge, who was helping out in the Consulate. Chinese graduates were two a penny during the war years. Severed from their families and private incomes, many had been reduced to picking tomatoes in the fens. Christopher and Tommy were all too glad to come to Liverpool for the smallest wage.

Opposite our lodgings was the Rialto cinema and dance hall. Fights often spilled out of the dance hall. Late one evening there was a bang on the door. When I opened it a big French sailor fell across the threshold. He had been stabbed in the back. I helped him on to a *chaise longue* and called for the West Indian-born Chinese doctor who happened to live upstairs. Blood was flowing freely over the patent leather sofa.

But as seasons and years progressed, work in Liverpool mostly fell into a routine of clearing up misunderstandings, claiming back outstanding monies due to the men and formulating new terms of employment. The formation of the union was something quite new to us all. Only communists had any experience of trade unions in China. Very few Chinese industries had ever offered security of employment, let alone fair play. We were sent an adviser from Nanjing. His name was Zhu Xuefan. He had been Secretary to the Postal Union, the best of its kind in China. The post office was one of the few large enterprises in China which offered any sort of regular employment.

I introduced Zhu to all the seamen leaders. With sailors constantly in and out of port it was difficult to track down a consistent body of men with whom to negotiate. Eventually they did manage to put together some kind of official union to be the negotiating arm for their employment contracts. Zhu was always very conscious of his refinement and education. He felt that it held sway with the men. He took his parental role very seriously. He also appreciated my academic background, especially as he couldn't speak any English and relied on me to deal with translation and interpreting. All in all we got along well and did finally manage to scratch together a model contract to protect the men.

When the war ended in 1945 the bulk of the Chinese in Liverpool jumped the first ship sailing east. They were all homesick. Within weeks Liverpool was deserted of Chinese. I, too, migrated south, for I felt that with the seamen gone life was draining out of the town. Before I left, the seamen from my own province threw a farewell dinner in my honour. The party was held in the Central Restaurant on the north side of Great George Square. I was entertained to an expensive twelve-course dinner by five tables of men. At the dinner I was asked to say a few words. Bearing in mind the Chinese consular officials in Calcutta, Rotterdam, Hamburg and other ports, who had been roughed up by the seamen on account of their high and mighty mandarin ways, I said that co-operation between bureaucrats and the common folk had never been easy throughout history but that, on the contrary, we had enjoyed a smooth and easy passage together. I raised my wine cup to drink to their passage into the future. Su Limoi, one of the leaders, brought me a sealed envelope and from a hidden table a range of solid silver cups and plates and a cigarette box were brought forward and presented to me. It was their last tribute in recognition of the thousands of hours I had spent helping them out of one kind of scrape or another. Many of the pieces of silverware were donated by people I had bailed out of prison for drug-trafficking! They must have been doing well. I didn't know whether to feel proud or relieved for having got by without being beaten up. When dealing with the masses, good public relations and sumptuous banquets are critical to your success. Whatever you have done must also 'be seen to be done'. Then only good, food and silver will come of it!

Before leaving Liverpool I must mention Poon Lim. Poon Lim was a pantry boy, barely twenty years old, but when he walked down the gangway at Liverpool, the Lord Provost of Glasgow and the Commander-in-Chief of the Western Approaches, Admiral Macnaughton, were there to salute him. Poon Lim's ship, the *Ben Lomond*, was sunk by an Italian submarine on 23 November 1942, with all hands assumed lost. He was not picked up until April the following year, after 133 days on the open Atlantic. President Truman had thought fit to make him an honorary American citizen, and, since he had served on a British ship, the British government wanted to award him an MBE.

As he ambled down the gangway he did not look like an unkempt pantry boy. He was well-dressed, seemed in excellent health and was sporting a glowing tan to show for his ordeal. He was immediately engulfed by Press. I shouted to him not to give his story away for nothing. I needn't have bothered. He didn't understand them anyway.

It was an October day of 1947 when I was lent the Chinese ambassador's car to drive Poon Lim to Buckingham Palace where he was to be invested by King George VI. I sat on one of the side seats to watch the ceremony. The King, also well-groomed, and crimson in the face, spoke to Poon. I did not catch what the King said as I was too far away; neither did Poon Lim, despite his energetic nodding.

After the ceremony we returned to the Welbeck Palace Hotel where I spent nearly ten hours drawing out of him the story of his remarkable journey. He had lost relatives from three generations when the ship had been torpedoed. Luckily Poon Lim was a resilient boy and instead of dwelling on his bad luck, he set about the business of surviving. Throughout those 133 days that he drifted, half naked, on the Atlantic, he survived on rain and condensed moisture, raw fish and tiny birds that he could lure on to his raft. Since I had extracted quite a lot of money from the Press for his story, on our return to Liverpool we had a banquet for thirty friends. That was the last rite that I performed for our boys in the Allied

Merchant Navy.

When I left Liverpool I knew that I would be able to obtain another three-year British Council scholarship to further my studies of English literature, regardless of having already completed five years' study at Cambridge. There were eight scholarships going begging. Chiang Kaishek, as temporary Foreign Minister, concurrently Prime Minister and Head of State, had insisted on signing all exit papers. With the inevitable bottleneck, almost no exit visas had been issued to students wanting to travel abroad. To help the British Council out of their administrative dilemma I claimed one of the scholarships.

I decided on London. After the freedom of Liverpool, a second period of monastic academia in Oxford, the other option, would hardly be tolerable. Dreaming up a title for my PhD dissertation, 'A comparison of Lord Chesterfield's letter to his son and the home letters of Marquis Zeng Guofan', I made my application. Apparently the assessor was more convinced of its merits than I was. I had chosen these two characters simply because I knew their work quite well. Zeng Guofan was one of the four great viceroys who took over China as the Manchu dynasty teetered. Although a militarist responsible for putting down the mid-nineteenth-century Taiping rebellion in China, he was also a reformer and a pure Confucian in spirit. As compared with Zeng Lord Chesterfield was a rogue. But the scholarship was worth £35 a month, so I embarked upon my research.

I'd thought that I had said cheerio for good to the Wirral, the Mersey Tunnel, the New Brighton Ferry, the Tower Ballroom and all the 'cool hands and warm hearts' I had hung on to in the north. But I had hardly been at University College six months when I was called into service again by the Embassy. This time I was to go to Manchester.

Manchester was in the grip of a very cold winter, so it was lucky that my office was well heated. It was on the fifth floor of the only skyscraper in Manchester. It was called, aptly, the Sunlight Building, and stood at the intersection of Deansgate and Opera House street. Mr Joseph Sunlight, the proprietor, actually operated the elevator himself. He probably wanted to keep an eye on his tenants. The building had a heated swimming pool and Turkish baths in the basement. Every afternoon I had a Turkish bath. It was a minimal luxury before I made the trek home to my cold suburban lodgings.

On coming out of the Sunlight Building in the late afternoons I would cross St Peter's Square and head for the Chinese Student Centre or the International Students' Club of the British Council. When I first arrived in Manchester, I held a party for the local Chinese community at the Student Centre. It seemed to be the gentlemanly thing to do and was in keeping with what I'd learnt about community relations in Liverpool. But in the immortal words of Mencius, 'the gentleman distances himself from the kitchen', which would seem to have automatically precluded my own ascent into his pantheon of heroes. However, Mencius was only referring to the messy business in the abattoir. But on that day his maxim was almost strained to the limit.

My intention was to give all the guests a bowl of chicken noodle soup. For the ingredients I asked one of my Irish Liverpudlian friends to provide six chickens. When I arrived at the club that afternoon I saw to my consternation that all six of them were still clucking in a crate. I was at a total loss. However, I remembered that among the Chinese graduates there was a surgeon and a dentist. Considering that their skill with the scalpel was likely to be at least superior to mine with the wood chopper when I had slain the duck in the lower kitchen at Lo Lodge, I immediately summoned them to perform the essential job. The dentist proved most capable in the matter of strangulation. The surgeon was more inclined to use the only knife available, a blunt penknife, and made lamentable work of it. It only remained for me to pluck and dismember the birds so I could stuff them neatly into a huge tea-urn, where they boiled for nearly two hours. In the end chicken soup poured into the forty-three expectant bowls of drained noodles with a simple turn of the tap. There was plenty left for seconds, and many thought my 'Chicken Noodles' unrivalled in the whole of Britain. That was probably the most bizarre performance of my whole diplomatic career, and it went off with hardly a hitch while I managed to remain respectably aloof from the tasteless slaughter.

At the British Council's International Centre I would search out stimulating conversation or robust girls for robust exchanges. There were never many bright intellects around, but there were plenty of girls. Perhaps I was more fastidious about conversation than physical attributes. I was seldom short of something to say, being more experienced than most students who thronged the bar.

As there were no Chinese restaurants in Manchester at that time – not even one – when I felt enamoured or just generous I would invite the lady concerned for a curried potato and rabbit at the Koh-i-noor Indian restaurant on Market Street. Who could resist such an invitation? Unfortunately the date would usually end there. It would be sheer madness to invite anyone home to the frozen, distant suburbs of Manchester even should she be willing. So I developed a casual, *laissez-faire* attitude to love and sex. I met some stunning blonde Scandinavians but I never fell in love in Manchester. I thought back to the nurses from Liverpool General and the redhead who worked in the Wirral co-op. Now there was true love, Liverpool style. Manchester seemed different.

There were other matters to attend to. I was finally able to renew contact with my parents and friends who had been marooned in Japanese occupied territory throughout the war. It seemed that the treatment of the civilian population had varied wildly from area to area, and I was anxious to hear how my family had fared. There had been terrible massacres in Shanghai and Nanjing.

I should never have worried about my father. He had been born under an eclipsed star and no-one ever noticed him much. Of course in Foochow we had been living next door to the Japanese Consulate for decades. The moment Foochow was invaded our house was automatically searched, for it stood strategically overlooking Japanese territory. On entering our drawing-room the officer in charge was astonished to find a display of Chrysanthemum ceramic bowls, the ensignia of the Imperial family of Japan. When it was explained that they were a present from Prince Ito, a classmate of grandfather's at Greenwich Naval College, the officer picked up a bowl with two hands and bowed low with undisguised reverence.

To celebrate the re-establishment of contact I immediately cabled home half of my first month's pay, and in addition I bought two expensive gifts from Aspreys, to reinforce the impression that I had 'arrived'. For my mother I bought a crocodile skin handbag and for my father, a solid silver cigarette case. Altogether I spent £62. I had bought them not so much for their usefulness as for the pride and gratification my parents would undoubtedly take in them and me. Although I was not as brilliant as Charles, their first-born, they would appreciate the sentiment and the quality.

Keeping abreast of Charles's movements had been difficult. After his expensive and tricky journey into the interior from Shanghai, via Hanoi to Kunming, he had spent about three years teaching in the South-West University before leaving for Chongqing to join Chiang Kaishek behind the front line. There he had found employment in the Department of Information in the Foreign Office. He never went into much detail about how he was and what he was feeling, but I gleaned that there had been terrible carnage during the Japanese bombing of the city. He had also fallen in love, but had left Chongqing without his girl. He had received the commission to go to America as Secretary to the Ambassador, Wei Daming, and had flown west down the

Burma road to Calcutta. From there, penniless, he jumped a Flying Fortress which took him all the way to America.

Mother wrote regularly, giving me general news of the family. It was Michael who really kept me informed of life and times in Shanghai. He was studying European history at St John's University in Shanghai and wrote elegant, informed letters, full of good observations that would help me piece together what was happening. He had grown to be a handsome young man, but had trouble with his ears and was sadly to become stone deaf before he turned thirty. Walter, at the Catholic University in Peking, was not a letter writer, and Father never wrote – maybe he had forgotten how. After a decade of immersion in the English language, even I found it too laborious to write in Chinese!

The year 1946 was a crucial one for me. In the transition from war to peace it had to be a year of decision. Many would have thought it was high time to be going home to embark upon a proper career in the foreign service. That would have been the normal course to follow. For a Chinese, educated in the orthodox way, I should have provided my parents with sound moral reasons for my career decision not to return to the fold. But I was still reluctant to return home and, besides, times were not normal, my parents were not orthodox and demanded very little of me.

I hadn't yet achieved what I had mapped out in my mind. I wanted to get a book published in the UK, I wanted to play tennis at international level and finally I wanted to settle down with a British girl. The last condition would never have been admitted as an admirable objective in the mind of any good Chinese, except perhaps my father, but he could hardly be held up as a model. I was fed up with one-night stands that seemed no more than the perpetuation of wartime experience. I wanted something of Britain to which I could hold on, something less transient, that could become more a part of my life than fleeting memories. I wanted more than to be washed up in Foochow with a closet full of handmade shoes.

Besides, I had my own analysis of how things were going in China. I remember once expressing it when invited to lecture at the City Library in St Peter's Square. I enjoyed that lecture, and found myself able to talk for one and a half hours without any notes. I told the assembled crowd that although Chiang Kaishek appeared to have the upper hand, in the long run Mao Zedong would turn the tables on him. I told them that whoever had the backing of China's peasant population would prevail. But I asked the representative of the local press not to put my view into print. As the Chinese Consul, representing the Nationalist government in Nanjing, I might lose my job for preaching its downfall!

My analysis took into account the soaring inflation that was raging in all of the major towns of China. The inflation was so bad that it was annihilating the flimsy urban middle class of China in one stroke. Without them there was no buffer between the small ruling class and the sea of discontentment and poverty that engulfed the rest of China.

After having ignored the social dimensions of their 'Three People's Principles' in my high school hymn, the three screws that held together the Nationalists' war machine were also more than a little loose. Their 'front was of brass and feet of clay'. Firstly the troops were billeted on the people, living largely off the land. This meant indiscriminate requisition and straightforward looting. The gulf between army and peasant was growing ever wider. Secondly, although the United States arms dumps in the north-west Pacific had been opened to Chiang, much of the artillery would require heavy transport and continual logistical support. In the hinterland of China, operations were mainly over paddy fields and it was of little use. Heavy equipment would merely bog down troop movements and rapid-firing guns merely exhausted a limited supply of ammunition. Finally there was no paymaster system operating in the Chinese army. The troops were being paid by the officers. Since corruption festered in the gap between commanders and men the final thread on the final screw was wearing thin. It was a wonder that they had the morale to fight when they met up with the Communists for the final showdown along the Longhai Railway Line of Central China.

From deep within Japanese-occupied territories, such as Manchuria, Mao's armies had emerged with their military capacity substantially enhanced by picking up Japanese hardware as they fled after Hiroshima and Nagasaki. In fact my sympathies had always leaned towards Mao, but I was loath to say so too publicly. I disliked Chiang's war-lord ways and had always felt the Communists to be closer to the earth of China. No doubt my ideals had also been shaped by left-wing intellectuals at Cambridge, and not a little by Edgar Snow's *Red Star over China*, a first-hand report of the Long March. I was deeply moved by Mao's vision of social equality and the commitment of the men and women who followed him.

President Truman was not unaware that if he managed to bring the civil war to an amicable solution it would be to America's credit. Even though America had been siding with the Nationalists and the 'Song dynasty' (Chiang's wife, Song Meiling, T. V. Song, her brother, and

H. H. Kong, her brother-in-law), their economic backbone, he sensed the danger in falling out with the CCP. So he sent General Marshall and the ex-president of my own college in Peking, Dr Leighton-Stuart, to initiate some kind of peace-keeping process. But it was far too little, too late. Wrapped in my cosy suburban life, I felt blessed to be out of it.

When winter loosened its grip on the northern city I moved from Victoria Park to the outer suburb of Didsbury. There I found accommodation with a back garden which opened out on to the Northern Tennis Club, the premier tennis venue of the north. It was perfect. As an ex-Cambridge Blue, I had no difficulty in getting myself introduced to the majority of the top tennis players in the region. Soon I had also beaten most of them on the court. Perhaps no-one had practised during the war and, with an easy job, I was playing five times a week. At weekends I frequently made the trip to London to play. Being still in my early thirties I had no difficulty in training myself to a peak of physical fitness. I was running at my best and proud that I could dash 100 yards without quickening my breath. In the final of the Liverpool West Derby tournament I beat the long-entrenched Lancashire Champion, A. T. England, in straight sets. I repeated a similar victory over the Cheshire Champion, Charles Hall, in Ripley.

One day news came from the Embassy. China was intending to field a team to compete in the Davis Cup, and I had been chosen as third player. There was little time to prepare and I was to go immediately to London to train with my two team-mates, W. C. Choy and Kho Sinkie. I also had to get measured for a national blazer and tennis clothing. I was raring to go. As a team we lacked neither prestige nor money. My team-mates were players of some stature: W. C. Choy, although far from robust, had won thirteen tournaments in a row. Our other team-mate, Kho Sinkie, had just won the Eastern Mediterranean Championship in Cairo. In fact, Kho and Chay had not long ago met in the final of the British Hard Court Championship in Bournemouth. The Chinese Ambassador had cabled to congratulate them with the words 'whoever wins today, China wins!' I felt honoured to carry their bags. During those few weeks of training, life could not have been better.

Although China was topsy-turvy, she was putting forth a brave face to the world. The military, naval and air forces all wore resplendent uniform. At the Allied Summit in Cairo, Chiang had sat with Roosevelt, Stalin and Churchill as one of the leaders of the world's four great powers. I was in a very junior post, but I could have been forgiven if I'd thought that I might move upwards within a matter of a few years. But I was taking a back seat to watch the progress of events. History was rolling on and I was going on a tennis spree in Europe.

The most unforgettable Davis Cup matches were played against Denmark and Belgium. The tie against Denmark was played in Copenhagen. China won by four matches to one. My team-mates won all their matches and I was responsible for our only defeat! We played on a sunken show court in a club called Kobe Hallen. Although I was at the peak of my fitness and was able to sprint up four flights of stairs, after the four-set match I had no weapon left in my repertoire. Unless I could generate greater control and power in my service, I knew I did not deserve a position in international competition. Although my tennis was a disappointment the trip was most enjoyable. The celebration banquet was held at the Vivex, a venue with which I was well acquainted from my previous visit to Copenhagen, a decade before. For dessert we were presented with a bouquet of the most beautiful flowers frozen into an enormous block of ice. In the top a deep bowl had been scooped out and filled with ice creams and coloured sorbets. The whole prize pudding was like a volcano with clouds of frozen breath erupting against the summer sky. The dark clouds of war seemed far away.

Brussels was a true cosmopolitan city. We crossed the Channel by boat to Ostend on a sunny afternoon. The short train ride to Brussels made the two cities seem continuous. We were shown to our respective suites in the Metropole, the top hotel. No expense was spared to entertain us. Everyone was celebrating the cessation of hostilities everywhere, and we were eager to catch the bounty. Our manager told us that the costs incurred would be paid out of the gate receipts received from the three-day match. They were expecting some 10,000 spectators at the Royal Leopold Club, where tickets would not be cheap. So we were, after all, earning our own keep and need not feel any reservations about extravagance.

Steak, ice cream and chocolates overflowed on the terrace of the Royal Leopold. China and Belgium battled it out on those perfect En-Tout-Cas courts which felt like silken powder underfoot. At one point the two countries were at level pegging with two matches each. It was only in the end that Belgium forged ahead and won the deciding fifth match which went to five sets. Hardly any of the spectators could remain in their seats. The Chinese Ambassador was on his feet and two Belgian Ministers, Messrs Van Sieland and Spaak, were so carried away in the excitement that they invited all the members of both teams to dinner. After changing into our smartest outfits, we met at the Asti Restaurant for an occasion of some splendour. In the middle of the dinner the roof over the long dining-table opened and we rose to toast each other. As we raised our glasses the night air was so still that the candles' flames barely flickered under the starry dome.

It was the pinnacle of my tennis career. I was fully satisfied in being just the third and reserve member of China's National Team. Here I had only sat beside the court and cheered. I had not even had the chance to lose! But I was just pleased to be on the team at all and to have participated in the resurgence of European life after the war.

We retired to train for Wimbledon. Tennis standards were patchy that year after four years of war. Anyone who could still serve power-fully was likely to go far. Among such a motley crew even I became a 'nominated player' and was fetched and carried in a Daimler. But on the day I was due to make an appearance disaster struck in the shape of my old friend Robert Li. He informed me that my match was published as third in the afternoon. I should not arrive too early for fear of exhausting myself. I should have learned my lesson in Paris. Robert didn't know about romance; how could he know about tennis? Neither had he ever taken my sporting life seriously. When I arrived at 4 p.m. I found that I had been 'scratched'. I should have been on court two hours earlier! I was not now to play Johannson of Sweden on No 4 court, but Washer of Belgium on an outside court. I tried to take heart. Above the Centre Court were two lines from Kipling, painted in gold letters,

'If you can meet with Triumph or Disaster
And treat these two impostors just the same!'

All the same it was a hard mistake to swallow.

Following my setback at Wimbledon, I retired north to play suburban tennis at the Northern Club and the new hard courts of the Jewish Country Club. Despite a poor season, the glamour of having just competed at Wimbledon and the Davis Cup gave me entrance to both clubs. Moreover, there were advantages to being Asian. Nobody could tell to which class you belonged. My job left me plenty of time to enjoy a good social life and my tenure was likely to be long. I wallowed in the cosiness of English suburbia, whether in congenial female company or simply the safety of the tennis clubs. Life was made up of morning coffee at the Kardomah, followed by lunch at Kendal Milne or at Finnigan's, where I'd wave at my tennis friend Brian Finnigan at lunch at the proprietor's table across the dining-room. My Jewish friends would take me to Blacks where the Chicken Soup with Noodles and Meat Balls was reminiscent of Wun Tun Noodle Soup. And towards the end of the day I would board a bus to trundle home to Didsbury where there was always tea and digestive biscuits before my blazing gas fire. What more could I ask for?

During this whole time only the occasional wave carrying the debris of the outside world would wash up on my doorstep. In those easiest years of my life each of those waves would seem like an intrusion. Luckily I was out when one of them came. Jiang Tingwen, Chiang Kaishek's commander-in-chief of the Eastern Front, was touring friendly allied countries, just as if he had won the war. He borrowed General Montgomery's limousine to tour the north. When he arrived in Manchester my English secretary told him that I was away playing tennis. He considered this a dereliction of duty, and was displeased enough to complain to the Ministry of Foreign Affairs in Nanjing saying I was not to be found anywhere. Fortunately nobody wanted my job and the matter was overlooked.

A couple of years later, when the confrontation between the CCP and the Nationalist Army was reaching a showdown, a notice was sent to all embassies, legations and consulates abroad, instructing them not to extend or issue passports to a list of people suspected of being 'left-wingers'. My good friend Zhu Xuefang, past Secretary of the Chinese Postal Union and our adviser in Liverpool, was on the list. Naturally, I reflected, he had known too much about workers' rights to be a true Nationalist. And within a very short time, there he was, in my office, asking to have his passport extended. Teddy Teh brought him along. Teddy (later Acting Solicitor-General for Singapore and business tycoon), an out and out capitalist, and Zhu were unlikely bedfellows. Far from the centre of conflict, friendship mattered more than political allegiance. I gazed at them, visualizing the firing squad I would face on my return to China. But Manchester was not China and there were plenty of places to hide in the Peak District if the going got rough. I whipped out my seals, signed the passport and did the bravest thing I had done during that whole wartime period. Zhu was able to travel to Prague and then to Moscow from where he eventually worked his way back to China via Manchuria. In due course he marched into Peking with the Liberation Army in 1949 and was immediately appointed Postmaster-General of China, the first of many illustrious posts.

Seldom in my life had I had so much time to spare. I couldn't help feeling it was just a little wasteful. In my grandfather's time students were said to commit the Webster dictionary to memory in their idle moments. For fear of being totally lulled into a suburban stupor I hit on the idea of translating the Works of Mencius. Of all the Confucian classics I loved the Mencius. He believed in 'People's Power' too, and in the days before I went to school I'd practically committed the whole text to memory. With my familiarity I was able to chant and translate simultaneously. It was a great advantage over western scholars who probably had to struggle through the text with a dictionary. I was also disdainful of the existing translation, for I felt that it lacked the spirit of the original. When the translation was complete I had it typed and sent to John Murray, the publisher. He kept it for quite a while, returning it to me with the explanation that he had only just published an abridged edition and was not ready for another. I lost all my enthusiasm there and then and consigned it to the bottom of a disused suitcase where it remains.

Over hot tea, the gas fire and digestive biscuits another project soon floated into view. I could assemble the scribbled notes that I'd taken during the five years of the war and put together a history of the Chinese seamen in Liverpool during the war years. That would at least document a little bit of history which might be of interest to posterity. I came across a printer, a partner in the *Padiham Advertiser*. He had enough paper in stock. I also met the distribution manager of W. H. Smith Ltd, north west. The cost of printing up 2,000 copies was quoted at no more than £200. I became my own publisher. The distribution was not a success. *The Forgotten Wave* was printed on very rough paper and had no coloured illustrations. The majority of the stories were fragmentary except for the 'Poon Lim Epic' which had already been published in the Penguin *New Writing*. Not long after I received a letter from the Imperial War Museum asking for a copy for their archives. At least someone was interested! However I was not disappointed at my lack of commercial success. In a ramshackle way I had achieved two objectives: I had played tennis at an international level and I had published my own book. There remained just one thing to do.

CHAPTER TEN
Anne Brown

My delight and thy delight
Walking like two angels white,
In the gardens of the night:
My desire and thy desire,
Twining to a tongue of fire,
Leaping live and laughing higher;
Thro' the everlasting strife
In the mystery of life.

My Delight and Thy Delight, Robert Bridges. 1844–1930

MY THIRD OBJECTIVE came bounding into view when I ran into Anne Brown. For me, Students' Movement House was a natural habitat. For Anne, it was work. She, the nineteen-year-old refectory manageress, had just graduated from domestic science college. I was struck by her clean features and her broad, cloudless brow. There was something very fresh about her, a briskness of movement and purpose that was instantly appealing. Unlike other women I had found attractive, she wasn't athletic. But she had a shapely body which, despite its speed, concealed a ponderous strength. Her legs and arms were impressive, made for hard work. She described herself as a Grecian vase, with 'sturdy underpinnings'. Had it been encouraged in Bedford boarding schools, I reflected, she might even have been a discus thrower.

But I was only one of a dozen boys milling around, drawn to

her infectious laughter and indiscriminate friendliness. Being four-teen years her senior my chances seemed remote, unless she could be interested by my experience and intellectual pretence. But Anne was not an intellectual, nor did she aspire to be one. I noticed that she often engaged in heated exchanges and always seemed very assured of her position. Here was a woman of certain reality. One who left little room for confusion and who was unlikely to be led into futile exploratory discussion. She could be a tower of strength. Soon after she had caught my eye, and then my full attention, Anne Brown disappeared.

Anne's departure left a vacuum in my life, but there were many matters that required my urgent attention. To return south had not been a big wrench because I had not formed any strong ties in the north. Neither was I stuck for somewhere to live, for throughout my sojourn in Manchester I had maintained a room in Belsize Park. The room had a bright and pleasant aspect and from the window I could watch the rush-hour crowds pouring in and out of the tube station. There was plenty of congenial company, as several Chinese friends lived in the same house and Monty, the landlady, treated us like relatives.

But soon the £450 that the Chinese Foreign Office had given me for my passage home had dwindled to £50 and I was forced to look for employment. Now I was entirely free to do as I pleased, the avenues open to me seemed quite limited. All I had was the spirit of optimism coursing through my veins. With the Globe tennis club behind the station I was naturally tempted to use the racquet as a means of making a living. At £1 an hour, there was no real money in it, but with £10 a week I could scrape by. However, my membership of Queen's Club left me with the impression that there was a clear distinction between being a professional and being a gentleman. It was slightly distasteful to make money from the game, like a groundsman. With Mencius and my father to support the prejudice that a gentleman should not drift too far from scholarly or leisure pursuits, I could not be allowed to take that option seriously. I had to broaden my horizon and find a more refined occupation.

A decade after my employment at the BBC, the Chinese section was manned by well-qualified Chinese. They wouldn't be needing the likes of me. Although I might consider myself the founding father of their department, should I have walked in they wouldn't have known me from Adam. I had toyed with the idea of becoming a journalist, but the only subject I could have written on was China and news since the revolution was becoming scarcer as the years went by. Besides, every established paper also had its 'old China hand'.

From time to time I wrote for Kingsley Martin's *New Statesman and Nation*. I went to see Kingsley in his spacious Buckingham Street flat, overlooking the Embankment Gardens. Kingsley, although warm and voluble, had no China desk on the *New Statesman*. But his wife, Dorothy Woodman, was producing and editing a quarterly magazine called *Asian Horizon* for which she required some help. It was not a properly funded journal and there was to be no pay. I was glad to accept a job that would mean work experience and might prove to be a lot of fun. For a while I was in and out of the flat, several days a week. I brushed shoulders with many Labour leaders of the day and of the future.

Of the British socialist interpretations of Mao's revolution that I read and overheard, many seemed to be overworked and highly theoretical. The revolution that they visualized was far from the one that I had seen brewing in the 1920s and 1930s. There simply wasn't a substantial proletariat class in China, so the idea that China could participate in an international revolution was a myth. Of course there were Russian advisers around, but I guess they were as frustrated and confused as everyone else! Mao's revolution was a home-grown affair and could be as much attributed to Mencius' ideas of the 'Mandate of Heaven' and the people's right to revolt against tyrants, as to Marx. Mao's great strength had been to win over the peasant farmers. There was no other way to win China. With simple notions of land reform and through humanitarian treatment at the hands of his armies, he had won the propaganda war. And he had had a large measure of luck when the Japanese surrendered, leaving him to pick up their arms in Manchuria. The increased artillery enabled him to fill the power vacuum in the north with hardly a fight. When Chiang Kaishek's élite forces re-grouped further south along the Longhai railway, Mao's massed armies were riding the crest of a wave and the game was largely up for the American-backed regime.

Those were the days before the Great Leap Forward, when Mao had yet to try to prove himself as a statesman, as well as a revolutionary. The British Left were enthused by Victor Gollancz publications, and all revolutions were good revolutions. What we heard of Maoism was about armies of brave, barefoot doctors, people's communes, and large scale attempts to solve China's substantial social problems. The fragmentary news left great gaps which could be filled with positive images of a new egalitarian society. Even news from home could be interpreted well. Though Lo Lodge had been confiscated by the Red Army and was now a dormitory for the Eastern Command Army, my parents had been given a smaller wooden house, further down the hill.

The house was basic but elegant and quite big enough for them. It also had a fair-sized courtyard. Michael and Yongyong, ever faithful, were looking after them. Mother wrote regularly, and her letters did not appear to be censored. She was a practical woman who would be able to make do whatever. The family had not been categorically classified as one of the hated landlord class and were not the brunt of anyone's resentment, so seemed to fit quietly into the new society. Old friends were re-installing themselves in the provincial bureaucracy and I felt confident that my parents were out of harm's way. Father had been demoted to the position of a road sweeper and was reported to be enjoying his new job! I could imagine him on Cangqian hill sweeping the ginkgo leaves into piles, just as if it were an extension of his own beloved front garden. The true pursuit of a gentleman.

Whilst working with Dorothy on *Asian Horizon* might have proved advantageous in the long run, it did not provide enough to keep body and soul together. I visited all my friends looking for inspiration. Brigid and Peter Thompson provided tea and sympathy. Peter had been under George Ye at the Chinese Ministry of Information but, after Liberation, became a BBC film producer. Brigid was at the British Council liaising with Chinese students. For a year I became a member of her flock.

At tea one afternoon I was shown numerous cultural items left over from the old Ministry. They were being used as Christmas and New Year presents – aids for disseminating Chinese culture. Two items were quite striking: the Chinese brushes and the black and white prints of prancing horses. I was certain that there would be a market for them. Above all the British public were animal lovers and I felt that they would also appreciate the strength and simplicity of the brush-work. The brushes themselves were handmade and mouth moulded – infinitely superior to the mass-produced brushes used by the average artist. There and then I decided to go into business.

The practicalities of business had to be confronted. My ex-Consul colleagues lent me £100 and I set about looking for some inexpensive offices. Mencius would have been as disapproving of my entering business as he was of my earning money from tennis. I had to put a distance between myself and the whole operation. Five rooms in a self-contained flat on the fifth floor of a building in Nassau Street provided the right venue. An absentee accountant had inherited the offices from some bankrupt advertising business. I took a room with a view over Mortimer Street and for a minimal fee also hired the services of the accountant's red-headed secretary, Megan Roberts. Across the main drag was Students' Movement House where I could lunch cheaply and meet young people from all over the world. It was an ideal vantage point from which I could launch my own Great Leap Forward.

Within a few months Anne Brown was back again, still smiling, but noticeably subdued. She was unwilling to divulge where she had been and went to her job with added dedication and efficiency. I reflected that women with a past were certainly more interesting. The mystery simply enhanced the appeal. Just around that time a programme of international cookery was being organized at the club. Students from all over the world were invited to stage a dinner to illustrate their national cuisine. There was a Malaysian night, an Indian and Nigerian night. Why shouldn't I stage an evening of Chinese food and cooking? All I needed was an extra pair of hands. I found a very hard-working pair of hands with Anne, and I simply needed to supply the crucial stir-frying, flavouring and heat control. Anne did 70 per cent of the work and I gladly played her consultant. We were a great success and the event naturally brought us closer. After that we took to meeting up several times a week and I spent even more time lounging around the club. Business stress on the west side of Tottenham Court Road was alleviated by tender thoughts of Anne. Even though we were not yet properly engaged I would regularly send azaleas across the divide.

Despite Anne's forward nature, it was quite a time before our relationship advanced as far as holding hands. I was full of respect for her and didn't want to crush our relationship in the bud by making a hasty advance. We had been to the Battersea Park festival and had trailed homeward along the Embankment for what seemed to be several miles. Walking hand-in-hand suddenly became natural. Confucius must have been intoxicated by the moonlight, or perhaps his whisperings of caution were drowned by the steadily rolling waves of Old Father Thames. The next day I wrote her a poem and posted more flowers.

For Anne, 'A Song of the City'

In the hot hubbub of this noisy city
Where dusty men clash for dustier motives,
and women are worn thin with nervous strife,
You suddenly spoke in the voice of an angel,
Turning, I recognize your face amongst many
that throng my day!

Remember our walk along the cool bank of that river . . .
It was midnight when you said, 'I cried to ease my pain',
and, 'what have I to lose?'
You said, 'those who smile often conceal deep sadness'.
And suddenly the moments congeal and the days
surge ahead.

Tonight over the steamy dance-floor you flit
like a tired flower, still light footed, beautiful,
vulnerable, yet brave, too charmed for innocence!
Suddenly – with definite clarity and how deep a pathos –
your soft lips are all that I shall ever know!

Alas, how poor the gifts of one in love,
For once to be a god becomes urgent, that I might bear
you gifts to stay you on your way.
But all I have are flesh, strength and
sweet, passionate words which men have always whispered.

Music plays, the dance goes on,
and you must finish your waltz; my dream of revelling
in a sunny haven has to fade,
for the cacophony will not yet end.
Elsewhere I may have to lavish life's treasures and just seize what
 bounty comes my way . . .
The quick step beckons you on to the jazzy floor,
to sing, weep, fight, dream, starve and feast in this bitter-sweet,
 life strewn city!

K. Lo, 1952

Time was ripe for pushing forward frontiers. I was beginning to feel
a success. First sales are also memorable. In my case it was the sale of
a picture print. Pictures had an immediate visual impact which didn't
require introduction. Of several horse prints by Xu Bihong, including
the 'Filly' and the 'Stallion', the 'Colt' was the earliest and the best.
I left the first Colts 'sale or return' with an antiquarian bookseller in
Great Russell Street. He placed them in the window and within ten
minutes he had sold two.

This was the first of some 200 accounts in London alone. I
opened accounts with practically all the London department stores:
from Gamages in the east, to Bentalls in the west, through
Selfridges, John Lewis, Bourne and Hollingsworth, D. H. Evans and
Fortnum and Mason in the centre; all were on my circuit. The stores

considered my prints 'fun purchases' and not one of them became a substantial account. Eventually I discovered that the biggest buyer of prints had its offices a stone's throw away, just behind the Dominion Cinema. It was the picture-buying offices of Boots Ltd, who had 260 galleries. After the first breakthrough with Boots Ltd, I found a good agent in Australia who began to buy in bulk. I was making frequent trips to Norwich where the pictures were being printed by Jarrold & Sons. Only six good pictures – two horses, two dogs and two cats – were rolling off their presses, but Mr Jarrold and his sons deemed it sufficient to honour me with a slap-up meal every time I visited. The popularity of my prints seemed to be attracting universal interest. Their cheapness meant that they were destined to decorate the walls of a large number of the bedsitters in the country.

Next came the Chinese brushes. I took my selection to Winsor and Newton, which was within walking distance from my office. They displayed mild interest and purchased a small number saying that they already had a stock. On my way back I passed another artists' supplier called Rowneys who were far more interested. My sales gave me courage although, in the end, business with these two companies never achieved any great volume. By distributing Chinese brushes in any quantity they would merely have jeopardized the sales of their own brands.

Soon I found myself posting parcels to well-known artists. Art teachers and students were enthusiastic about the brushes, but business at the colleges didn't achieve any volume either. Ironically my biggest buyer was Max Factor (Hollywood) Ltd who wanted only tiny wolf-hair brushes for ladies' lashes!

With our increased turnover, there were many more telephone calls and letters to be written and Megan Roberts became more my secretary than the landlord's. Unfortunately our turn in fortune was not sufficient to keep Megan in the style to which she aspired. I often had to accompany her to a pawn shop in an alley off Oxford Street.

I was really getting to know Britain. I had never driven, so every account had been solicited on foot. If the British were 'a nation of shopkeepers', then to get to the bottom of the national psychology you had to understand the retail trade! As a travelling salesman, trotting on foot from one account to another, I not only had the opportunity to explore uncharted sales pitches, but I could also feel that I was adding another facet to my family's exploration of British culture that had begun in the nineteenth century with my grandfather!

To reach a wider public we began to produce greetings and

Christmas cards. In the run up to Christmas, Christina Foyle invited me to put up a stand in the entrance of Foyles. We were such an instant success we had to replenish the stock twice a day!

Emboldened by the aroma of commercial success, my trips to Students' Movement House became more frequent. All along Anne was smiling and easy-going, a great encouragement to me. For fear I might lose sight of her in the young international crowd, I wondered if I should not 'pop the question' sooner rather than later. One evening on the way to a Cypriot restaurant with a gang of friends, I did just that in the middle of Tottenham Court Road. I suppose she said yes, but I was lost in waves of traffic and noise that surged around us.

Then one thing piled in after another. We bought a £70 engagement ring on hire purchase in the Burlington Arcade. Then I was given the once over by Aunt Anne at tea in the Bonnington Hotel. Then Aunt Anne brought Aunt Connie for a second opinion. I had to tangle with a gaggle of silver-haired, elderly aunts, all of whom were practically indistinguishable from one another at first, wore brown lace-up shoes and had an aroma of Earl Grey tea. Aunt Connie, said to have been a very handsome young woman, turned out to be the *grande dame* of the family. I guessed she had the most money and had heard that she had married into the Cadbury family. Aunt Anne was more accessible. She wore clouds of blue chiffon as well as brown lace-ups. Being fortified by country walks and having had her horizons broadened at spiritualist meetings, accepting a Chinese was no problem to her. But a report had to be sent to mother.

Mother cried. She lived in a little village called Shefford in Bedfordshire, where marrying a foreigner would be taken very seriously. Despite my good pedigree and qualifications, acceptance could not be automatic. She knew that when Anne had made up her mind there was little that would sway her resolve, but that didn't make it any easier. We had to go and win her over. I prayed that my intrusion would not be resented by the Brown family in its quiet corner of rural England, where life had been chugging along with the same peaceful monotony for generations.

Mother was boiling chicken for supper, stooped over the kind of portable kerosene stove used for economy during the war. The whole room smelt of plain boiled fowl. Anne introduced us and then fled outside where she spent the rest of the time digging furiously in the massive back garden. Throughout my visit conversation was cordial enough, although not conducted with the same ease as over tea with Aunt Anne. By the end of the weekend I felt that she had resigned her daughter to her fate, although I could never tell what she was really thinking. Probably the occasion was held up by a very stiff upper lip.

Anne had been born on a farm called Rosehill in Shillington, an attractive village built around a hill north of Shefford. She spoke nostalgically of her early years when the farm was still ploughed by a team of shire horses, of catching moles to make moleskin gloves or trailing around after her strong, silent father. But her father had died when she was five, leaving them to the mercy of his brother's family. Anne was sent away to boarding school where she was very unhappy and, eventually, she and her mother were both driven out of the farm and cut out of the Brown brothers' inheritance.

Perhaps her mother had been the problem. Apparently, coming from a large, well-established bureaucratic family, she had married late and someone who was considered to be below her 'station'. She gave birth to Anne, her only child, at forty-five. Having been well-educated and having enjoyed a full and sociable life before her marriage, life at Rosehill might well have proved too basic. In her youth she had accomplished a great deal. She had been a governess, run a pack of Brownies and ridden the first penny-farthing in Bedfordshire. She was also not as English as might be assumed. In the family photo album Anne showed me the Anderson strain, the Da Costas, a family of Sephardic Jews from Portugal, and the Tanquery-Guillaumes, Huguenot silversmiths from Alsace who had come to England during the seventeenth century to avoid persecution by French Catholics. Despite the rich and varied influence, Anne's mother remained a devout Christian and this, not ancestry, might have been the cause of her concern about me.

With such diverse religious and philosophical heritage, discussing the virtues of different kinds of wedding ceremony was bound to be controversial. I was concerned that Mao's administration would not accept a Christian affair – we would have to have a secular wedding.

Anne's whole family naturally favoured a church wedding. In the end we decided to have both. If we had to have a church wedding I knew exactly where it was going to be held. It had to be St Martin-in-the-Fields. Memorial services for both my Davis Cup partners, W. C. Choy and Kho Sinkie, had been held there. Choy had died of leukaemia and Kho of pneumonia. Even Edward Li, our team manager, had died in a plane crash. As the last remaining member of the Davis Cup team, I felt that I had to carry on the spirit of our endeavour. I had promised the Vicar that the next time the Chinese Community turned up it would be a happy occasion. I didn't expect it to be my own wedding!

It was a beautiful summer's day when we ascended the steps to the church. Anne looked perfect in her wedding trousseau. I wore a morning coat from Moss Bross. And despite their reservations, most of Anne's relatives had turned up to give us their support. With a large contingent of my friends we had a substantial number of guests. Crowds of onlookers had gathered in Trafalgar Square. Even though they had probably turned out for some royal occasion, it was easy to imagine that they were clamouring to see us. St Martin's vergers had to close its heavy iron gates to prevent the mob from flooding our wedding party. It felt like a real 'society wedding'!

Anne's mother paid for the reception, which we had at a restaurant called the 'Asiatic'. I had originally negotiated for the premises on their behalf with a Mr Chaudhuri, another journalist from Dorothy Woodman's *Asian Horizon* set. So the Asiatic put on a grand feast at half the listed price. But all along I couldn't help wondering what Anne's mother thought of it. I never asked her and she didn't venture an opinion.

After a night in Brighton we spent our honeymoon in Paris. I couldn't fund the honeymoon entirely by myself and had written around the Chinese community asking for handouts. I had even tried out the Tan family in Singapore. In the end I scraped together enough money to go in style. I felt that we were a good-looking couple, well-dressed and cosmopolitan, and I conducted the tour with pride. We visited all the places I had known as a student. We went to the Sacré Coeur, Moulin Rouge, Eiffel Tower, Versailles.

Once back in London I was all ready to settle into a comfortable, married routine, with Anne around to help on the domestic front. But my first memory of married life was sitting at the window of my bedsitter, watching her marching off to work. She had found receptionist work looking after luncheon trade at Egon Ronay's 'Marquee' restaurant. I couldn't help feeling that it was not quite right that Anne went out to work so soon after our wedding. I had still to appreciate that Anne's natural philosophy was to find purpose and consolation in work, and work for its own sake. She immersed herself in ceaseless activity.

It had been devastating having her move in. She had flown around my room, packing, unpacking, cleaning my cupboards and drawers, sorting out my preciously ordered messes to make room for her own debris. I stood and watched, paralysed by the cyclone that was threatening my inner sanctum. I had the most unsettling feeling of foreboding and had to steady my nerve by making endless cups of tea.

It was largely through Anne's ethical influence that I was to turn my back on the old influence of Father and Mencius and to start to coach tennis in earnest. She made it clear that work had to be found, for Cathay Arts was not yet self-supporting. Some days I coached for ten hours on the trot and came home barely able to stand up. Egon Ronay's two daughters, Esther and Edina, were among my pupils. Anne's work at the Marquee had sparked off a long association with Egon. In the post-war years British catering needed creative venues like the Marquee to bring a renaissance to British food. I was invited for a bowl of bouillabaisse at the restaurant and, when Egon discovered that I was a natural food critic, I became his unofficial guide to good Chinese food for several decades. I was sent up and down the country to eat free of charge and write reports for the *Good Food Guide*. It was a pleasing job for me.

To keep Anne happy and to ensure my ascent to her heaven, I also took up an old profession. I could lecture on contemporary Chinese events to anyone, but it turned out that it was private girls' schools that wanted me! As a filler in the long haul during the last few weeks of term, I would be invited to such establishments as Roedean, Cheltenham Ladies, Dartmouth Naval, Epsom and Eastbourne colleges. I must have visited 200 girls' schools.

My usual lecture took the assembled girls through all the different stages of contemporary Chinese history, from the Boxer Rebellion through the 1911 Revolution, the great Northern Expedition, the Civil War, Japanese Invasion, Long March and Liberation. There was plenty to talk about and I would illustrate the march of events with personal episodes. For most it was probably 'in one ear and out the other'. But when the girls were writing historical projects, the debate could become quite lively and lead to fresh explorations. Of all my different employment lecturing was the easiest. I felt confident at speaking on China and things Chinese and there were so many avenues to explore. Sometimes a school lecture would start with current affairs, degenerate to a practical Chinese cook-in and end up as a coaching session on the tennis court!

While sitting in the bar at Queen's Club, I was confronted by one precocious sixteen-year-old called Buster Mottram. He invited me to have a drink with him. In a flash he began interrogating me about Yuan Shikai, Li Yüanhong, Hong Guozhang and Cao Kun. I was taken aback. Hardly one in a million Englishmen knew of these people; how could a teenager be so well-informed? It turned out that he too was doing an extended essay on the early Republican presidents. I put them into historical perspective for him and told him that Yuan

Shikai was my grandfather's blood brother, Cao's daughter married the elder brother of a friend and that Li Yafu, a contemporary of mine at Cambridge, wanted to join Queen's! Buster was suitably impressed.

On the odd occasion I addressed massive audiences. At Luton's Savoy cinema I gave a lecture with Robert Donat who was dressed as a knight in armour. He gave a rousing talk declaring, 'he who lives by the sword, dies by the sword'. I was a little more low-key. After the talks we had tea with his mother. Another time I was invited to talk to a literary circle at the Winter Garden at Eastbourne. The cosy literary gathering grew mysteriously to over 750!

All through those early years in London, when I was relying on my spirit of free enterprise, it wasn't as if a grand plan was shaping my life. I was drifting with the tide and when I accidentally washed up against a project that looked promising I could always find the energy to rise to the occasion. With Anne behind me, bursting with enthusiasm, I always had someone to give me a kick start. It was in that same spirit that I took my first excursion into food writing. It was an excursion that was meant to be a 'day trip' but turned out to be more of a 'Long March'.

Not far from my offices were the offices of the publishers called Arco. One of the proprietors was a young gentleman by the name of Bernard Hanison. He wasn't a great intellectual, rather a secondhand bookseller in the East End who would amuse himself by driving backwards down Fitzroy Street. He could talk non-stop and would always hail me in the street, 'Ken, why don't you write a Chinese cookbook for me. Can you do it?' I would reply 'Simple!', and with confidence, 'When I find a moment!' I had assumed he was joking but, one day, he pressed five crisp £10 notes into my hand. 'I want you to write that cookbook for me. This is the advance – sign on the dotted line and complete by Christmas.' That was springtime. By December I still hadn't begun and Mr Hanison was complaining to Anne that I had pocketed his money.

My bedsitter had become too cramped for married life, let alone literary enterprise. And I was finally driven out by the arrival of four young boys associated with my tennis partner, W. C. Choy's, family. They had been sent to school in Britain and I had accepted responsibility as their holiday guardian. All together we moved across the road to Professor William Empson's Studio House, where the rooms were large enough to contain us all. The shake-up gave me the incentive to get cracking on the book.

That first Christmas holiday was memorable. After a day in the office I would come back to cook for my four wards. The preoccupation with cookery got my adrenalin moving. I learned to be quick and inventive, and my charges were well-qualified to be discriminating judges of the result. To satisfy them I had to combine all my experience of years of watching Qingqing and Kuozui (Big Mouth) in the lower kitchen at Lo Lodge, as well as forty years of eating out in China and Britain. The dishes had to be both quick and easy. In that first cookbook I simply tried to introduce two concepts: stir-frying for minutes over a high heat and with little oil, and red-cooking in soya sauce and stock. Any dish that seemed to please the gang of four would gain instant access into my manuscript.

Between washing up and midnight, with speed and concentrated effort, I was able to work for one and a half hours. After an undisturbed sleep I could pack in another one and a half hours before rushing off to the office. After three weeks of dedicated application I began to see daylight. The last chapter was in sight. By Christmas morning I tied the completed manuscript with pink ribbon. Bernard Hanison was astonished. He had thought that I had barely begun!

Studio House was an extraordinary place to live. Not only was the Professor a recognized poet and a great literary critic, he was also a mathematician of some standing. William was one step removed from contemporary reality and seemed to stroll through life unhindered by its troublesome details. The secret to the success of our relationship was that I didn't bother to try and find out what he was thinking. Just contemplating the title of his book, *Seven Types of Ambiguity*, was enough to set my mind adrift. There were plenty of people keen to discuss the meaning of life and literature with him, without my adding my amateur thoughts. In fact literary luminaries were a part of the furniture, all milling around, consuming vast amounts of alcohol and stubbing out their cigarettes on the Henry Moore sculptures, at the endless all-night parties.

But perhaps the main attraction at Studio House was Mrs Hetta Empson. She was a tall South African who was at least as handsome as Ingrid Bergman. Her main room, the Studio itself, was two storeys high and difficult to heat. Hetta built a huge brick bed, big enough for ten people to stretch out on. In North China such a construction was called the 'kang', a bed at night that doubled as a living platform to eat and sleep on during the day. Heat was generated into the brick-bed cavity by burning straw in an outside oven connected to the bed by a primitive flue. Unfortunately this was not to be in Studio House. Such practices were forbidden under Hampstead by-laws.

Having been thwarted by the Camden fire officer, Hetta, not one to be daunted, erected a tent in the centre of the studio. By placing a smokeless fuel stove opposite the tent entrance, the radiating heat warmed the tent in no time, without having to heat up the cavernous room. Hetta was trying to recreate Inner Mongolia in NW3. William and Hetta had lived in China for several years, when William had been Professor of English at Peking University. Hetta had given birth to their two sons, Mogador and Jacob, there.

Studio House was all a little avant-garde for Anne. People didn't appear to do any real work there! She was alarmed by the excess and noted, with sympathy, that while the adults slept off their hangovers, Mogador and Jacob could often be found on tiptoe in the kitchen, trying to reach up to the cooker to make themselves breakfast before setting off for school.

Our own twin boys, Robert and Michael, were born while at Studio House. Anne wanted six children and I, despite protestations from my own mother in Foochow, was only too happy to try to indulge her. I had no idea what it meant to have children without the back-up of a team of servants and cooks. But faced with two hungry babies in the middle of the night, I soon learned. And to create even more havoc – Anne wanted a castle to call her own.

Early in the summer of 1955 we set out house-hunting. Behind high walls, the gardens were ablaze with flowers as we pushed our double-pram through the lanes of Hampstead, dreaming of where we might settle. The most beautiful house was called 'Blue Tile'. It stood on the side of the hill overlooking North London and a rustic unpaved roadway led to the door. It had five en-suite bedrooms and a huge Spanish fireplace in the lounge. Even though the property was once owned by Gracie Fields it was going for no more than £10,500. Our hearts were set on it and I went about the business of arranging a mortgage. With a deposit lent to us by Anne's mother we could just about afford it. A couple of days later we returned to find to our disappointment that someone had put down cash. We had been gazumped!

Our next find was a three-storey, four-bedroom house in Perceval Avenue, a short residential street not far from my old bedsitter in Belsize Park. It didn't inspire so grand a vision as did Blue Tile, but it was a family house with some merit for us. It had a front garden, a garage and drive-in at the back. At £7,500 it was a bargain and we had money left over for furnishing.

Once there Vivienne and Jennifer were born in quick succession. All our children were a mixture of Anne and me, although Jennifer was the only one to be easily identified as Chinese. The other three were mongrels that would have been as inconspicuous in Israel as in Italy. With two au pairs, Katrin, the wild one from East Germany and loud and boisterous Gerd from Norway, we had our family of six and it was time to stop! When I wasn't pushing a pramful of laughing monkeys past the string of ponds on Hampstead Heath or down Primrose Hill to London Zoo, I was cooking for the au pairs who had insatiable appetites. Katrin could wrap herself around a leg of pork skin and fat in a few mouthfuls.

Mother, now graduated to Granny, was living on the third floor. She was happy with me as a son-in-law now, having decided that I couldn't really be Chinese. 'Kenneth's really English you know!', she would be overheard to say. Vivienne was always upstairs feeding the pigeons or hobnobbing with Granny's cronies who were all pushing eighty. I often saw Vivienne guiding them gently on their 'constitutionals' around the block.

The boys were too rough for elderly ladies. What they loved was Hampstead Heath fairs, where the merry-go-rounds, dodgems, giant swings and slides would whip up their excitement and ignite their imaginations. Then they would go home and tell Jennifer about huge spiders and multi-coloured snakes that they had seen in the grass. Jennifer was still the baby and, although the most adorable looking, was probably quite left out. Through deprivation she made her mark by developing a stubborn streak that manifested in only eating fried egg and bananas.

In spite of being enmeshed in her domestic responsibilities Anne was soon at it again. With a Belgian designer as her sidekick and a German seamstress, she founded a couturier house called 'Cathay Couture' in the back garden shed. There they produced a range of high-collared, split-legged traditional cheong sams in gorgeous silks and satins. At the height of their success they made the costumes for *The Inn of the Sixth Happiness*.

One summer's afternoon in the late 1950s Charles came strolling down the garden path. He had been naturalized as an American, and for the first time could leave without fear of not being able to return. We looked at each other with slight disbelief and some amusement. How could twenty years have gone by since he was chasing my train along Peking railway platform? Sitting together in the living-room at Perceval Avenue, that gap seemed to dissolve and neither of us was inclined to recreate it by filling in the details. So we sat in silence. Charles's arrival provided me with a link to a time that, since my arrival in Britain, I had confined to pre-history. For a while it was all that we could do to re-absorb the world that we had opened up for each other. From time to time, as an elder brother should, he recited a line from a Tang poem or the Spring and Autumn annals and tested me to match it with the next. It was like going home to the verandah at Lo Lodge and the heat of a Foochow summer.

Of course everything had changed. And Anne was puzzled by our behaviour. Charles was also not sure what to make of her or my swelling family. He was living a bachelor's life in New York where he had found a job teaching Chinese language, modern and classical, to undergraduates at Columbia University. His taste in women and lifestyle was more academic and less robust than mine. The more discordant he found my new family, the more he retreated into the past. In fact the first thing he wanted to do was to ride on the 13, 113 and 2 buses from Willesden Lane to Maida Vale, to revisit Fitzjohn's Avenue, Eaton Square and Gypsy Hill. When we found our old houses he would march up to the front door and announce that we had lived there forty years before and 'could we have a look around'. We had to eat in the restaurant that mother used to take us to in Piccadilly Circus and it was all I could do to stop him going to a matinée at the State Cinema on Kilburn High Road.

I had less of a taste for digging up the ghosts of the time gone by. Nor was I much interested in family archeology. But I was struck by one piece of family history that Charles brought to my attention. Anne was not the first A. Brown to be associated with the Lo family. In fact H. P. Lo, a cousin who had grown up around us in Foochow, had a mother called Alice Brown. His father had met her in London at the end of the last century. They had married, had H.P. and returned to China together. Unfortunately H.P.'s father had, in an arranged marriage, been betrothed as a child to an older woman. His first wife proved to be the classical first wife tyrant and being childless, she claimed H.P. for her own and drove Alice away. Tradition and the family was on the first wife's side. Alice had no choice but to abandon her son. She fled, never to be heard of again.

At first Charles, the only representative of my family, didn't seem too keen on my A. Brown. He left, suggesting that I should join him in New York. It wasn't clear whether he was inviting me over for a trip or providing me with an escape route from my crazy family. Of course it was out of the question and with his subsequent annual summer visits, bit by bit, he came to be fond of us all. He, too, became an important part of my own nuclear family.

CHAPTER ELEVEN
Drifting with the Tide

In Moving, like Water
In Stillness, like a mirror,
Respond like an Echo.

> Chapter 33, *Zhuang zi. Circa* 4th century BC

THE RAPIDITY WITH which I had managed to market the Chinese prints gave me the impression that it was easy to join the ranks of successful capitalists: all that it seemed to need was a range of commodities that could readily be promoted. Sooner or later you were bound to make a breakthrough.

With new-found confidence Anne and I embarked upon a series of carefree holidays. We had taken our first family holiday when the twins were just babies, renting a large white-fronted Regency house in Lewes Crescent, Brighton, next door to Moira Shearer. It belonged to a Norwegian shipping magnate but, through a mutual friend, we rented it for a token sum for the whole summer. The boys spent three months rolling on a blanket on the lawn in the square. The air was clean and life seemed restful after the hustle and bustle of London. Although I commuted by Pullman to London every day, to return to such luxury allowed me to feel that I was enjoying a well-earned holiday.

At the peak of Cathay Arts' commercial success we were encouraged to go further afield, and booked a holiday at Blanes, a small fishing village north of Barcelona on the Costa Brava. The poverty that still existed in Spain made the landscape and lifestyle quite similar to that which I had known in South China. At the height of summer the sun was so fierce that it drove us indoors to siesta after midday. And at night I had to draw on my childhood experience to build the wood and charcoal fires we needed to cook on. And then there was no food. The butchers had no more than a couple of emaciated chickens hung up for sale. Customers would come into the shop to buy a pair of chicken feet for soup. But most memorable was diving through the gigantic waves of San Francisco Bay to get out into the open sea and the great splashes of colour from the bougainvillaea against the dazzling expanse of white walls as we trekked around the hillocks of the town.

We even took a luxury holiday. It began with a flight to Nice. I was amazed by the sudden change of climate. The palm trees were so tall that they mounted to our second floor hotel windows and the sea water was warm enough to enjoy swimming in. It must have been pure bravado that had seduced me into booking an expensive hotel next to the Negresso. It wasn't really a grand hotel, but it was big enough for us to walk tall when, after breakfast, we strolled out along the length of the Boulevard des Anglais. From Nice we took a train to Diana Marina, following the Côte d'Azur, passing the high cliffs that tower above Monte Carlo and the ripening oranges that peep through their dark green leaves and line the Italian boulevards.

Those were dizzy, hazy days when our marriage and children were young and full of promise – Belsize Park provided a cosmopolitan lifestyle and we felt part of its varied and interesting world. Many and different were the people that wandered through our lives. Apart from the au pairs we also took lodgers – most notable were the identical twins Dick and John Contigulia, two concert pianists who, coincidentally, shared the same birthdate as Robert and Michael. They were studying with Dame Myra Hess and would play opposite each other on two enormous grand pianos. When they were around Perceval Avenue was full of music.

It was not very much later that Michael, the younger of my twins, had his first bump. He walked into a lamp post and a lump immediately swelled up on his brow. He swallowed hard, refusing to admit the pain. It was his first day at kindergarten and, being a brave boy, he knew it wouldn't do to arrive crying. Robert, the older by twenty-six minutes, had an even greater aptitude for swallowing back emotion and did not readily admit defeat.

But the boys had a natural communication between themselves which made them disinclined to share their feelings with anyone else. With all the bumps life had in store for them it was lucky that they were born warriors. The only time that Robert really let himself go was when I took him on a ride on the Hampstead Heath Fair. When the roundabout reached its fastest he shouted 'Scared! Scared! Scared!' and that was all!

Walking with the children, holding their hands, was one of the most intimate times of my life. I enjoyed that gentle feeling of giving guidance and protection while, at the same time, feeling appreciation and love pulse through their soft, warm hands. As I walked with them through the winding lanes of Hampstead I always chanted sentimental tunes like:

> Walking with you through the world today,
> Wind, and rain, and sunshine light our ways!

My years in the West were allowing a slow displacement of lines from the Chinese classics by the lyrics of popular song!

But our dream bubble was soon to burst. Christmas and greeting cards were the source of both our success and our failure. Success came in the sense that they allowed us to open innumerable accounts and expand our business. Had there been only myself, a junior and Megan Roberts, we would have been fine. But once we had a properly staffed office, a sales team on the road and huge print runs, decline began to set in. But the vision of El Dorado kept leading me on and it was several years before I would admit that business was grinding to a halt.

We had one big splash, which was at the International Art and Craft Exhibition at Olympia, before we finally sank. The new Chinese government had begun to exhibit abroad and, occupying a whole floor of Olympia, was ostentatiously rivalling the Russian stands. As the government exhibits were for display and generally not for sale, I saw the chance to take an adjacent stand where everything could be purchased! When the exhibition opened, the public flooded in. Drawing credibility from the Chinese government stand, we sold huge quantities of greeting cards, Chinese brushes and art prints among other miscellany.

But that killing was not enough to arrest the general decline. At the time the exhibition merely kindled our interest in the import and sale of other Chinese art and craft products. The Chinese organizers of the exhibition were only too pleased to leave us goods on a 'sale or return' basis. These we placed in two retail shops we had acquired, one in Heath Street, Hampstead, and the other adjacent to South Kensington Station. The loan of such exclusive stock only served to encourage us to keep on the leases which we could ill afford.

As I watched our revenue diminish I knew, with sinking heart, that we could not sustain our lifestyle. Perhaps there had been no basis upon which to begin living as we had been. In any case Anne was feeling that the country would be a better place to bring up the children, and she determined to give them the benefits that she, herself, had enjoyed as a child. So we sold our Hampstead haven and Anne, Granny and the family moved to 'Little Gables', in a Surrey village called Fetcham.

When Anne chose a property you could be assured that it would make a solid home. The house stood in half an acre of ground with a front garden and a drive big enough for several cars. A lawn stretching away at the back ended in a small orchard of apple trees. Viewed from the garden the house was a beauty. Not half a mile up the Ridgeway, the village gave out upon the North Downs overlooking the Mole Valley. From the top of the hill the valley swept away before you towards Boxhill, Dorking and on to the open stretches of Sussex and the South Coast. Altogether it seemed a healthy environment to bring the children to, not to speak of Shane the poodle, the cats, hamsters and family of guinea pigs.

Despite the country comforts they were lean years. Anne went to work, scraping a living in catering wherever she could. The children began their education at a private Junior school until we could no longer afford it. Anne, with some inheritance left by Aunt Connie, purchased a small cottage in Snowdonia, where the family spent all their holidays. Gone were holidays in Spain. I did not follow the family to the country straight away, preferring to remain in London to mind what was left of the shop and to concentrate on trying to rebuild our source of finance. With the demise of Cathay Arts, the departure of my family and faced with yet another spell of impoverishment, my spirits had taken a battering and it was a while before I recovered my natural sense of direction.

Apart from sending the odd cheque in response to my frequent SOSs, Charles made one significant contribution to my well being and sanity: he paid my annual membership to Hurlingham. It was there that, while the world outside might be collapsing around me, I could still feel that there was some dignity and grace left in life. One says of Oxford that it is 'That sweet city with her dreaming spires'. Well then, Hurlingham must be the club with 'the dreaming tree tops'. It is distinguished in having an enormous stretch of parkland along the Thames where many mature trees grow. For its ageing members, to sit by the grass courts after an afternoon's match and watch the winter's sun fade slowly over the tree tops is peace itself. For me the feeling was always reminiscent of the approach of evening on Yanjing campus, when the luminous northern skies seemed even more bright with the expectation of a good evening meal. The evening meal at Hurlingham was also good.

Even more memorable than the dreaming tree tops and the well-manicured lawns, the croquet championships or the pre-Wimbledon garden party, were the pots of hot tea expertly prepared and served by the elderly dressing-room attendants in the tennis pavilion. They could be a grumpy lot, but if you were courteous and left a good tip they would provide you with a service to make you feel the gentleman. Tea was not in the statutory provisions of the pavilion, but if you were on the right side of them they would even serve biscuits and cakes from Fortnum and Mason. If you were a favourite, the attendants might put your smalls and tennis gear through the laundry after every game. As I was courteous and generous with tips, Anne was spared my laundry. Nor did I ever have to use the crowded bath at home; there was less of a rush in the tennis pavilion.

Hurlingham provided me with the sense of ease and the tennis that I needed to maintain my sanity. I have always taken the easy option, followed the course of least resistance. When I failed to follow Charles into a technological subject at Qinghua, I settled for English, the subject where I already enjoyed a natural advantage. Like my father, I was motivated by pursuit of leisure. Even at Cambridge, when faced with having to sit a Classics paper, instead of choosing Greek or Middle English, I chose Chinese Classics where the papers set by the examiner were no more difficult for me than ABC is to the native undergraduate.

Of course at times, when inspired by a project, as in digging Madame Petoello's trench, I could put on a spurt of adrenalin and work hard, with pride and joy. But the real joy to me was always doing what came naturally. In the same spirit my first excursion into Chinese cookery writing was meant to be a 'day trip' from which I would return as if from a picnic. I never dreamt that the excursion would turn out to be my personal 'long march'. Hence my writing always made light of the complexities of translating the Chinese kitchen to a British setting. Western gourmets have always equated the exotic with the most authentic. Consequently I have had a difficult time convincing the serious aficionado that he didn't have to make a bee-line for those dubious establishments which serve up pig's stomach, congealed chicken blood, ox's penis, fish lips or fresh monkey brains, opened at the table, in order to taste authentic ethnic Chinese cuisine.

The best is usually produced from run-of-the-mill materials, cooked in the simplest manner.

The two Chinese vegetable dishes distilled in my memory are very ordinary dishes. The first is Braised Chinese Cabbage, simmered in the finest stock and the best soya sauce with a trace of dried shrimps and a little sugar. The second is Plain Stir Fried Spinach. The spinach is cooked with nothing more than half a dozen cloves of roughly chopped garlic, a teaspoon of fermented beancurd, two tablespoons of soya sauce and four of hot vegetable oil. The stir frying is conducted over a medium heat so that the vegetable neither dries nor burns but becomes tender and very juicy. The result is a dish of deep green, glistening leaves, chunky enough to be a main dish and flexible enough to complement any combination of dishes.

Spare Ribs, Sweet and Sour Prawns and Superior Fried Rice, the well-known Chinese standbys that have made an in-road into the domain of fish and chips, are not so bad if cooked from good raw materials, and with the addition of a special dish can be the basis for a delectable banquet. Communal eating is surely the one great difference with Chinese food. At an ordinary family meal each diner may select from half-a-dozen different dishes. How different from the confines of western appetizers, main meal and pudding. At a banquet the menu could easily run to a dozen dishes. With such a variety to be had, no wonder the Westerner is intrigued.

Stir frying – subjecting the raw materials to high heat for a very short while – demands that the ingredients should be of the highest quality. With vegetable dishes the process is akin to making a western salad, except that we use hot oil. And we would first impregnate the hot oil with additional flavour by flash frying ginger, shallots, garlic, chilli or whatever other taste is required. The vegetables are first of all tossed in the flavoured oil before anything else is added. It is this 'double-layer' of flavouring that creates tastes of such high quality.

Chinese chefs will talk more about 'controlling and harmonizing the heat' (he huo) than making sauces and in every restaurant's kitchen there is more than one fire chef. With approximately fifty established firing and heating techniques, each with its individual name, it could take a lifetime to learn how to cook. However, over the years, it has been possible for me to produce most dishes with just three – stir frying, long cooking and braising. To go further only complicates matters and is entirely superfluous to the ordinary western cook. So while many of my fellow authors tended towards making a serious study of all the subtleties of Chinese food, I was always more inclined to under-emphasize its peculiarities in favour of making it accessible to the British public at large. This approach, of course, suited my general light-hearted attitude towards writing on the subject. But the area of Chinese food, like China herself, is too big a territory to wander in and out at will, and once I was in, whether serious or not, it was not easy to extricate myself.

In the aftermath of the Second World War, Chinese food rapidly gained popularity in the West. Westerners had gone East in unprecedented numbers and brought back a taste for the Orient. The troops may only have had time to gulp back their food, but even that experience left them in no doubt that the Chinese chefs had more to offer than their counterparts back home. With large scale migrations of ethnic Chinese, prospecting for a better life overseas, following the Gold Rush, fleeing from Communism, the decades after the war saw hundreds of thousands moving westwards and bringing with them all their culinary expertise. Wherever they had passed you could always find a bottle of soya sauce or a root of ginger to track the migration. And, where the settlement had put down deeper roots, Chinese restaurants sprang up as tangible staging posts for the progress of that tide.

In earlier centuries, when the Han and Tang dynasties were expanding their empires westwards along the arid trail of the Silk Road, if an innkeeper could produce a large bowl of steaming noodles after a day's journey through biting wind and sand, he could bring untold joy. So it was and is when any Chinese, student, business man or refugee, travels anywhere. The eating houses provide a beacon to guide the weary and alienated traveller to safety. Just as I had found board and lodging at 'The Nanking' restaurant in Berlin after leaving the Olympic village, so, decades later, I could still find refuge and identity in a Chinese eating house.

And as the network spread, British and Americans were breaking through their prejudices about Chop Suey and Sweet and Sour Pork. Not far from Piccadilly Circus the Allied troops had poured out of the Rainbow Rooms to eat in the largest and most prosperous Chinese restaurant in town, the 'Hong Kong'. The proprietor, Mr Yang (actually Chang Moon Hsiung) and his English wife, Betsy, became very prosperous and Betsy soon opened the Hong Kong Emporium, a Chinese supermarket in Rupert Street. Betsy and Mr Yang were old friends and I often stopped by to join them in a late lunch.

I enjoyed their Steamed Fish made from a whole fish, perhaps sea bass, or simply a thick cut of a big fish or a fish head. It was part-buried under a pile of shredded root ginger and spring onion and steamed for twenty minutes. After steaming, the shredded ginger and spring onion were removed and replaced by a fresh layer of the same. At this point two tablespoons of soya sauce and several tablespoons of boiling oil were poured over the full length of the fish, passing through the shredded ginger and onion so as to drum the aromatic flavour into its tender flesh. The result was a fresh and pure tasting fish awash with a clear savoury stock, ideal to be eaten with plain boiled rice. For someone who hails from the fish-eating southern coastal region of China, their Steamed Fish was more than adequate to make a centrepiece for any banquet, regardless of whatever else might be served.

Another of my post-war favourites was 'Ley-Ons', situated in the northern section of Wardour Street. Mr Ley-On was more flamboyant than Mr Yang, very warm in his welcome, but less generous. As I always had to pay for my meal I was careful what I ordered. Hence I was more familiar with the basic dishes in his restaurant. I often ate Wo Mien, a noodle dish mixed with shredded meat, prawn and the 'Trinity' of Chinese cooking, ginger, garlic and spring onion, to make an irresistible savoury treat. The pleasure I derived from the simple elegance of run-of-the-mill Cantonese dishes must be the reason that Cantonese Onion and Ginger Lobster with handmade noodles remains one of my favourite dishes. It is by far the most succulent dish available in London and combines a vibrant colour with freshness of taste.

A third and most important beacon in Soho was the 'Fava', owned by Zhang Kaichang, a native of Foochow. Before the revolution he had become a teenage chauffeur for the Russian financial attaché in Peking. Following his boss back to Moscow, he married a white Russian woman and was eventually posted to London where he settled. For several decades, Zhang worked in Italian restaurants. The couple had a handsome daughter called Mary. Mary was the toast of the town. She was truly beautiful, and when her father opened the Fava in Frith Street, a whole generation of us would gather there to pay tribute to her and simultaneously eat Mr Zhang's spaghetti bolognese. Just as Mary's beauty blended the elegance of the Orient with the solidity and strength of the Russians, there was something indefinable about Mr Chang's spaghetti bolognese. I believe that he made a few minor additions – a dash of soya sauce and a sprinkling of ginger.

Messrs Yang of Hong Kong, Zhang of Fava and Ley-On of Ley-Ons were the three Chinese culinary 'musketeers' who laid claim to the heart of London. But within a decade or so the number of Chinese outlets in and around Soho had exploded from a handful to a few score and then a few hundred. And the quality of the Chinese establishments changed as well, from basic eating houses to elegant restaurants.

Following hard on the heels of the three musketeers came a new brand of proprietor and another three Chinese to develop the restaurant scene. These three, Mr Michael Chow of Knightsbridge, Mr Fu Tong of Kensington High Street and another Mr Yang of Richmond, all catered for a fashionable and wealthy clientele. They were responsible for changing the face of Chinese food in Britain, and paved the way to making it acceptable as a highly esteemed international cuisine.

Only one thing remained to be done. There was hardly a book which could introduce the essential meaning and preparation of Chinese food into the British home. Apart from my own first effort there was one published by Faber & Faber and written by a colleague of mine, Li Mengbing, who had worked as a secretary at the Chinese Embassy. It was a rudimentary book, designed to be effective during the years of wartime rationing, which recommended the use of Marmite as a substitute for soya sauce. As soon as the war was over it became hopelessly inadequate. Faber licensed the book to Penguin, but then took it back when the licence expired. So Penguin were on the look out for a Chinese author who could write a cookbook in English.

Thus, almost ten years later, my second 'excursion' into Chinese cookery writing was, for my part, almost as accidental as the first. I was invited out to eat at the 'Lido' in Gerrard Street by an old friend, Dr H. M. Lo, from Canberra University. He was engaged in writing a dissertation documenting the life and times of an eminent Australian journalist called Morrison, who had been *The Times* correspondent in Peking from the turn of the century to the mid-1920s. To this end H.M. was rooting through some 200 boxes of documents that Mr Morrison had left. It transpired that this Morrison was the father of Ian, a contemporary of mine at Cambridge. Ian had also become a Times correspondent in the Far East but had sadly been killed while covering the Korean war.

That dinner time I was introduced to Ian's daughter, who was keen to meet me on two counts. Firstly she was eager for contact with anyone who had known her father in his youth. I told her that while I was at college in Peking during the 1930s there was a girl called Han Suyin. Han Suyin had later written a novel which had been made into the film *Love is a Many Splendoured Thing*, starring William Holden and Jennifer Jones. Her hero, also a foreign correspondent, had been modelled on Ian Morrison.

Later our conversation settled to the subject of Chinese food and the second area of Miss Morrison's interest in me. It transpired that she was an assistant to the food editor of Penguin. The lease was about to run out on their existing Chinese food title and she wasted no time in commissioning me. I accepted with alacrity. Over the years I had arranged and attended innumerable banquets and dinners and consumed thousands of dishes. What remained in my memory were the occasions themselves, the people and places and not the dishes. My palate does not seem to be retentive. Once consumed, a dish is soon stored away in one of the backrooms of my culinary memory. To hold the memory I would need to wrap it most carefully in the most appropriate words to allow it to be easily retrieved. Otherwise those dishes that were indeed a delight could easily slip into semi oblivion. To maintain any clarity I needed to build a well-documented library of favourite dishes.

Before long I found myself in a small building off the Theobalds Road, more like a boarding house than the offices of a famous publishing company. I was to discuss my ideas about structuring the book with Jill Norman, the editor. The outcome was that I would write a Chinese cookbook, called *Chinese Food*, with a strong introduction followed by twenty recipes for the most popular Chinese dishes to have established themselves in the West. Then I should address regional fare by culling dishes from each of the culinary areas of China: Peking, Canton, Sichuan and Shanghai [Lower Yangzi]. I felt that six dishes for each of the four seasons of the four main regions would be suitably representative. Such a strong framework could provide me with the basis to bring out the local colour of the dishes and increase their authenticity. Although over 100 recipes seemed an enormous task, I remembered, once I had begun, how easily I had written my first book for Arco, and I took heart.

The result was a great success. Despite the uninspiring cover of cooked meat and offal hanging in a Chinese restaurant window the book was almost a perennial, having been reprinted annually ever since. From this point I went from strength to strength until writing cookery books became just a way of life. I remember calling in on all my different publishers. There was Pan off the Fulham Road, Phaidon in Oxford, Michael Joseph in Bloomsbury, Elm Tree and Hamish Hamilton in Russell Street, Hamlyn, at first in Feltham and later as Octopus in Grosvenor Street, Granada, at first in Golden Square and later as part of Collins in Grafton Place.

Of all the publishers that I have had dealings with I am most grateful to the slapdash, easy-going Bernard Hanison who never bothered to have me sign any elaborate contracts, thus leaving me free to pursue a writing career. By the time I had become a relatively successful cookery writer I didn't need to sign away my writing career to any one publisher. So I collected many cookbooks and publishers.

Of my editors, I am most grateful to Katie Stewart, whom I met when she was a consultant cookery editor at Hamlyn's. At the time she was overseeing the production of a series of cookery books, while, simultaneously, being cookery editor for *The Times* and *Woman's Journal*. Under Katie's domain was a well-staffed and well-equipped kitchen where all the recipes that she published were thoroughly tested. Many of my own recipes were copied from Chinese language cookery manuals. As I had simply identified and translated them, making alterations where I felt that the ingredients or procedures were not accessible to the British cook, I was naturally anxious about how they would stand up to Katie's scrutiny. Very few of them had undergone the sterner test of actually being put together on the stove. Even though the blending of flavour, the measure of seasoning, balance of heat to duration of cooking and relative quantities of the ingredients were largely 'figments of my imagination', my imagination was very precise.

To a traditionally trained cookery writer such levity of approach would seem criminal and I cringed when I saw my name listed among the Master Chefs. But I soon became used to it. The fact was that I made very few bloomers and such that there were were caught out by Katie in the kitchen! In fact that first book for Hamlyn was shelved for a number of years on account of a publishing takeover by Reed. When the book eventually arrived at the eve of publication I enquired of Katie as to whether my recipes had stood up to her scrutiny. She said, without hesitation, that all 144 had worked very well! I was relieved and invested even greater faith in my source material, coupled with extensive experience as a consumer and garnished with the odd flourish of imagination. Katie gave me added confidence and inspired me to write even more quickly than I had done previously. Eventually, when pressed to complete a book to tie in with a Thames Television series called *A Taste of China*, it took me just five days. I was commissioned on Monday and handed in my script on the following Friday.

It was accidentally and over two decades that I seriously developed my writing career, and on the way I did develop a sense of mission. All along I had felt that Chinese food and cooking had something significant to offer to the western way of life. For of all the labyrinth of Chinese culture, Chinese food could most easily convey the power and subtlety of Chinese civilization without it being necessary for the consumer to master the complexities of a skill beyond the wielding of chopsticks. And even that wasn't really necessary. It could take decades to appreciate Chinese literature, philosophy, painting, music or dance, but it took no special skill to appreciate good Chinese food. The important thing was to allow easy access and not to make heavy weather of obscure ingredients and methods.

I felt that it was a mission worthy of my grandfather. After all, he had come as ambassador to Britain with a burning ambition to plumb the depths of western civilization, to take back to China the secrets of western power and development. A century later I could find meaning in my mission to bring the fruit of several thousand years of Chinese civilization to the widest possible audience in the West. To demystify the basic techniques and to encourage people to look a little further than Sweet and Sour Pork would be enough. And I just might kindle the interest of some to look further and explore the richness of the Chinese cultural heritage.

Slowly, over the decade, I became the hub around which most matters concerning Chinese food and cookery revolved. At different times I was the inspector for both the *Egon Ronay Guide* and the *Good Food Guide*. As a result I ate in more Chinese restaurants than anyone in his right mind would care to do. Often time was short and the quantity of indifferent Chinese food that I had to process through my palate was quite alarming.

Once I was trying out a new restaurant in Liverpool's Bold Street. I had ordered a spread of eight dishes and had waited for quite some time. When the meal finally arrived each dish was garnished with a mountain of chips. Merseyside was hitting back at Chinese culinary imperialism. I still had many friends left in the north-west and I always took the opportunity of a tour of inspection to invite them to eat out. It relieved the tedium of consuming quantities of third-rate Chinese food and often made it great fun. On my last visit north for the Guides, I had quite a sizeable retinue. Unfortunately someone at head office must have noticed that as my restaurant bills were growing ever larger, there was a parallel growth in the lightheartedness of my reports. I was relieved of duty for 'eating too much'! Egon Ronay and I have, however, remained good friends. He decided that a better use of my talents would be to have me edit the reports made by other western inspectors. How clever are the Hungarians!

There had hardly been any cash to make reviewing for the Guides and there was even less in editing. When all was said and done there was nothing left in the kitty to treat family or friends to a good meal.

I sent the odd begging letter to Charles, who was now a professor at Columbia University, but he couldn't support my family. I had to think of another way to make a living. From writing, reviewing and eating, by the 1970s more and more people were drawn to enquire of me as to what to eat, what Chinese dishes to choose and where to go for good food. Anne, who was originally trained as a home-economist, was inevitably drawn into the periphery of my activities, arranging meals and menus. And out of these activities eventually grew the Chinese Gourmet Club.

During its early days the Club attracted the attention of food critics such as Egon, Fay Maschler, Christopher Driver and Quentin Crewe. For a time when Quentin was writing a column in the *Standard*, he ran a similar club for European food. After a while his club proved too much trouble and as, coincidentally, our Chinese Gourmet Club was expanding rapidly we purchased his membership list for the small sum of £50.

The fresh block of membership injected life into our club. Between 1975 and 1980 Anne and I organized as many as ninety Chinese Gourmet dinners a year in all parts of London. Sometimes we even made excursions as far afield as Birmingham, Manchester or even Alderley Edge. The strength of our club lay in my familiarity with the restaurant scene and in Anne's willingness to work hard without necessarily being paid. For every ninety restaurants that we ate in there were another ninety that I had sampled and rejected. That was also hard work.

The highlight of the Chinese Gourmet Club year was undoubtedly Chinese New Year or the Spring Festival which, ironically, is held in Britain's cold and dreary month of February. Our Spring Festival was always a gastronomic event of heroic proportion. Not one of the ten that we must have held consisted of less than 120 people and several drew crowds of over 200 diners. We would take over a full floor of one of the largest restaurants in Chinatown, preferably with a good view down on to the street entrance where the Lion Dance would come crashing around. When we ate at the Lido our party took a full three floors and once we had to hold two parties simultaneously as our guests outgrew the first restaurant. That day the crowd of festival-goers grew to such proportions that, in the end, it was impossible to pass through without risking being squashed or trampled. Nevertheless, Anne pressed back and forward until it was no longer possible to move.

It was into this kind of melée that we would throw our army of unsuspecting diners and I would always feel a tug of nervousness in my breast. Perhaps the reservation had not been confirmed and without tables what would we do? It was difficult enough to find the space for one person to sit down at the New Year, not to speak of two hundred. And where would we find an unreserved gourmet dinner?

On such occasions Anne would simply march through the crowd and start to place name cards of our guests on the appropriate tables, regardless of whether there were other guests already seated or not. Following hard on her heels was often our youngest daughter Jenny. Anne had ten times more courage than I ever had. One time, with the aid of the proprietors, she uprooted several score of seated diners before we could claim our reservation. Anne always felt that dining in Britain should be an orderly affair and, left to me and other Chinese, we would pile the people in, willy nilly, as we might do back at home. I was always in awe of her ways and was left in no doubt as to where the real might of the British Empire had lain.

Our club dinners were held in Chinese restaurants of all shapes and sizes, all degrees of luxury or sparsity. We ate our way from Ealing in the far west to India Dock Road in the East End, from Watford to Wimbledon. My personal favourites were the 'Rendezvous' group owned by Mr Yang Zikong. Mr Yang had taken the torch for promoting Peking food from Guo Delü, the chef who defected from the Chinese embassy in Portland Place during the 1950s. Guo was an excellent chef but did not make a good employer. Yang was more of a kindly patriarch and his empire stretched all the way to Eastbourne where he escorted me once or twice in his Rolls Royce. Of his half-dozen Peking restaurants, I most frequently used the Soho Rendezvous in Romilly Street or the Richmond Rendezvous which was his very first. Unfortunately his success was curtailed at its height due to a hiccup with Customs and Excise.

The Rendezvous restaurants served a very good Peking Duck and Mr Yang was largely responsible for introducing the dish to the British public. I had had many Peking Duck dinners during the 1930s and was well qualified to discriminate between one and the next. The most famous Peking Duck restaurant is the 'Quan Ju De' where I have eaten over half a dozen times. Over a thousand ducks are roasted in nineteen brick kilns for the table every day. Each kiln, fired by burning logs at the entrance to its stove, produces twenty ducks at a time and is manned by a chef and two assistant cooks. The temperature in the kiln is high even before roasting begins and the whole process is completed in thirty-five minutes – half an hour shorter than the prescribed time for roasting in a British oven at gas mark 7. If a bird is unevenly cooked then it is browned over the open fire that blazes away at the mouth of the kiln.

All this mass production is still not enough to produce the 'perfect' Peking Duck. In fact the best one I have had was served in the old Bubbling Well Road in Shanghai where the 'Jing An' restaurant managed to cook the skin to a perfect crispness while maintaining the tenderness of the meat. The pancakes, the sauce and shredded vegetables were also prepared and arranged with pride. Against these models the Rendezvous Duck stood up quite well. But the tastiest duck that I have ever come across was to be had at the Peking in Westbourne Grove. The duck was not really authentic 'Peking'. It was first smoked in tea and camphor wood before being subjected to the usual Peking Duck hanging, steaming and roasting.

Many restaurateurs have tried to emulate Mr Yang's success, using either Sichuan cooking or various combinations of Japanese and Indonesian hybrid menus. The spiciness of the kind of well preserved food to be had in landlocked Sichuan, adjacent to where the Yangzi River rises, was introduced to New York by Craig Claiborne of the *New York Times* during the 1970s. Since then it has become a runaway success, perhaps an overreaction to the background of tasteless Chop Sueys and Egg Fuyong. The unique hotness of Sichuan food is created by adding heat to heat in varying qualities. For example, the addition of Sichuan pepper, the delayed action incendiary bomb which blazes at the back of the palate, gives an unsuspected depth to chilli heat that focuses at the tip of the tongue and makes itself known on contact. The heat of the Upper Yangzi is best appreciated when contrasted with plain rice or the aromatic quality of crispy barbecued dishes of the North or the succulent long-simmered dishes of the Lower Yangzi and the fresh savoury seafoods of south-east coastal China.

At its height the Club had a membership of 1,000 and I must have personally taken 20,000 people out to dinner in London. But we lacked Mr Yang's natural business acumen and couldn't find it in ourselves to exploit our market. We were charging next to nothing for the annual subscription and collected it erratically. On top of this we were disinclined to place a good margin of profit on top of what the restaurants had charged us. The net result was that there was not enough in the till to pay for the cost of postage, packing, secretarial and printing costs. The bank manager never failed to remind us of our overdraft. In the end we couldn't even settle our accountant's annual bill. Anne ploughed on regardless and I followed suit, as a gentleman should, without being too perturbed by money matters. I hoped that in the long run my earnings from the numerous books would paper over all the small cracks.

The Chinese Gourmet Club, when viewed from the profit and loss account, can only be considered a dramatic failure. But when viewed with a wide angle lens over a longer period it has been a very important commercial asset. Didn't Confucius say that 'those bent on money-making cannot be altogether kind, generous or superior people; those who are kind, superior, generous and benevolent and not bent on money-making will never be wealthy'? Things were going badly again, and it looked as if we couldn't generate enough immorality to put it straight!

Those were busy times – not only from the point of view of managing the Club – but also the early 1970s were my most productive writing years. The children were also time-consuming. Day-to-day their growth had been imperceptible, but suddenly a decade had gone by and they were no longer naked shrimps but full-blooded, sinewy teenagers.

Perhaps because we were separated from Monday to Friday, we created separate lives which bore little relationship to each other. I was not inclined to do what was unnatural to me, nor to force my children to follow in my footsteps. They were uncomfortable on the tennis court just as I was on the football stands. Anne watched my apparent lack of interest with dismay.

My own father had barely commented on my development or adolescence and had left our upbringing to my mother. Anne seemed perfectly competent at the job. She came across the *Classic of the Way and the Virtue* and began to understand that philosophical daoism abhorred unnecessary intervention with the world around you, or that perhaps there was a legitimate philosophy behind my laziness.

With hindsight, despite the freedom of the countryside, Surrey was no place for children of mixed blood with a bad dose of 'missing identity'. A cosmopolitan life in Belsize Park would have been much easier on them. But growing up as Number 2 in a very clear family hierarchy did not equip me to understand teenagers whose place in their own society is not guaranteed from the start. It was even more impossible to give them guidance.

Throughout their turbulent teenage years, however wide the gap of lifestyle and aspiration, I could always feel an inner core of warmth that linked me with my children. That was never displaced. Confucius and Reggae may be worlds apart, but they share the underlying principle of common humanity.

Anne and I were great believers in holidays. Anne spent every holiday at the Snowdon cottage with the family, hoping that they could work out their frustrations climbing rocks and walking mountains. For a while it was just what the doctor ordered but, for me, the cottage could not be compared with our summer residence on Drum Mountain. I took little pleasure in its primitive appeal. Without a tennis court in sight and with the interminable sound of rain dripping off the slate roof, I fled after twenty-four hours, never to return. A holiday wasn't really a holiday unless we'd at least crossed the Channel.

To help widen the horizons of our team of teenagers we decided to take them on a Grand Tour, as any nineteenth-century British family would do, except that Anne had acquired a Volkswagen Dormobile to make do for travelling and to save spending money on unnecessary fares and expensive hotels.

Our first epic journey took us over the Alpine pass via Conte de Ampere. In midsummer we were surprised to see the mountain gulleys still full of snow. Within a few days we had driven the length of Italy, stopping briefly in Rome to see the Colosseum and listen to the splashing fountains, rounding the Bay of Naples and climbing Vesuvius on the way. Anne drove for long hours, and once fell asleep at the wheel, crossing the central reservation of the motorway. Finally we arrived safely at Amalfi where we had booked a chalet on a hillside overlooking Capri. We spent five days there resting and swimming. Capri was more romantic in song than at close quarters. It was spoilt by boatloads of tourists and litter that crawled all over the island. And Gracie Fields wasn't in when we visited her far-famed restaurant.

On the way home we passed through Venice which, just as it had been in the 1930s, lay steaming and putrid in the midsummer heat. At Florence we stayed in a hotel by the dry riverbed. We listened to recordings of the background to the Pontevecchio Bridge and potted histories of the town. And best of all we sat in the shadowy squares with locals and other tourists, sipping iced drinks from huge, coloured glasses. Charles, now a regular visitor every summer, flew to meet us in Salzburg. I moved from the cramped VW to join him in his hotel, leaving the family to go about their own business. He treated me to dinner at a luxury restaurant while the family ate sandwiches on the street. There just wasn't the money to treat everyone!

In 1974 *Quick and Easy Chinese Cooking*, being a decade in advance of the wok, had failed to impress the British market, but was an overnight success in America and became the 'Alternate Choice' to the book of the month. To celebrate we planned another European odyssey. Our destination was a Spanish castle in Andalusia where some American friends, Francis and Jenny Guth, were keen to stage a five-day cookery experiment. The return journey would be a good 2,000 miles. Anne, always rooting for a challenge, was delighted.

Our initial progress was slow. We had failed to take the French national holiday into account, and tried to cross the Pyrenees on 1 August. By the time we had crawled across the border and arrived in Burgos it was getting dark and the statue of El Cid stood menacingly in the city square. It reminded me that the Europe of the Middle Ages was a dark and menacing place, just like China under war-lord rule.

But there was greatness in Spain, a greatness that was apparent the moment you crossed into the Iberian peninsula. Behind its crumbling decay there was a huge history and empire that unfolded itself not only through such historic buildings as the Escorial, but through glimpses of life behind the intricately carved and huge wooden gates which guarded the entrances to private mansions. There was nothing provincial about Madrid. At every turn there was something redolent and reminiscent of the great empire now past. It was like a huge sleeping giant that reminded me of Peking in summer time. It seemed by accident that the Industrial Revolution had taken place in northern Europe and not in Spain or China.

Madrid was hot. The stone walls and concrete steps absorbed heat all through the morning and radiated it all through the afternoon, just like in Foochow. While travelling there had always been a breeze to cool us, but now on the plain the heat descended heavily on us and it was merciful to check in to the Velazquez Hotel. But the Velazquez Hotel was more expensive than I had been led to believe, and the children emptied the refrigerator in the hotel room overnight. It was time to get on with our journey. Travelling south through La Mancha, it was easy to feel as though I were back in the Min River valley basin. But there were fewer people hawking their wares by the roadside. Both places grew olives, but I missed the lychees, watermelon and sugar cane.

Our host and hostess, Francis and Jenny, were having a siesta when we arrived at the Andalusian mountain village, so we had time to explore a little. Their home was more of a secluded mansion built behind high walls than the Norman castle with turrets and battlements that we had imagined. Viewed from above, terracotta roofs fell away in every direction. Inside, the rooms were dark and cool, the doors heavy and solemn. The girls headed directly for the bedroom with the en-suite sunken bath with golden taps and then threw off their clothes to go swimming. When Jenny and Francis came around they gave us a conducted tour of all the kitchens – the town kitchen, the country kitchen and the Chinese kitchen. Apart from the woks, the steamer, and huge chopping board and choppers there was the cover of my book *The Chinese Cookery Encyclopedia* pinned to the kitchen wall. I could tell Francis was serious and that I was not going to get away with any Egg Fuyong.

Francis was a serious gourmet. Before long we were settled into deep conversation about the exotic: the beef tendons, duck's webs and sea slugs. Six hours later we realized that it was too late to buy any ingredients and the family were all starving. The next day Anne and I went shopping while Francis supervised Vivienne and Jenny who had been given a pig's head to pluck clean for brawn. After a tentative meal they complained they were still hungry! It was a little hard to find appropriate ingredients in the small Spanish town, but eventually I managed to put together some 'eternal stews' – my variation of a red-cooked dish, eaten with rice and served with lightly stir-fried fresh vegetables. It was a wonderful meal, not to be rivalled by any elaborate dish from the Imperial kitchen.

After a few days Anne and the girls, always lovers of their freedom to wander, began to feel stifled by the confines of the castle walls and were itching to go south. They were also fed up with gourmet food, and desperate for something basic to eat! We cranked open the gate, waved goodbye and aimed the VW towards Granada. Once on our way we went in search of paella. After borsch and brawn it seemed to be a wholesome dish, and with its seafood, chicken and rice, even a little reminiscent of the Min River. Granada had much to offer. We stayed in a cheap *pensión* close to the Alhambra and spent a few days wandering around the palace, cooling ourselves by the fountains and in the bathrooms. I was impressed by the elegance of the palace, the first great testimony to Moorish culture that I had ever seen.

The rest of our journey up the east coast was less cultured. We hopped from camp site to camp site making rapid progress along the Costas Brava and Sol to avoid spending too much time eating fish and chips. The remaining highlights were strolling along Las Ramblas in Barcelona, the lush green as we passed the foothills of the Basque country and those medieval hill towns on the way north through France.

That was the last of our epic holidays with the children, as children, in tow. The 1960s and 1970s passed by in this way – the children came and went and very slowly my life's path was finally taking shape, more by accident than by design. A career in cookery writing had been the last course on my mind and one which, at first sight, I had hardly been prepared for. But, 'whatever shall be, shall be', and the most appropriate response was to bring the best of my skills to bridge the gap between my two cultures – diplomacy, communication and a love of eating and socializing – and to see where the next tide washed me up. Confucius smiled benignly.

CHAPTER TWELVE

Sailing to Byzantium

An aged man is but a paltry thing,
A tattered coat upon a stick, unless
Soul clap its hands and sing, and louder sing
For every tatter in its mortal dress,
Nor is there singing school but studying
Monuments of its own magnificence;
And therefore I have sailed the seas and come
To the holy city of Byzantium.

Sailing to Byzantium, W. B. Yeats. 1865–1939

JAPANESE COMPANIES are far more efficient than their western counterparts. With their company songs, flags, morning drill and exercises they pump up the adrenalin and promote corporate loyalty. Their empire was run with the same zeal. At the opposite end of the scale I know of few businesses organized in a more random way than the Chinese catering trade. China herself was always too big to be run with the same attention to detail and her trade is correspondingly haphazard – more dependent on all the family mucking in than on the spirit of efficiency. Yet, in the true spirit of private enterprise, the Chinese catering trade has galloped its way throughout the western world.

In the course of the next decades Chinese food will develop in all directions. In the past Chinese cuisine lacked capital, organization and recognition. Now it has some recognition and, before long, the

Chinese resources from the Pacific rim will flood forth to promote Chinese food in all corners of the West. I can see that it has the potential to be used at many levels of society. It can be incorporated into western family cooking, adapted for cocktail parties, banquets, fast food or even to meet the requirements of cooking in the Third World.

The Chinese are extremely lucky to have one of the largest culinary ranges in the world, with most dishes prepared from inexpensive food materials that are easily available in most of the continents of the world. Although the talented Chinese chef can cater for sumptuous banquets for the affluent, the rice and noodle dishes, prepared in bulk with all manner of vegetables and minute amounts of meat, are tasty, nourishing and cheap enough to produce for the exploding populations of the Third World. By the same token, with slight upgrading and refinement, it can be used for mass catering in the form of cheap convenience or fast foods.

I have always welcomed the opportunity to act as consultant to large international companies who plan to produce a range of Chinese-style dishes for the mass market. When sitting in with half a dozen executives from Marks & Spencer or Heinz & Co and mapping out the area of operation for convenience food development I have always felt a great satisfaction. I can readily muster the sum of my experience in Chinese food in Britain. Whether from eating with the Chinese Gourmet Club, the Good Food or Egon Ronay Guides, I find that I know how far Chinese food has penetrated into Britain and what potential there is where. When making plans to market it on such a scale I really feel as if I am systematically pumping the essence of one culture into the veins of another.

Although the Chinese restaurant trade, taken as a whole, is a trade of considerable scope, no single company has tried to harness its momentum, no Fukien Ken has leapt ostentatiously on to the high streets of Britain to challenge the likes of Colonel Saunders or Ronald MacDonald. If I ever had a catering ambition it would be to feed the thousands both cheaply and well, to have a chain of popular noodle houses serving up good food to the masses. But that was not the way it happened.

It was within the Chinese Gourmet Club that we first conceived of opening a restaurant. The prospect had always seemed vexing to me. But with Anne no longer working in school meals and the children more or less off our hands, she had to find a new project to harness her energy. Our Club clientele was rich and varied enough to have sampled the up-market restaurants already established in such trading centres as Taiwan, Hong Kong and Singapore, and thinly spread in the western capitals, and it was at this upper end of the market that our thrust was aimed.

The first wave of enthusiasm came in response to a general call to subscribe to the company's capital. We collected a myriad of shareholders, many old friends and friends to be, each contributing greater or lesser amounts of money and help, but all of them adding their own special colour to the fabric of the enterprise.

But when it comes down to brass tacks, the establishment of any business is never a simple and easy matter, unless one has unlimited capital to play with. That we never had. Indeed, despite illustrious contacts, in all my businesses I was always about 50 per cent short of basic capital. Apart from gathering the 'critical mass' of capital, there is all the boring bureaucratic and legal procedure to wade through which takes the persistence of a saint. Drifting with the tide could never be enough. But Anne was born the farmer's daughter and in the matter of ploughing on irrespective, one furrow after another, she was the expert. After a while when we looked back it was amazing how much distance we did cover.

It was not unlike the process of writing my longest book, the Collins *Encyclopedia of Chinese Cookery*. When it was complete I was amazed that it ran to 650 pages and well over 120,000 words. All the agony and pain of creation fades with the memory of completion and all the small triumphs on the way. I remember choosing the name 'Memories of China'. Many names had been suggested. Most lacked the spark or poetic appeal to propel them along while others were just banal or vulgar. The British invented too pretty a name, which did not do justice to the range and power of Chinese food. The Chinese suffered from a limited acquaintance with the English language and could not break away from well-worn clichés, such as Mandarin this or that, Happy Garden, Pearl the other. When Memories of China popped into my mind I felt that I should stick to it. It was unpretentious and charged with nostalgia, a name for the sanctuary that would transport every Chinese in exile back home.

So we had a good name to pin to our restaurant. In choosing our location we did not prioritize busy sites that would attract passing custom. With the combined publicity of my numerous cookbooks (by that time I had sold in excess of a quarter of a million copies) and the many contributions I had made to almost all the national papers – from *The Times* and *Country Life* through *Vogue*, *Punch*, *Honey* to the *Sun* and the *Mirror* – and not forgetting the invaluable support of the

1,000 members of the Chinese Gourmet Club, we felt confident that we could set up in Bermondsey or Battersea and still make a go of it.

Anne played the scout, driving around non-stop to view a host of different places until she found one which pleased her. The site was to be in Ebury Street, SW1. Although this was not the most fashionable street in Belgravia and no restaurant in that street had enjoyed any remarkable success, it was a stone's throw from the residential areas of Chester, Eaton and Belgrave Squares. It was more than good enough for us.

Apart from making up the name, my other contribution was the theme of Tang dynasty horses. To have them etched on to enormous panels of smoked glass for the front windows was Anne's stroke of brilliance – a very extravagant stroke of brilliance. Although naturally frugal I supported her, remembering the saying that 'when an Empire was glorious and in the ascendancy, defence was conducted beyond the distant frontiers'. Hence in the great dynasties, such as the Han and Tang, the horse has always played a big part. The horses were grand and we were on the ascent. The rest of the restaurant was designed by our architect and shareholder, Derek Irving. He came up with a sparse design: bare whitewashed walls graffittied with Tang dynasty poems, seals and a few carefully chosen classical pictures, a quarry-tiled floor and natural pine lattice screens to divide the tables. Anne added the exotic touch with fresh purple orchids on every table. It was the prototype for a new generation of Chinese restaurants – a far cry from the wall-to-wall carpeting of Hong Kong-inspired 'luxury' glitz and perfect for the understated, elegant look of the early 1980s.

Behind the swing doors at the far end of the restaurant was the biggest Chinese kitchen in London with a burly northern Chinese chef to fill it. Kum-Po But's cooking was head and shoulders above that of his contemporaries. We had first noticed him when he was cooking at the Golden Duck in Fulham. But's family came from the province of Shandong, where Shanghai used to recruit most of their policemen. But But's big heavy hands had a very delicate touch that worked with precision and great care. Although trained as a Dim Sum chef in Hong Kong with an intimate knowledge of the seafood traditions of the south, he could faithfully reproduce the northern Peking flavour too. By far his most celebrated dish was the long-braised knuckle of pork, which needs to be slow-simmered for hours in soya sauce, sugar and wine until the meat falls away from the bone and has the same jelly-like consistency as the gravy. It is a dish best eaten with steamed buns and spinach, flash fried with loads of garlic. And among all the London chefs, But was easily the best 'noodle thrower'. He brought along a young chef called Yang with him. Yang had swum across the straits from mainland China to Hong Kong with the aid of a car tyre inner tube. With such dedication he was bound to be an advantage!

But this is to jump the gun. Before we had enough hard cash for the bricks and mortar I was invited to Hong Kong to join in the shooting of a Chinese cookery film. The film was designed to indicate that many of the well-known traditional Chinese dishes can easily be cooked in a British suburban kitchen. I was to play the part of compère with a young woman called Anneka Rice. When I arrived in Hong Kong I stayed at the Lee Garden Hotel.

The proprietor of the Lee Garden, J. S. Lee, was an old friend who dated back to my early university days in Peking and later to wartime London and Liverpool. He was also the Hon Treasurer of the 1946–7 Chinese Davis Cup Team. On noticing my sojourn at his hotel he took me to a dinner party with our mutual friend, Mr Y. H. Kan, then Chairman of the Securities Commission of Hong Kong.

Mr Kan's dining-room opened out on to a hillside garden. In the hot Hong Kong summer the situation was breezy and cool. We dined at a vast round table with more than a dozen people. Most of the meat dishes were cooked in light clear broth, rather than the more common rich sauces generally considered to make up a banquet. Indeed the guests were no peasants. There was one lady present who owned forty-nine cake shops and employed 900 people in her printing plant. On hearing that I wanted to launch a Chinese Cookery School in London she volunteered to take me to see her cookery school.

In fact, these were the 'top-cats' of the booming colony. At some point J.S. mentioned to the small congregation at the dinner that I was starting a restaurant in London and that I could do with some additional investment. I can't remember whether a hat was passed around, but a sum of £18,000 was collected instantly. That sum represented the last brick to be slotted into place before the name, 'Memories of China', was pinned to the entrance of our Belgravia restaurant. On returning to the hotel I telephoned Anne to tell her the happy news. We determined to open on 4 July – American Independence Day. It would be auspicious. We could capitalize on the celebrations of all our American friends.

In the morning I was informed that the whole filming project was cancelled as the publishing company which had initiated the filming had run out of cash, due to having too large a crew sitting around in hotels waiting for visas and local government clearance for the shooting of the film. At that juncture in my life it was an insufferable encumbrance to be tied up with a filming contract and I was delighted at the news. The director was trying to mould me into an actor and every time he used the words 'body language' it made me cringe. I was on the point of walking out anyway.

As soon as I heard of the cancellation I checked the balance of travellers' cheques and found that I still had more than enough to make a return trip to Peking. I nearly shouted with joy. For ten days I had money and time at my disposal – a rare freedom in my life! My first stop was the China Travel Service where I found a girl who arranged my visa and the next day I found myself on a Trident, taking the twenty-two minute flight to Canton. The flight was so short that it felt like riding a bus down the King's Road without any traffic jams.

On touching down in China, my first impression of this post-war revolutionary country was the lack of normal western trappings: a railway ticket office appeared like the window of a half-opened bedsitter and a banking hall like an undermanned canteen, where half the staff were munching at their dinner. In such an environment I was not surprised to find that the air ticket for the second leg of the flight to Peking could not be purchased at the airport where I had just alighted and where I was to commence my flight north a few hours later. That would just be too convenient. I had to go to the town centre to purchase it. I reminded myself that there was no point in fretting and that I should exercise my renowned Chinese patience. As I waited I noticed numerous lychee peddlars squatting on the ground and occasionally moving around a little to interest the queuing passengers in what they had to sell. Their lychees were still attached to the branch which had been roughly chopped from the tree. There were also sugar canes, washed and cut into six-inch segments. It was a small reminder of summer in Foochow.

When I got back to the airport with my air ticket the two large planes were already on the tarmac. This time I wanted to get down on my knees and kiss the good earth of China to mark my return after fifty-four years. But before I could do anything so ostentatious I was hustled towards the plane. Two handsome girls in blue shepherded the passengers behind the barriers where they should await the signal to board. These were the new women. They were taller than I remembered and there was that 'no nonsense' attitude in the way they pointed out their commands.

As the plane swept north all the historic geographical land-marks of China appeared below. I could make out many of the battlegrounds of history – the high water levels where the Japanese tide had advanced into China, where the Communist and Nationalist armies had engaged along the Longhai railway. No sooner had we crossed the Yangzi than we were crossing the Yellow River and I could make out the plains where all the classical battles took place. And then we were already descending towards Peking.

Peking airport was disappointingly small considering the size of the capital city. There was a moving pavement to conduct the traveller towards the heart of the airport. Otherwise the veneer of modernity disappeared rapidly, especially as the taxi sped towards the city centre. China was still the old China I had left – a poor, industrially-backward Third World country. Though when I sharpened my focus I could make out that more people were shod, and more burdens were carried on carts rather than on the backs of stooped women.

Both Walter and Michael seemed to find little difficulty in locating me at the Overseas Chinese Guest House near Wangfujing Boulevard in the centre of Peking. In the midst of the splendour of one of Peking's top luxury hotels, both my brothers looked like the stragglers of tat-tered battalions, ageing survivors of the Cultural Revolution. At that time I did not know how much trouble they had gone to with their appearance for that occasion. Both of them were bachelors. Within moments Walter asked me if he could have a bath in my en suite bathroom. Michael followed the reunion handshake with the same request. A private bath was a luxury neither had enjoyed for many a decade and the unlimited hot water in my rooms brought them back every day throughout my stay.

In contrast Walter shared a flat with a family of five in a red-brick compound that backed on to the Boulevard of Eternal Peace. The district was quite central, only half-a-mile from Tiananmen and close to the foreign embassies and the Friendship Stores. But the estate was very cramped and ill-lit. We had to light a match to find the key hole. The family of five lived and slept together in one room and Walter had been sleeping on an unupholstered bed base, without a mattress, in the small next door room for two decades. They shared their kitchen and toilet. Walter used his room as a bedsitter.

A bare light bulb hung from the ceiling and lit up his desk where stacks of books lay undusted among broken tea cups, the old Underwood typewriter I had sent him years previously, and a radio sent by Charles from Hong Kong. A few boxes of Lipton's tea, a small pile of Knorr chicken stock cubes and a bottle of Nescafé represented the only intrusion of Western creature comforts into the bare essentials of life in Peking. Despite the long and bitter northern winter, I could see no source of heat.

Walter scraped a living by teaching English here and there. He had a bevy of young girls who were desperate to improve their foreign languages and promote their chances of graduating to better jobs or even leaving China altogether. Most he didn't even charge, treating them as if they were his own daughters. At sixty he needed a family to look out for him and it was these girls, ever grateful for their tuition, that came to help him wash and cook and watched over him on a daily basis. Every week he would teach at an Agricultural College more than twenty kilometres out of town where he stayed for a couple of days. This was all new to me. Walter was not a great letter writer so I had had very little news of him over the years. All in all he had not only survived but he was one of the most cheerful people I have ever met. He had endless tales to tell of life in Peking and was at his happiest when torrents of events and facts about China were tumbling out of his mouth 'like beans from an upturned jar'.

It was dark when we left his room. Peking was dusty, but not as dusty as it used to be. We returned to the centre of town and entered the hutongs, the residential lanes of the old capital. At night many of the residents of the tiny cramped lanes were sitting out in the open to catch whatever little breeze there was. They were also out for the gossip and engaged in animated conversation. There seemed to be all the time and leisure in the world and I imagined the same voices to have murmured on through every summer night of peacetime in the heydays of the Yuan, Ming or Qing dynasties. It reminded me of summer nights of long before, when I used to lie in bed and listen to our parents talking away to the early hours after the mahjong parties on the verandahs below our bedrooms.

As we strolled Walter talked on. Every now and then the subject turned to politics or analysing Chinese society. He was very well informed from reading daily newspapers and listening to 'Voice of America'. He had a gentle American accent. What fascinated Walter was figures and he had the GNP, population, foreign debt and agricultural input all readily at his command. But every time he had something important to say his voice dropped so low as to become barely audible. It was a habit he had cultivated during the Cultural Revolution, when the 'walls had ears' that were ever peeled for those who harboured 'counter-revolutionary' sentiments. I looked around us and saw how many cigarette ends were glowing in the darkness and how closely we were being shadowed on our leisurely stroll. Other cigarette ends were moving faster through the gloaming as chain-smoking cyclists wove through the dark streets, magically able to avoid colliding with bicyclists or pedestrians. In the residential hutongs there were people everywhere.

I had to remind myself that this was 1980 and that a decade had passed since the end of the Cultural Revolution. The crime rate was almost non-existent. In fact China was one of the safest countries to stroll around in after dark. 'Law and Order' had been effective at the grass roots since early Imperial days when the bao jia system had been invented. Each community was divided into groups of ten, a hundred and a thousand and had been made responsible for its own 'security' through a network of vigilante-like head men. If law and order broke down with an individual their whole community could be held responsible. Many punishments were meted out to the nth degree of relationship, meaning that if you had committed a capital offence your wife, parents, siblings or cousins would be exterminated with you. This system, created 1,500 years ago, could have been the envy of the KGB.

Walter's natural frugality had undoubtedly contributed to his survival through the hard times of the revolution. But he told me that to keep up an easy and pleasant relationship with everyone immediately around you was the most critical factor. You need only maintain a strictly correct relationship with the authorities. To ingratiate yourself might prove fatal when the locus of power changed. When the Red Guards came knocking in 1966 Walter had invited them in and given them a cup of tea and a warm bowl of water to wash their feet in. Then he had enquired about their day. After all they were only children, and being revolutionaries was exhausting work! All along he was polite and courteous but never ingratiating. Given that, as a teacher, he was a prime target for 'correction' by the Red Guards his survival was remarkable. To add the Lo preference for colonial habits – drinking Earl Grey tea and wearing expensive leather shoes – his survival was a miracle. In fact not one of the Los suffered as desperately as many around them, despite being teachers. It seems that they were just ignored.

Many of the Wei family, with their passionate likes and dislikes, their strong opinions and outbursts, had been buried under the rubble of the Cultural Revolution. Uncle Long, who had taught me martial arts and swimming on my first return from the West, had perished in the family's coal-mine in Henan. Uncle Tong, mother's number two brother, was the chief executive of the joint Anglo–Chinese

Kailuan Mining administration, employing 150,000 people. After liberation he had managed the mine to such success that he was virtually given freedom of movement in China. But his patent leather shoes and dancing proved too decadent for the Red Guards. His second daughter, Wen Lin, a pretty 'debutante' type, had gone with her husband, Tommy, to run a hospital in far-flung Ulumuqi. After prolonged hounding by the Red Guards she, sadly, committed suicide.

We wandered almost at random through the hutongs. Peking was immense but we were never in danger of being lost. In Peking the streets run north–south, east–west and the principal avenues traverse the city. Walter walked several miles every day and knew the city like the back of his hand.

When we returned to my hotel we went to the canteen dining-room which served popular family dishes until fairly late in the evening. Walter's cheerfulness began to crescendo as we entered the canteen. If there was anything he liked better than a good conversation about the state of the country, it was a good feed.

Michael was altogether a different kettle of fish. He had travelled all the way from Shanghai to be with me. Although I knew that Michael had begun to lose his hearing in his youth, it was more than half an hour before I realized just how deaf he was. Everything had to be written down, partly in Chinese and partly in English, in order to communicate. I already knew that Michael's English was quite charming from his letters. He had graduated in European history from St John's University, Shanghai and was extremely well read. That was before his deafness set in. His conversations read more like those found in nineteenth-century novels than contemporary English, which he probably had never heard!

I soon realized that the formality of communicating on paper actually reduced, rather than increased, any social embarrassment we might have felt after such a long separation. Each thought had to be carefully considered: should it be Chinese or English, how simply and eloquently could it be translated into an easily digested communication, written down and passed over? Michael would nod and acknowledge when he had understood and the process began again. There was no question of awkward silences, it was all conducted in silence!

We soon fell into a comfortable companionship and I was surprised how familiar it felt. I was suddenly struck by the familiarity between this meeting and the mid 1920s when he returned to Foochow after growing up in London. I remembered that lonesome little boy, barely five or six and speaking a strange mix of pidgin Foochow and English, pointing at the goldfish and saying, 'fish, fish!' There was no question as to how he had survived the Cultural Revolution. He was far too complex and disabled to incriminate and, besides, his tragedy was all too obvious in the way he looked and communicated. No-one would have added to it even had they sensed the sophisticated mind that lurked behind his shabby exterior!

Most of that week I spent eating out and revisiting old haunts. That naturally meant a trip to Yanjing campus where Professor Daisun was now living in the Yin Qun Yuan, (The Garden of Eternal Spring). I calculated that he was well into his eighties and was expecting him to be worse off for the revolution, and his advancing age. Not a bit of it! Daisun's uncompromising six foot, erect and unbending body came quietly out to meet me and his hair was less grey than mine. As a sportsman still able to compete at a national level, albeit in veterans' tournaments, it came as a shock to me. Daisun's gait was even more sprightly than mine and with his long legs it was still an effort to keep up with him.

The Garden of Eternal Spring was a modest scholar's residence which Daisun shared with a family who had been moved in with him during the Cultural Revolution. Although this was now a decade later Daisun had not taken any active steps to ask the university to have them removed. The half of the house that he occupied with Chen He, a lady cousin who looked after him, consisted of two bedrooms, a front room and a study. By any ordinary Chinese standards they had plenty of space. But bearing in mind that Daisun was the single senior Professor of Economics in the country, who would often represent the government in international matters, it seemed a little strange that his whole house had uncarpeted, concrete floors and that his salary was no more than a manual labourer's (about £20 a month).

Cousin Daisun was not one to complain. Walter was always hypothesizing about how people survived the Cultural Revolution unscathed. Daisun should have been a prime target, being a teacher in Peking and one who espoused economics that definitely had a Keynesian rather than a Marxist flavour. How had he managed to stay clear of the Red Guards, and survive successive turns in economic policy and Communist dynasty so totally intact? Walter's conclusion was quite simple. At a theoretical level no-one understood his theses and, not wishing to expose their ignorance, they declined to criticize him. On a personal level Daisun was always so erect and straight, so unmistakably fair in his dealings, that he had never made the kind of enemy that would seek revenge amid such turmoil as the Cultural Revolution. I think he was also quite lucky.

Happy and satisfied with all my meetings in Peking, I returned home for the opening of Memories of China, Ebury Street. As anticipated, we had crowds of Americans who came to celebrate Independence Day. The Americans were clearly in the majority despite the opening having been written up in almost every British paper and magazine. It was an American journal that gave us the biggest recognition. Their top American travel and leisure magazine, *The Gourmet*, gave us a four-page write up. The same writer, John Bainbridge, followed on some years later with another marathon write up when he recommended two places to visit in the capital, the Queen's Gallery in Buckingham Palace and Memories of China.

I became a regular visitor to China. Once I took a veterans' tennis team and personally played with Wan Li, a survivor of the Long March and the then Deputy Prime Minister of China. Wan Li played a steady game but lacked international experience. I had to pull my punches. Between 1976 and 1984 I had won the Mens' Doubles event at the veterans' Championships of Great Britain five times with my partner, Tommy Anderson.

Another abiding image of one trip to China is of Arabella Boxer snooping around Walter's kitchen trying to imagine how anyone could cook amid such squalor with one pan! As I remained in the capital and major cities, playing tennis with old friends and family, Anne was keen to go on more intrepid adventures and took tours into the hinterland, even as far as Tibet. Most memorable of all was the televized Gastronomic Tour of China in the early summer of 1986.

The trip was designed to take me home on the first leg of the journey. We set out from Hong Kong on a Scandinavian-built, Chinese-run coastal steamer. As we steamed out of the harbour I stood at the stern of the ship and watched the jagged skyline recede into the distance. Hong Kong may have been created by a mere two or three generations of western and Chinese co-operation but it has become a manifestation of twentieth-century China. The few years under British rule will pale into insignificance when seen against the future that it has to come.

I had just heard from Charles, who had been travelling in China and had visited nearly all our relatives. I could never share his fervour for archeological explorations of our own family. His exile had definitely turned him into a 'roots searcher', one who finds solace in the past, the culture and the extended family. Perhaps it was because he had no family of his own. He found that in spite of all the turmoil and revolution, the students and young people of China were still much more courteous to the elderly than in the West. And as a teacher at

Columbia and New York Universities he should know the youth of America well. The lives of the elderly in China were incomparably better than the misery of isolation and alienation that he too often saw among the old folk in New York.

I could not share Charles's nostalgia, but the entry back into China has always been a dramatic moment for me. Quite apart from my own memories I have always been keenly aware of China's geography and history and returning to her both reminds me of the cultural identity that I miss in the West, and also makes me feel very small when set against the enormous scales involved. People often ask me whether I feel more Chinese or more British. After all, I have spent far more of my life in the West, and have a British wife and mixed-up children! But the memory of chanting Confucian classics is almost a part of collective memory. It is shared with every generation of Chinese scholars' children throughout the millennia, which irrevocably connects you to the umbilical cord of Chinese history. And of course there is the food for which I will remain forever Chinese.

We sailed up the Guangdong coastline, through the offshore islands of Fujian, passing the statue of my childhood hero, Zheng Chenggong, defender of a Han China against the Manchurian horde. All along I was being interviewed by Hilary Minster and filmed by Bob Bolt, the cameraman. We were in the company of many distin-guished gourmets including John Salvi, Oz Clarke, Kathie Webber, Al Davidson and Maurice Riverly. Our first port of call was Xiamen or Amoy, the university town where the famous Amoy soya sauce comes from. With such a guest list we were under pressure to provide some tempting travellers' fare.

The vegetarian dinner that we had that night at the Nan Putuo temple, three miles east of the town, came as a surprise. I don't know how we came to be there or whether we turned up on the off chance. The meal seemed to have required intricate and lengthy preparation, when in fact it had been quickly thrown together by a neatly turned out and very composed lady chef. She was reputed to be the top vegetarian chef in all of China, and had prepared banquets for such personalities as Deng Xiaoping and many others. Since many of the Politburo were octogenarians they preferred to eat easily digestible vegetarian food.

I was relieved to see that none of her dishes was the crass reproduction of poultry and meat dishes to which many vegetarian cooks are inclined to resort. Instead they were works of art created to make best use of the flavour, colour and texture of the ingredients and called such names as Setting Sun on the Yellow River, Crescent

Moon Behind the Willows, or Spray of White Petals on the Motion-less Lake. There was no conflict between the poetry and the flavour of these dishes. They were all light and easy to eat, a relief for both the palate and the belly after the multi-flavour banquets of Hong Kong and a good start to our gastronomic tour. We finished with a dessert of almond doufu in a light syrup.

Along the coastal roads from Xiamen to Quanzhou where, in my time, people have travelled by sedan chair, and where, a very few years ago, motor transport was unheard of, today streams of home-made lorries send jay-walking chickens scattering to the roadside. These green Chinese-made lorries look like tiny ancient Dodge trucks. But the mini bus in which we travelled was a Japanese-made Toyota which flew along bumping over pot holes in the road, much to every-one's consternation.

When I awoke, from a snooze, at dusk we were already arriving in Quanzhou. Quanzhou was originally known by foreigners as Zaytun, the busy trading port from which Marco Polo set sail for home in the fourteenth century. It has a glorious history, but these days the harbour is silted up. The town was reputed to be an old and sleepy medieval provincial capital, renowned for its classical temples and archeological remains from the Song and Yuan dynasties. Instead, through my half-closed eyelids, I could make out technical colleges, libraries, gymnasiums, stadiums, indeed a whole modern city looming all around us. It was most unexpected.

But as we travelled into the centre of town, the old city sprawled out before us. The next morning at 4 a.m. the full roar of traditional China came swelling up through the windows. It sounded like a foot-ball crowd bursting out of a stadium and filling the streets below. I peered out of the window but could see nothing. It took some time for me to realize that this was the pre-dawn gathering of market traders setting up their stalls. Since there was no distinction between food-types sold on this central market, what I could hear was a case of Smithfield Market, Covent Garden and Billingsgate all rolled into one. In fact, when we went to investigate, it was not unlike those markets. Most markets are a little medieval and, in the half-light, Marco Polo would hardly have known the difference here. The only sharp difference for our sensitive and contemporary western guests was that the chickens and ducks were alive and trussed up in a manner that would be totally unacceptable to the RSPCA.

Having been away from my hometown for fifty-four years I wondered how I would feel as we approached by road from the south. Would my pulse quicken as our bus drove across the broad

Min River on which the city stood? Most Chinese count themselves lucky to return to the place where they were born in a wooden box. They buy plots on the hillside for this purpose. I imagined that our family's hillside plot had long ago fallen into disrepair. Who would tend it now at the Gravesweeping Festival? I felt lucky that after all these decades I was still able to return wielding a tennis racquet, and that there were also eager tennis players among my cousins to meet me.

Because I was dusty from the long drive from the south I simply wanted to have a quick wash and feel clean before facing the thirty-odd relatives and schoolfriends who were waiting to greet me in the hotel lounge. These were people whom I had left behind as young men and teenagers and who were now seventy or eighty years old. A few jokes later I found that they were still the same old rascals in spite of all the wars, revolutions and lifetimes of changing fortune.

To my surprise I felt entirely matter-of-fact about everything I saw. Perhaps I had been away too long to be able to feel sentimental or perhaps that is how I am made. There was little to remind me of home. It would certainly have been different if Lo Lodge had still been there, or if my mother and father had survived to welcome me home. But Lo Lodge had been razed to the ground leaving only the giant tree, still visible against the skyline, to mark where it had been. My mother had passed away after a long and debilitating illness in the 1950s and my father, who had survived hale and hearty into the Cultural Revolution, died of old age in the late 1960s.

The following day I went to visit the new Lo Lodge that had been allocated to my family after Liberation. Naturally it was not a patch on the grandeur of the original one, but it was comfortable enough, a red brick and wooden building, still on Cang Qian hill, set in its own walled garden with flats for four branches of the family. In the garden, beneath a stone bearing the inscription 'Imperial Servant of the Qing dynasty', lay my grandfather and my parents. There I took incense and bowed as I would bow as a boy to the ancestral tablets placed on the shrine on the upper landing.

I could not pass by Foochow without taking a trip up to the Bubbling Spring Monastery on Drum Mountain. It was also an opportunity to retrace the journey to the vicinity of our old summer house. The monks' dinner on offer at the monastery was probably the roughest vegetarian meal I have ever had and was in stark contrast to the fare at Nan Putuo temple. It embodied the basic elements of the Cultural Revolution – by the peasant for the peasant – a combination of two bean curd dishes, one dried, one stir fried, some boiled cabbage, salt pickle and stir-fried celery, mustard green and sweet potato served up with plain boiled rice. I supposed that it was nutritious enough, but led a posse through to inspect the kitchen. There, as I expected, were nothing more than a bunch of farmhands being bullied and shouted at mercilessly by one head chef who seemed to be acquainted with the rudiments of cooking. I recalled the basic fare, sixty years before, at the farmer's shack on the mountain where, in early summer, we would wait for our parents to join us before moving on to the summer house. At least food at the monastery was better than it had been when we went to see the lambs, goats, ducks and geese that were allowed to live out their natural lifespan or when we accompanied our grandmother to gold leaf the petalled seat of the Buddha.

Shanghai was impressive for its congestion. When we poured out of the train at the station we felt in danger of drowning in a sea of humanity. But out of that sea came Harry Li, beaming his broad smile through the decades. It was a treat to see him, for nothing seemed to have changed apart from the health of his legs which were not up to playing doubles with me on that occasion. He spoke perfect English with an American lilt, for his children had emigrated to the States and Harry had spent some time with them.

The rest of our time in Shanghai was spent trying to expose our guests to the flavours of Shanghai. A distinctive style and character of the food of the Lower Yangzi area does not stand out as readily as that of Canton, with its profusion of seafood flavours, or that of Peking, with its roast and barbecued dishes, its pronounced taste of garlic and thick soya-paste sauces. In fact, the cuisine of the region is in direct contrast to that of the Upper Yangzi, Sichuan. Where Sichuan food is hot, highly spiced and strong-tasting, the eastern emphasis is on dishes which taste fresh, pure and full of natural flavour.

The Lower Yangzi is full of flowing water and the land is criss-crossed with innumerable streams and studded with ponds and lakes. Since the cooking of any region must reflect its geography, it is natural that the character of Shanghai cuisine should reflect the purity of the water and incorporate a host of freshwater products: shrimps, crab, duck and a wide range of vegetation which flourishes in the area, especially with plants growing in and beside the water. There is a tendency in Lower Yangzi food towards vegetable and vegetarian cooking. Bean curd, in all its various forms, is widely used in East China. Sometimes it is dried, at others used as a skin for 'paper wrapped' dishes and at yet other times it is shaped into replicas of ducks, chicken or fish – an unnecessary indulgence.

Although in China we usually eat rice plain – boiled or steamed

– in Shanghai green vegetables are sometimes cooked together with the rice. Of course the Yangzi is the greatest rice-producing region in China. All the rice-based products exist in abundance, among which Yellow Wine, including China's well-known Shaoshing wine which comes from the town of the same name, give rise to dishes with names like Drunken Chickens, Drunken Crabs, Drunken Spare Ribs, and so on. Parallel to the use of wine in cooking, the region is well known for its quality vinegar, the best known being the Jingjiang aromatic vinegar. This is used in the famous Westlake Whole Fish in Vinegar Sauce of Hangzhou.

In contrast to the use of freshwater products, unrefined crystal sugar and honey are used for the richer dishes such as Qing Hua Ham with Honey Sauce and for this reason the people of east China have a reputation for their sweet tooth.

It was with this memory of Shanghai and East China cooking on my mind that we returned to Britain with a new vision of a Shanghai-style restaurant on the river, with a maritime theme. The chef for this restaurant was introduced to us by an English lady called Joy Larcomb, author of *Salad Garden*. She had made her own tour of China and had her eye on vegetable and vegetarian dishes. While staying at the New Asia Hotel in Shanghai she had enjoyed a vegetarian meal of excellent standard.

I penned a respectful letter in my best Chinese to Mr Tang, the head chef at the New Asia. To my astonishment the reply came back in faultless typewritten English. The chef had graduated from university in English. One day in the summer of 1988 Anne and I drove to Heathrow to meet him, a tiny southerner, whom we immediately christened Tim.

I am not familiar with the whereabouts of Byzantium, but sailing up the Thames to Chelsea Harbour reminds me of the poem *Sailing to Byzantium*, which I've heard many times. I imagine Byzantium to be everything brilliant in an ancient civilization. It was this vision of a 'New Byzantium' on the Thames which originally attracted Anne to the Harbour. It would be a riverside town of the future, the best of the West to which we could bring the best of the East.

Viewed from our new house near Battersea Bridge, along the broad sweep up river, the Belvedere Tower seems to project straight into the sky like some mystical obelisk proclaiming Levantine power. Closer at hand and following the river between home and the Harbour the Embankment is filled with historical homes of people such as Turner and Whistler and Carlyle. In front of them the Thames was the main thoroughfare of the City along which waterborne traffic carried many distinguished people between the Tower of London and Hampton Court.

From the top of the lock, which separates the Harbour Marina from the open waters of the river, the cluster of brand new white buildings to the north shines in the sunshine like a vast canvas by Canaletto, a brilliant alabaster city towered over by the gleaming Conran Hotel that seems to drink from the Marina itself.

To complete this 'mirage', the monument to modern civilization must be combined with the infinite resourcefulness of the culinary arts of Cathay. If we could combine and contrast the chilli and pepper hot dishes of the Upper Yangzi with the abundance and freshness of the Lower Yangzi and all its freshwater products, we could produce a jewel on the great river.

But as usual our vision had to be capitalized. We had to find £300,000 before we could sign on the dotted line for a twenty-five year lease. This we managed to achieve through a Rights Issue based on the Business Expansion Scheme. From then on 'Sailing to Byzantium' turned out to be a rough ride and many would-be participants jumped ship at the last moment. But Anne and I jumped in in customary style and left the future to take care of itself.

In a piece which I wrote for my fellow directors I recounted:

> During the past fifteen weeks I can't remember a single day when Anne worked less than fifteen hours a day. She would leave home at 9.30 a.m. and be back home again at past midnight at the earliest on the following morning except for an hour's break between six and seven when she returns for a quick bath, a change and a mouthful of food. There hasn't been a single Sunday during the past couple of months when she didn't go into one or other of the restaurants to attend to essential repairs such as plumbing, gas supplies, electric or water. I believe the original builders fixed the water supply at a volume far below the requirements of an average restaurant half our size.
>
> On one unforgettable occasion, a couple of days before our opening day, 30 May, she worked through the day and night and never came back until the late afternoon of the following day. Soon afterwards she rushed off again to do another full evening's work. We were scheduled to hold a gala charity banquet and had a full house for lunch. In addition there was a full dragon boat crew of twenty-two men to feed for supper. To our utter dismay we discovered that the three custom-built Chinese wok stoves would not be ready in time.
>
> It was rumoured that the metal-workers were on the verge of

bankruptcy. I said to Anne that if bankruptcy threatened those who were actually on the factory floor they would be very responsive to ready cash. If she were to go over personally to their workshop with four £50 notes they would deliver that same day. She drove up to North London with the necessary cash that very evening. I waited for her return. I fell asleep fully clothed and when I awoke it was 2.30 a.m. She still hadn't come back. I knew that she would stay to the bitter end at the workshop sitting probably under one of the railway arches to make sure that the work was done. It was daylight when I awoke and Anne still hadn't returned. I became agitated. It took me a quarter of an hour to ascertain the telephone number of the metal workshop. When I eventually got through to the foreman to my great relief, he said, 'Mrs Lo has just gone off in one of our trucks with the first Chinese stove on board, and the two remaining ones will follow on.'

Anne didn't come back, even for a few moments, during the rest of that day. She had two appointments in the morning in Victoria and three more in Chelsea in the afternoon. There was no time for her to drop in. It was like that legendary Emperor Yü who, in striving to tame the Great Antediluvian Flood of China, never entered his own front door in three years, although he passed it many times. Anne didn't return until quite late on the second evening after thirty-eight hours in one stretch.

Time sped on and soon the first Chinese New Year was upon us. The noise that we made reverberated throughout the Harbour. When the Lion danced it reared up to chew up and spit out the cabbage and snatch away the red envelope of lucky money that we lowered from the balcony above. Children shouted and the cymbals clashed. There was a three-piece Chinese orchestra and a Chinese girl singing traditional Chinese songs. Children were also riding the two rickshaws which ran between the Harbour Yard and the Garden Market, taking a turn around our Dragon Boat which was parked in the centre of the Atrium looking like a beached Viking long boat.

During the celebration luncheon we had to turn away thirty customers. Those were bumper days. A couple of days before we had held a wedding reception worth £3,500 of business to us. On the first floor alone we took £2,500 and with a large outcatering on one of the speedboats and our normal luncheon takings we totalled £7,000 for the whole day. This sudden spurt of business was a morale booster in a dull season, but it did not amount to a great deal when measured against all the requirements of the weeks and months ahead. It was, however, an undoubted assurance of the potential of the restaurant. But the capital we deployed was only a third of what it should have been. However, behind any darkening cloud there was always the silver lining and we were hopeful of getting to a plateau in business when we could glide home to Byzantium.

CHAPTER THIRTEEN
The Peach Banquet

In the middle of the garden are 1,200 trees, with double blossom and sweet fruit. They ripen once in 6,000 years. Whoever eats them can rise like the clouds and fly and never grows old. At the back of the garden are 1,200 trees. The fruit has purple patterning and pale yellow kernels. They ripen once in 9,000 years. Whoever eats them will live as long as Heaven and Earth and is as ageless as the sun and moon.

> Chapter 5, *Journey to the West* (*The Monkey King*),
> Wu Chengen. *Circa* 1500–82

EVERY CLOUD HAS a silver lining, but empires also rise and fall and some, as with the first Emperor of China, fall after a very short spell of glory. The economic success of most of my ventures also seems to be short-lived. 'Memories of China' enjoyed nearly a decade of glory before the recession and the Gulf War came to spoil our fun and we realized how under-capitalized we had been for our expansion into Chelsea Harbour.

For a while the economic depression seemed to be affecting my health. I no longer wished to venture out into the cold to play tennis throughout the winter and struggled to keep warm. I was finding it difficult to sleep and getting up six or seven times a night to urinate. By May 1990 I found myself trussed up in St Mary's Hospital in Paddington.

It was the second time that I had been hospitalized. The first time was in 1924 in Foochow when I had my tonsils and adenoids removed. I remember it quite clearly. I went with mother in our family rickshaw, pulled by Damei (Elder sister), our most robust male servant. It was summer time and the roads were shaded by the leaves of the ginkgo tree. The light flickered as the rickshaw sped from one sunny patch into another. We ran past the Foochow Club where the foreign taipans were basking on the first floor balcony, their rickshaws parked below like shining limousines. From there we wound our way down the hillside to river level where the streets thronged with people buying spice powders, cooking sauces and pastes.

I wasn't sure why my tonsils and adenoids had to come out. I didn't feel the least bit ill. It seemed customary for people who believed in the modern way of living. The Japanese-run Tating hospital boasted the best equipment in town and that was our destination. We crossed the Great Stone Bridge where, between the huge stone girders, I could see the waters of the Min River swirling and pouring downstream in summer flood. Once on the north shore we were at the hospital, next door to the city's power plant which belonged to a relative of ours called 'Electric Liu'. My mother told me that after the operation I could just pick up a rickshaw at the rank parked in front of the hospital and ride home. She gave me a dollar piece for the fare.

Her matter-of-fact attitude towards the operation was infectious and I felt as if I were merely paying a visit to the dentist. At the entrance to the hospital I passed into the charge of a lady nurse, then surrendered to the Japanese surgeon who confronted me. I was told that the Japanese were very precise, especially at sword play and, in my eyes, the surgeon could just as well have been a samurai.

The operating table was laid out with trays of instruments. I didn't see clearly which knife he was going to use. It wasn't like one of the heavy triangular Chinese razors which was sharp only at one edge. Nor was I quite sure whether he used anaesthetic or not. He made swift work of it. I had to gurgle up great mouthfuls of blood before being allowed to get up, weak at the knees, and fall into a chair to recover for a few minutes. On the way out I was issued with a small packet of permanganate to continue gargling with when I got home.

That was my only close encounter with a Samurai. In the war they were confined to the Pacific and I was buried in the Cambridge library, fire watching, with nothing more offensive than a bucketful of sand. Nowadays when we meet up, it is in the aisle between the restaurant tables. We bow most politely and I cede the way.

When Anne drove me to St Mary's, she was quite as matter-of-fact as my mother had been. I was so scared of being admitted to hospital, of dying under anesthetic and being committed unknowingly to oblivion. I was going in for tests, otherwise I would never have agreed to go anywhere near the hospital that wintry afternoon. I began to feel quite ill as we approached Paddington. It loomed before us, the most depressed and the most depressing area I had ever seen. I limped from the car park to the hospital entrance.

Within moments I was confronted by Dr A., a friend of my daughter, who appeared to ram something as big as a rolling pin up my backside. All the while he was talking about a simple 'plumbing job'. I had the vague sense of being set up, but by this time I felt that I had in some way committed myself to my fate. Once in the ward among cheerful and kindly sisters, I surrendered myself to their care and all anxiety seemed to drain away.

The hospital routine soon took over – my pulse, temperature and blood-pressure were taken regularly, my urine was checked and different tablets administered at different times. All the rituals seemed to create a life rhythm and *raison d'être* that induced a subliminal state within which anything was possible. A few days later, when I was being offered a day's break before the operation, I strenuously declined. I had been lulled into a sense of security and did not want to face the world when I was only half way through my ordeal.

Vivienne came on the morning of the operation. As an acupuncturist, she would never have condoned an operation unless she felt it to be absolutely necessary. Together we saw the surgeon and the anesthetist. The surgeon was not a Samurai. He may not have been wielding Excalibur, but he assured me that his electric lance would be even more potent. By the time they wheeled my trolley downstairs to the anesthetist we could hardly stop laughing. It was crazy and curious. No time seemed to pass at all before I was back up in the ward and feeling fine. In speed, elegance and consideration of my feelings, the operation was light years ahead of my experience at the Tating hospital.

All along there had been a continual coming and going of visitors. Anne, my children, grandchildren, employees and friends brought basketfuls of fruit and bouquets that piled up until they became embarrassing. In the end my 'get well' stream of traffic had to be slowed as it was not conducive to convalescence. Towards the end of my stay a senior member of my staff confided in Anne that if we were short of cash for a private hospital, he would be only too pleased to contribute £5,000. How many company chairmen could expect such generosity from their staff? But the specialist care which I received at St Mary's was quite the equal of any in the world.

Within six weeks I was back on the tennis courts playing Sunday tennis with three generations of the family. By the time Charles arrived in the late summer I was completely recovered and could put up a good match. It was not long since I had competed in the Crawford Cup, the Davis Cup for the Over Seventies. The average age of our team was seventy-three, with myself as one of the older members. At that time I had written four books during the previous winter and was sitting up every night till midnight at the Ebury Street restaurant which was bulging with customers. My lifestyle was certainly not conducive to peak physical fitness and when I heard that I had been selected I immediately began to get in training.

Every morning I spent fifteen minutes limbering up with free hand exercises based on the Tai Jiquan. After that I would go for a one and a quarter mile jaunt along the Embankment, interspersed with the occasional brisk trot. I slowly increased the amount of trotting, until after four weeks I felt perceptibly fitter and after six I felt like a ball of unsprung muscle. It was a feeling I had not experienced for over half-a-century. When over seventy, it is important that you never overstretch yourself, otherwise the recovery period is too protracted. But the daily exercise regime must be consistent, so that you gradually build your strength and stamina. After six weeks of unbroken training I could do twenty-five squats without even breathing heavily.

That summer of 1990, after his vacation jaunt to the East, Charles, as usual, ended up in London before returning to New York to teach in the Fall. He was not his usual self. His constant companion, our cousin, Cecee, had passed away the previous year and, to add to his misery, he came bearing news of my sister's death. Anna left Foochow for Taiwan before the Revolution and, that summer, Charles had accompanied her back home to China for the first and last time in forty years. On returning to Taibei she took ill, was admitted to hospital and never emerged again. Within a year Charles had also gone. That was the greatest shock to me. He died the following summer. He had just won a tennis match and was sitting beside the court with his tennis racquet in his hand, like a warrior with his boots on. In the face of absence and decline, I no longer have the heart to play tennis. I would rather cherish the memories of my best tennis matches than sit forlornly on the park benches at Hurlingham Club that bear sad inscriptions in the memory of my old tennis partners.

When I do look back over the years, I rarely feel either anger or regret. I have never hated any period of my life so much that I would prefer to close my mind to it. Most times are quite pleasantly memorable. But I seldom look back. For as each period drew to a close, it was to be followed immediately by another which seemed to promise so much excitement that I was sucked into the future without time to ruminate on what was passing.

I always remember the fortune-teller who came to Lo Lodge. He predicted that fortune would smile on me at different stages of my life. He said I should both arrive early [zao da] and mature late [wan cheng], two terms that remain clear in my mind. Early arrival was ambiguous. If it meant that I would arrive on to the academic scene then the fortune-teller was off the mark. My academic progress was erratic. But if he meant that I would reach my optimum age early he was spot on. I was a natural teenager – in love with life and youth.

Of course of my early education I still remember the classics. I also remember the Last Will and Testament of Sun Yatsen, the hymn that we chanted daily in united response to the Headmaster at the Anglo–Chinese College.

> For forty years I have devoted myself to the People's Revolution. During those forty years I have come to the conclusion that to achieve this purpose it will be absolutely necessary to arouse the political awareness of the people at large and to ally ourselves with all the other people and nations in the world who are prepared to treat us on an equal basis and for us to ally ourselves to them to pursue our common cause.
>
> At the moment our national Revolution is not yet accomplished. We, comrades, have yet to make great effort to apply ourselves to this purpose. My latest aim is to convene an all-nation conference, and to abrogate all the Unequal Treaties which have been forced upon us by Foreign powers.

Having been educated in the democratic tradition, I was naturally inclined toward the ideal of one man, one vote and the principles which inspired the French Revolution: Liberty, Equality and Fraternity.

But how to achieve national unity was always uppermost in my mind during those years of idealism. What was at stake was the very independence of China. Not since Genghis Khan had China's independence been so precariously held on to. There seemed little use to moan and clamour about equality at home when there was a good chance that there would be no homeland to call our own.

In the late 1920s when Communism was only a tiny germinating force, land redistribution and social equality all seemed rather remote and totally theoretical. In fact in the days when Zhu De and Mao were in the mountains on the border of Jiangxi and Fujian provinces they were designated the Zhu-mao bandits. That's all we knew of them. And I was not about to go and join up with any bandits.

It was only later that Communism gripped the imagination of young intellectuals. Espousing the theories was like a faith which became faith in youth itself and in the ability to decide one's own destiny. But when more and more young people drifted from the Nationalist camp to the 8th Route army, I did not follow them. It was an act of faith that I was not prepared to make.

There was always so much to live for. In China in this or any subsequent twentieth-century period, if you wanted to survive it was important not to be too headstrong nor to create too many enemies. I had no intention of inviting the attention of 'the Blue Shirt Contingent', Chiang Kaishek's secret police. What was the point of fighting for a cause if you weren't to be around to see the fruits of your labour?

Against such a panoramic sweep of modern history, any one individual's thoughts amounted to very little unless that individual happened to be called Mao or Zhu. I was always conscious of my own impotence when measured against the enormity of China's problems. With China's changing fortune one must count oneself lucky to be able to wear a pair of shoes and eat two meals a day. To have the chance of an education to Junior and Middle school standards was rare indeed.

There seemed to be two choices: one was to be reckless enough to pull up all the anchors of life and plunge, idealistic and adventurous, into some uncharted movement, vaguely aimed toward the regeneration of China. The other was to look after yourself so that you survived to see the flags fly.

I remember Zheng Weixing, a thin, sallow-faced classmate who was shot besieging the local police headquarters. I remember his brilliant command of contemporary Chinese. He was a weak boy, always pushed around in ball games, but once converted to Marxism an explosion of energy was released in him and he became quite fearless. His glory burnt furious and bright, but was snuffed out like a flickering candle. And so too were the lives of those children protesting for democracy at Tiananmen Square on 4 June 1988. For what did they make that sacrifice?

Physically I have never been able to run any great distance – a quarter of a mile at the most, but I was always able to walk twenty miles in a stretch. Mentally I was trained to commit 500 words to memory in one morning or to recite twice that amount in a day. I was made with the stamina and caution to stand the distance.

Perhaps this is what the fortune-teller meant by 'late arrival'. Unlike many of my more courageous contemporaries I survived my youth. I was over forty before I began my family and it took fifty years for me to establish a lasting profession.

This is perhaps the destiny of a family cut adrift from its roots twice in two generations. After the removal of the seat of bureaucratic power to Nanjing all the political influence in China shifted into the hands of the graduates of the Central Military Academy and the (T.V.) Song dynasty. Unless you could plug into the 'circuit' by re-aligning your network of 'connections' you were not likely to land a decent job. Our 'old school tie' connections were so tenuous that they could hardly be tugged without fear of snapping. In fact any family glory was beginning to recede into the long gone mists of the Manchu dynasty. There was only Uncle Yi, Becee's father, who stood anywhere near the centre of control at the Ministry of Foreign Affairs.

The Confucian concept of government was meant to be 'platonic' in the sense that Plato meant the government of a country to reside only in the hands of people who were educated for that specific purpose. Bureaucratic succession was expressed in cogent terms: 'the responsibility of office should follow in hereditary succession'. My grandfather was clearly educated for the job and my father, despite being no genius and in most ways unsuitable, was probably better placed to negotiate with the Westerners than some illiterate lackey of a war-lord.

At the time I failed to understand my father's political outlook. He appeared to display hardly any concern for the destiny of our country. Later on, when I was severed from any contact with China by geographical distance, I felt more sympathy towards him. Without an immediate confrontation, and deprived of a ready structure to channel political fervour, idealism, politics, nationalism, even the whisperings of Confucius, seem to drain slowly away.

What matters in life? For me it must be life itself. There was once a philosopher named Yang Zhu who suggested that the most precious possession was your own body and your primary duty was to maintain it. Being a natural youth, I am not happy with decline and would resist it. However, one has to be a little realistic and these days I rarely play tennis or walk too far.

In fact it is always people who give meaning to my life and the more alive and lively they are the better. On 12 September 1990 the sun was shining as usual on my birthday. The telephone rang soon after 8 a.m., I picked up the receiver and heard the strains of the harmonica floating down the line. It was Larry Adler wishing me Happy Birthday. Downstairs there were several birthday cards from my children and grandchildren.

Later on, as I took Anne her customary morning tea, I said, 'Let's go to the Belfry for lunch.' Anton Mosimann had opened up a new restaurant a short walk across the square. Anne was pleased as she had great admiration for his style of cooking. He did not do anything spectacular or elaborate and his strength was in quality and simplicity.

For entrée Anne had a fish cake and I had calves' liver. My calves' liver was both crunchy and tender. I noted that, although liver is almost always featured in oriental menus, we didn't have it in our own restaurant. It was high time to remedy the situation. For dessert I wanted Bread and Butter Pudding, but it had to be forsaken for the chocolate gateau which Mosimann had had delivered to our table complete with one tiny candle. Not even I could face Bread and Butter pudding on top of chocolate gateau.

In South China on a birthday, for an ordinary peasant family, we would be served a bowl of soup noodles topped with a hard-boiled egg, painted bright red. The egg denoted auspicious rebirth, the long noodles continuity of life and the heat of the soup the warmth in every corner of life. For me the combination of family, friends and food has to be the very essence of life. Food is generally not memorable unless there is an occasion to go with it – then it has the power to flavour the whole occasion. Food may impress one differently at different stages of life; if there is anything or anyone to recollect in life it can be done through the food that was shared. Food threads together the whole of life.

As I approach my eightieth birthday it is inevitable that I should reflect on the places, people and foods that I have held most dear. And for a celebration dinner I should weave them all into the feast of my life – with each dish recreating a place, a people and a time. To my birthday dinner I would invite my wife, children, and my eight grand-children – Gary, Pearl, Louise, Ria-Mae, Aaron, Kelly-Rose, Billy and Eleanor. This dinner will be called the Peach Banquet, for it will recall the banquet of the Immortals when the Monkey King stole the Peaches of Immortality. It will have all the ingredients of immortality, all the food to remind me of the best homes, the best people, the best tennis matches, times of my life and my family, who, if they continue to breed as they have, will easily keep the Lo family alive for another forty generations and ensure the immortality of my soul!

For the very earliest times – all my brothers and sisters – and winter at Lo Lodge we must have barbecued oysters, preferably on bamboo sticks – a dozen or more to a stick. To supplement this rustic delicacy we must have cold savoury kebabs of jellied meats. Included in this range are chicken's and duck's feet, wings, livers, drumsticks and other bits of their gizzards. These should be stewed in soya sauce complete with their skins and then cooled and eaten inside a plain bun with a hole in the middle, just as the street vendors would sell them in the lanes around our home. To garnish this cold Foochow *charcuterie* we should add hard-boiled eggs that have been simmered for a while in soya sauce and wine and cut into thin slices with a cotton thread.

Baked Crabs in Steamed Rice will remind me of the superior food available on the Isle of Snails, of Daisun and his mother, Auntie Ying, who were such an inspiration to me. Each crab is chopped into quarters, sprinkled with garlic, ginger and spring onion, before being steamed for fifteen minutes with the rice. The whole casserole is then transferred into the oven for a further fifteen minutes. An essential feature of this dish is that the whole table should end up covered in mounds of pink and glistening crab shell.

One delicacy unique to Foochow cuisine is a dough wrapper for pork dumplings called 'Swallow's skin' (yan pi). The wrapper is made of lean meat pounded with cornflour, which makes it much more savoury than the usual flour dough that is used. Swallow's skin dumplings were sold in the cafés and restaurants all around Foochow. They are commonly eaten in a clear stock and this will provide a light and warm soup for the course.

To return to those moonlit nights skating on Beihai lake in Peking, the cold sunlight and clear windswept skies of the north, we must have a barbecue of Mongolian lamb. Each slice must be wafer thin, so that it will cook in a flash on top of a blazing brazier. The lamb must be eaten with two dips, first coated in beaten egg and then dipped into a sauce of vinegar, soya sauce and sesame oil.

Of the finest dishes available in Soho during the war years I must select steamed salmon heads, just as Mr Yang would serve up, free of charge, if I arrived early to partake of their family meal in the basement of the Hong Kong restaurant on Shaftesbury Avenue.

To go with the fish, Chef But's Knuckle of Pork should be served as the main dish. This is a speciality of our first restaurant in Belgravia and is best appreciated when eaten with steamed silver thread buns which soak up the incomparable gravy like a sponge.

Such a carnivorous dish must be accompanied with something delicate from Chef Tang of the Chelsea Harbour Memories of China. As a chef from Shanghai he is an expert at vegetable cooking and sculpture. To balance But's meaty flavour I would choose his 'Spring Colours Fill the Garden', a riot of colour made up of stir-fried mangetout, baby corn, carrots, young leeks and Chinese cabbage. To complete this course we should have the plainest dish of spinach strongly flavoured with a liberal portion of garlic.

To finish we must have the fruit salad on ice from the Vivex restaurant in Copenhagen to remind me of our Davis Cup victory over Denmark in 1946. The sorbets should be flavoured with peaches of immortality, preferably those that Monkey stole from the Jade Emperor's orchards. We should also add fruit to recall the harvest from Foochow, piled up waist-deep, as if it were autumn in the village temple courtyards. Autumn, when all along the canal and river banks the golden oranges and yellows of tangerines and pomelos, purples and reds of lychees and longyan (dragon's eyes) filled those orchards of my youth.

> You came, Sir, from my old home
> and should know the village affairs.
> The day you left, before my silken window,
> was the winter plum in flower?
>
> Wang Wei (AD 699–759)

Index